The Railway that Helped win the Crimean War

The Railway that Helped win the Crimean War

The Story of the Grand Crimean Central Railway

ANTHONY DAWSON

FRONTLINE
BOOKS

THE RAILWAY THAT HELPED WIN THE CRIMEAN WAR
The Story of the Grand Crimean Central Railway

First published in Great Britain in 2022 by

Frontline Books
An imprint of
Pen & Sword Books Ltd
Yorkshire – Philadelphia

Copyright © Anthony Dawson, 2022

ISBN 978 1 52677 555 9

The right of Anthony Dawson to be identified as
the author of this work has been asserted by him in accordance
with the Copyright, Designs and Patents Act 1988.

A CIP catalogue record for this book is
available from the British Library

All rights reserved. No part of this book may be reproduced or
transmitted in any form or by any means, electronic or mechanical
including photocopying, recording or by any information storage and
retrieval system, without permission from the Publisher in writing.

Typeset in 10.5/13 pt Palatino
by SJmagic DESIGN SERVICES, India.

Printed and bound in the UK by CPI Group (UK) Ltd.

Pen & Sword Books Ltd incorporates the Imprints of Aviation, Atlas,
Family History, Fiction, Maritime, Military, Discovery, Politics, History,
Archaeology, Select, Wharncliffe Local History, Wharncliffe True Crime,
Military Classics, Wharncliffe Transport, Leo Cooper, The Praetorian Press,
Remember When, Seaforth Publishing and Frontline Publishing.

For a complete list of Pen & Sword titles please contact

PEN & SWORD BOOKS LTD
47 Church Street, Barnsley, South Yorkshire, S70 2AS, England
E-mail: enquiries@pen-and-sword.co.uk
Website: www.pen-and-sword.co.uk

Or

PEN AND SWORD BOOKS
1950 Lawrence Rd, Havertown, PA 19083, USA
E-mail: Uspen-and-sword@casematepublishers.com
Website: www.penandswordbooks.com

Contents

Acknowledgements		vi
Foreword		vii
Map of the Grand Crimean Central Railway, 1855		ix
Introduction: The Crimean War		1
Chapter 1	Allied Logistics in 1854	4
Chapter 2	The French Army	22
Chapter 3	Supplying the Troops in the Crimea	34
Chapter 4	The Military and Railways	60
Chapter 5	Building the Balaklava Railway	68
Chapter 6	The Railway Starts Work	107
Chapter 7	A Transport Revolution	119
Chapter 8	The Ambulance Corps	142
Chapter 9	Running the Railway	152
Chapter 10	The Second Winter	193
Conclusion	A New Weapon?	219
Notes		223
Select Bibliography and Sources		248
Index		253

Acknowledgements

The writing of a book is never a solo task, even though at many times it may feel like it. Firstly, I should like to thank my partner, Andy Mason, for his continued support of my writing endeavours and accompanying me on research trips across the country. Secondly, to colleagues in Russia and in Turkey: Vladimir Serdiuk a PhD Student in Moscow for searching for Russian sources, and Yunus Emre Adin for accessing Turkish archives in Istanbul concerning the sale of the Balaklava Railway. To them I shall be eternally gratefully. Thirdly, to Dr Stephen Summerfield for proofreading and editing this text.

Foreword

By Major (Retired) Simon Walmsley MBA MA,
Director, The Royal Logistic Corps Museum

The advent of then new technologies, use of the telegraph network and photography, allowed harrowing stories and images of the terrible conditions endured by the army in the Crimean War to reach the breakfast-table newspapers of their readers back home. The public's increasingly hostile opinion of the war eventually forced the government of the day to act and this became the catalyst for change that led to the modernisation of logistic services within the army.

The British army's shortages of equipment and the privations under which it struggled during the Crimean War managed to transform the way the army sustained itself in the field. These difficulties paved the way for major changes in how Parliament governed the army, together with the creation of new responsibilities for procurement, supply and transport – with many of these changes remaining broadly recognisable and enabling today's Royal Logistic Corps soldier to trace their history in an unbroken line back to the Land Transport Corps soldiers then raised.

This book describes the momentous Crimean War events in clear detail, explaining how the British army was sustained, before, during and after the war, and showing just how challenging these changes were in their delivery. Further, it explains the army's need to improve the capability and resilience of its supply line and, thus, why a purpose-built railway was constructed, detailing how it was funded, erected, operated and ultimately how effective it was.

Additionally, this book compares the British army's method of supply with that of the French, enabling the reader to contrast the two approaches and draw conclusions on their relative values. This book will be rewarding, not only to the serious scholar who seeks an in-depth analysis of the changes as they unfolded, but also to the more casual reader with perhaps a lighter interest in the subject.

Anthony Dawson should be congratulated for capturing this story brilliantly, with his evident use of extensive research from primary sources as well as from a wide range of historical and contemporary references. It is thoroughly researched and well executed, easy to read and logically laid out.

Editor's Note

The Royal Logistic Corps Museum tells the story of army logistics from medieval times to the present day. One of the key milestones on this extensive journey is the Crimean War.

Simon Walmsley has been the Director of The Royal Logistic Corps Museum since 2016. He initially saw service with the Royal Artillery and subsequently joined the Royal Logistic Corps on its formation in 1993. During his thirty-two-year military career, he deployed to the Falklands War in 1982 and also saw service in Bosnia, Kosovo, Iraq and Afghanistan. He holds a Master's degree in Business Administration and a second Master's degree in Museum Studies.

Map of the Grand Crimean Central Railway, 1855

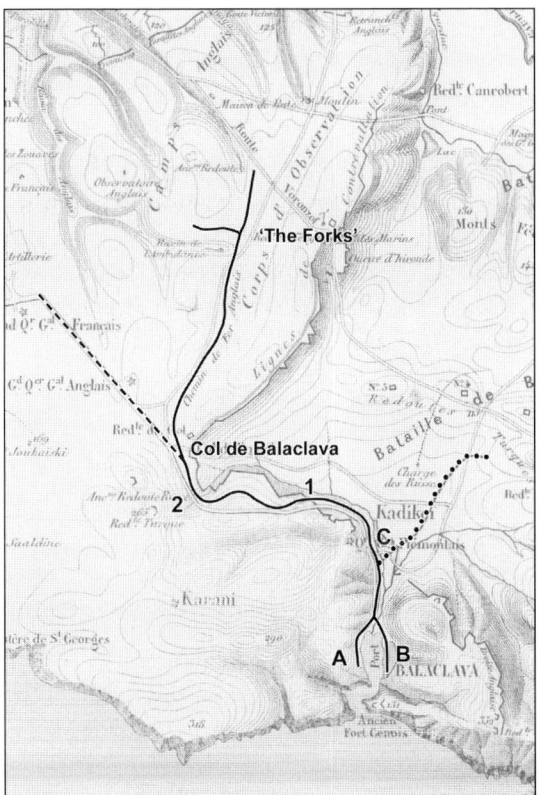

The Grand Crimean Central Railway, showing the main line and French (dashed) and Piedmontese (dotted) branches. The line was worked by locomotives from Diamond Wharf (A) and Ordnance Wharf (B) to the Commissariat Depot at Kadikoi (C) before making its way up the heights via two inclined planes. (1) Powered incline of 1:15, (2) Horse-worked incline of 1:25. From the Col de Balaclava the line was worked by horses. (*Andrew Mason*)

Introduction

The Crimean War

The Crimean War was fought between 1854 and 1856 by an alliance of Great Britain, France, Piedmont-Sardinia and Turkey against Russia. It was characterised by the eleven-month siege of the Russian naval base of Sevastopol. It was the first modern war; not just in terms of its scale – the French army mobilised a million men – but also the technologies employed, seeing the mass use of rifled muskets and artillery for the first time, the electric telegraph, the typewriter, steam ships, iron clads and, for this study, the steam railway.[1]

Distrust of Russia and her ambitions in the Near East had rumbled throughout the 1820s and 1840s. Considered land-hungry and reactionary, the Russo-Turkish War of 1827–8 produced the spectre of Russian control of Constantinople and the eastern Mediterranean. The trigger for war with Russia finally came in 1852 over the issue of the 'keys to the Holy Places' of Jerusalem. Since the Middle Ages France had claimed the right of guardianship of the 'Holy Places': the Church of the Nativity in Bethlehem and the Church of the Holy Sepulchre in Jerusalem. During the French Revolution and Napoleonic Wars this claim had gradually been allowed to lapse and Russia – which viewed itself as not only the champion of the Orthodox Church but also the Slavic people – assumed the mantle of guardian. Thus, when Napoléon III (1808–74, r. 1851–70) renewed the traditional French claim of guardianship and had a silver star engraved with the Arms of France placed in the Church of the Nativity, Russia was outraged. Thanks to pressure from the French Ambassador, La Valette, and French warships, in November 1852 the Sublime Porte, ruler of the Ottoman Empire, granted France the right to hold the keys to the 'Holy Places'. This was a policy that was supported in Britain and by the virulently anti-Russian British ambassador at Constantinople, Lord Stratford Canning.

In February 1853 Tsar Nicholas I (1796–1855, r. 1825–55) dispatched his own special envoy, Prince Alexander Menshikov, to Constantinople to negotiate with the Sublime Porte. Supported by Britain and France (and their warships), the Porte rejected Menshikov's terms, which would have resulted in the Tsar assuming authority over the Porte's Orthodox Christian subjects. Upon the failure of Menshikov's mission, the Tsar sent troops into the Danubian principalities of Wallachia and Moldovia. The British Prime Minister Lord Aberdeen had no desire to intervene in what was perceived to be a local squabble, whilst the bellicose Home Secretary Lord Palmerston urged for war. The Sublime Porte, however, was cautious and conciliatory, but in September 1853 he was presented with an ultimatum by radical Muslim imams to either abdicate or declare war, and chose the latter. Britain and France were content to observe what was a small, localised war until on 30 November 1853 the Turkish fleet was sunk in a naval action at Sinope; exaggerated newspaper reports of 'the Massacre of Sinope' pushed the public mood in Britain and France toward military action against Russia. Thus, on 27 February 1854 Britain and France declared war with Russia, a war that none of the armies of either of the key players were really prepared for.

Objective: Sevastopol

The suggestion to attack Sevastopol and therefore neutralise Russian naval power in the eastern Mediterranean was made by Napoléon III in February 1854 and this became France's central war aim. It was to be a war of limited scope with clear objectives accomplished by a single knock-out blow. The British Cabinet, however, was divided in its war aims. The Prime Minister wished to maintain the status quo in Turkey through a limited war, whilst the sabre-rattling Lord Palmerston clamoured for a 'popular' European war and wanted Austria to join on the side of the Allies. The First Lord of the Admiralty Sir James Graham, Sidney Herbert (Secretary at War) and the Duke of Newcastle (Secretary of State for War and the Colonies) all agreed with Napoléon III and wanted to aim a 'decisive blow' against Sevastopol. Yet even the belligerent Palmerston thought an attack on Sevastopol was too ambitious and 'too large an undertaking'.[2]

The plan of campaign against Russia that eventually emerged was limited in its scope and aims: to curb Russian naval power in the Baltic and the eastern Mediterranean. As Sir Hew Strachan has identified, it was a policy created by the navy but enacted by the army, to maintain the naval hegemony in the Mediterranean. However, because of weak leadership and lack of an effective means of communication, the army was unable to express its own doubts and inadequacies.³

The invasion of the Crimea was envisioned as a 'Grand Raid' – a rapid descent on the Crimea and capture of Sevastopol by *coup de main*. Speed was of the essence: Sevastopol was to be knocked out and occupied by winter so that the Allied troops had winter quarters. But, as the French commander-in-chief *Maréchal* Jacques Leroy de Saint-Arnaud (1798–1854) noted, by the time the plan had been finally formalised in August 1854 it was much too late in the year to plan a major campaign, intelligence was inadequate, no suitable landing ground had been identified and there was no effective means of supplying the armies over such vast distances or evacuating them in case of a major defeat. Furthermore, no one seemed to know how many Russian troops were in the Crimea, let alone garrisoning Sevastopol. It was expected by the politicians that Sevastopol would quickly fall to the Allies, and indeed many, if not all, of the subsequent failings of the transport and medical services of both the British and French armies was entirely due to this belief: there was no expectation of a winter campaign.

Neither the British commander-in-chief Fitzroy James Henry Somerset, 1st Baron Raglan (1788–1854) nor his French counterpart Saint-Arnaud were in favour of the invasion of the Crimea; indeed, Saint-Arnaud expressed his own grave misgivings about the scheme to Napoléon III. He felt he had been compelled by the politicians in Paris to invade the Crimea 'in deference to the English plan' to maintain the alliance between Britain and France. Raglan expressed similar sentiments: 'The descent on the Crimea is decided upon, more in deference to the views of the British government than to any information in possession of the naval and military authorities, either as to the extent of the enemy's forces, or to their state of preparations.'⁴ Nor was it just the commanders-in-chief who had misgivings about the invasion of the Crimea; three of Ralglan's five divisional commanders, as well as his Chief Engineer, General Tylden, were opposed to the plan. So too many of Saint-Arnaud's senior commanders. But despite these reservations, the invasion went ahead driven by the politicians in London and with the adulation of the domestic press.

Chapter 1

Allied Logistics in 1854

The *Oxford English Dictionary* defines military logistics as 'The activity of organizing the movement, equipment, and accommodation of troops.' This chapter will examine the logistics and support services of the British and French armies in the Crimean War. Although the French are traditionally thought to have been far superior in terms of logistics than the British army, as the present writer has described, this is based on a largely emotional response to the human drama in the Crimea which created a skewed perception of French relative success, and one which was not based upon detailed study. Both French and British soldiers went hungry and without shelter or boots, and in many respects the commissariat arrangements of both armies were not fit for purpose.[1]

The British Army

Placed in command of the British 'Force in the East' was Fitzroy James Henry Somerset, 1st Baron Raglan. He was 66 years old; he had been appointed to command because of the available candidates he was the only one below 70. Raglan had last seen active service at the Battle of Waterloo in June 1815 where he had lost his right arm and had to learn how to write again with his left hand. He became the Duke of Wellington's secretary in 1819, and with Wellington becoming General Commanding-in-Chief of the British Army in 1827, Somerset became Military Secretary at Horse Guards until Wellington's death in 1852. In that same year he became Master General of the Ordnance and was created Baron Raglan. From his long association with Wellington, it was felt that some of his genius had 'rubbed off' on Raglan and that he was the best-qualified man to command the British forces in the field.[2]

Above left: Lord Raglan, commander of the 'British Forces in the East', had not served in the field since 1815 and had never held a command, having spent most of his service life behind a desk at Horse Guards. (*Library of Congress*)

Above right: Sir George Brown, another Peninsular and Waterloo veteran, commanded the Light Division. He was much in favour of pipeclay and strict attention to regulations. (*Library of Congress*)

Right: Sir George De Lacy Evans commanded the Second Division. He had seen service in the Peninsular War but also during the Spanish Civil War (1834–40) meaning he was one of few British senior officers to have recent command experience. (*Library of Congress*)

Beneath Raglan, his five divisional commanders included the cantankerous Scot General Sir George Brown (1790–1865), in command of the Light Division. Brown was a veteran of the Napoleonic Wars and had fought in the Peninsula and in Canada during the War of 1812. He was a strict disciplinarian who believed in the benefits of pipeclay and the leather stock. Command of the First Division was vested in the young HRH Prince George, the Duke of Cambridge (1819–1904), a cousin of Queen Victoria who had never seen active service; the irascible 'radical general' Sir George de Lacy Evans (1780–1870) commanded the Second Division; Sir Richard England (1793–1883) the Third; and the headstrong Sir George Cathcart (1794–1854) the Fourth. Command of the cavalry was vested in George Bingham, 3rd Earl of Lucan (1800–88), 'a hot-headed nitwit Irishman', as one officer under his command described him. Raglan's chief engineer was Sir John Burgoyne (1782–1871), another Napoleonic veteran. Other than the Duke of Cambridge, these were all men pushing 60. Brown, Cathcart, England and Evans had all served during the Napoleonic Wars with Evans later commanding the 'British Legion' sent to intervene during the Spanish Civil War (1834–40). Cathcart had in fact served alongside the Russian army during 1813–14 as an observer, whilst Lucan had gained his only combat experience as an observer with the Russian army during the Russo-Turkish War of 1827–8.

If there was a lack of recent campaign experience in the higher echelons of the army, then the same was true of the army as a whole. Only a single battalion of the British force sent to the Crimea – 1st Battalion the Rifle Brigade – had seen any recent active service other than unpopular policing duties during times of unrest such as the Chartist disturbances. The army was going through a period of transition; much-needed reform had been held back by the Duke of Wellington as Commander-in-Chief at Horse Guards. Upon his death he was succeeded by the energetic Henry Hardinge (1785–1856), much to the disappointment of the future Baron Raglan, who was offered the Master Generalship of the Ordnance and a peerage as compensation. Hardinge was a favourite at court but had considerable military and political experience thanks to long service in India, and it was under Hardinge that a limited scheme of reforms was introduced.[3] One of the leading reformers was de Lacy Evans. He was a fierce opponent of flogging, the purchase of commissions and poor enlistment conditions of the common soldier.[4]

Where reform did take place, which included the re-arming of the infantry with rifled Minié muskets, barrack building, the Chobham 'Camp of instruction', this was primarily a reaction to a threat of disorder, both internal and external, leading to increased military spending. Existing British Russophobia was fuelled by the British press following the escape of Hungarian liberals to Britain in 1849, and the domestic and military press were fed by paranoia of a strong France under a Bonaparte and the re-establishment of the French Empire, which prompted anti-French feelings. The military budget was also increased due to growing internal security issues, such as the Chartist demonstrations of 1848–9. These perceived threats led to Britain's armed forces being scrutinised and generally found lacking, leading to limited reform.[5] This in turn released money to the army in order to improve the national defences, most of which was spent on emergency repairs to south-coast forts and on the Royal Arsenal at Woolwich, to counteract a perceived, but ultimately unrealistic, threat from France.[6]

Moreover, thoughts turned to administrative reform including abolition of the ancient Board of Ordnance which included the merger of the Army and Ordnance Medical Departments, a proposal first mooted in 1851. Sadly, this reform also did away with the Field Train Department of the Board of Ordnance, which meant that the Royal Engineers which hitherto had had its own militarised transport had to rely upon the commissariat to move its stores. Importantly the commissariat, then a part of the Treasury, was to be transferred to the new War Department, which came into effect in December 1854.[7]

Command and Control: The Staff

The administrative and operational needs of the army were handled by the staff, which included the Quartermaster General, Adjutant General, and their assistants, as well as the Judge Advocate General and finally the various aides-de-camp (ADCs). The position of Quartermaster General, responsible for all the supplies, provisions and logistics of the army, was at first filled by the eccentric and entirely unsuitable Lord de Ros. He was succeeded by the hard-working General Sir Richard Airey (1803–81), who had been military secretary to Lord Hardinge. In charge of the discipline and administration of the army, including publishing of orders, correspondence and personnel, was General James Bucknall Bucknall Estcourt (1803–55), the Adjutant General. Estcourt, who was more interested in travel and exploring, had no prior experience of staff work and was thus completely new to his job.

Rather like the commissariat, which was not a fixed or permanent organisation, so too the staff had to be organised for every campaign. Although the staff were expected to be learned, experienced officers

General James Bucknall Bucknall Estcourt served as Raglan's Adjutant General, despite having no previous experience of staff work and being more interested in travel and exploring.

who showed aptitude for their positions, the formal training for the staff was paltry at best. Lord Panmure raged that, 'We have no way of making General Officers or of forming an efficient staff'.[8] The 'Senior Department' of the Royal Military College at Sandhurst offered a 'Staff Certificate' designed to train a young officer for staff duties. But, out of the 216 officers who earned certificates between 1836 and 1854, only 20 of them ever held a staff position. Author and social commentator Charles Dickens raged that of the 135 staff officers with the army in the Crimea, only 9 had attended the Senior Department at Sandhurst, making a mockery of the existence of the Staff Certificate. Not that possessing a Staff Certificate meant that the duly qualified officer would be any good at staff work. Nor did it mean that they would be respected; in the anti-intellectual atmosphere that pervaded the army, the Royal Military College was 'all very well for Frenchmen and Germans, and even for those officers who were unfortunately obliged to think of the army as a career' but 'it did not do for *gentlemen*'.[9] Some reform-minded commentators noted that a French corporal had probably had a better military education than a British officer with his Staff Certificate. In no way could the course at Sandhurst compare with the education provided at the *École d'Application d'État Major* (special staff school) in Paris which every French staff officer had to attend.[10]

In order to serve on the staff, a Line officer had to go on what was known as 'half pay', whereas officers from the Guards did not. Staff officers still held regimental commissions even though they did not do any regimental duty and were thus still eligible for regimental promotion, effectively blocking the 'ladder of promotion' to those junior than themselves. Furthermore, some of the best trained officers in the army – artillery and Engineers – were denied access to staff positions. This led to a lot of friction and animosity between officers of the Line and those on the staff; they were considered to be spoiled and lazy and that the Guards had a monopoly on 'comfortable' staff appointments. Furthermore, senior officers were at liberty to appoint their own staff and ADCs, the latter usually being 'bright young things' who were relations or sons of friends. Indeed, one staff officer, Arthur Griffiths of the 63rd Regiment, admitted that he spent more time in Paris drinking champagne than on active service in the Crimea and that the staff was a route to a comfortable lifestyle of 'flaunting and philandering'.[11] Members of the staff were almost universally viewed as 'effete officials', 'inactive ignoramuses', 'snobbish' and 'frightful'.[12] Captain Maxwell Earle raged:

> Let us succeed to find men possessing good education . . . Let it no longer be said 'my helper is useless to me on my staff, but I must keep him up for my sister's sake.' Generals ought to chose [sic] men who are of use to them, if their relative so much the better. But if that relation is useless have him off the staff. Why should poor soldiers suffer because the son of a nobleman taking high office has the entire management of the Quarter Master Generals' Department and is unfit for post![13]

To make matters worse for Raglan, Airey and Estcourt were constantly feuding, each believing themselves to be de facto Chief of Staff, resulting in 'mischievous delay and inconvenience'. Indeed, the situation would grow so bad from the number of complaints about Airey and Estcourt that it was proposed to recall them both in spring 1855 due to their alleged incompetence, particularly Estcourt. The position of a French-style Chief of Staff to take overall charge of the staff did not exist until Sir James Simpson was despatched in spring 1855. However, when Simpson duly arrived in the Crimea, he quickly found he was 'the fifth wheel of the coach, without power of working' as there was no mechanism or custom for a Chief of Staff, and he was well aware of the 'impotence of his position'. Furthermore, he, like Raglan, was too much an affable gentleman and unable to impose discipline upon the staff. Staff officer Anthony Sterling remarked 'war and amiability are not compatible' and that the Staff had become a 'cushy number' for well-connected officers; even General Airey agreed with this assessment. Thus, to many reform-minded officers the staff was full of 'malingerers and skulkers' which rendered it inefficient in its duties of managing the army.[14] Not only were Estcourt and Airey squabbling with one another, but there was friction between the Quartermaster General's Department and the commissariat. Deputy Commissary General William Drake wrote how:

> The whole of the Misery of the Army has been attributed to two things, the 1st Not knowing we were to Winter here & that when Lord Raglan thought of it he did not communicate with the Commissary General to procure supplies of every thing necessary for Winter & 2ndly The gross neglect of the Quarter Mast: General. Dept. in not making a road from this to the Camp, in fact that Dept. have proved quite incompetent & useless – There are some very gentlemanly clever fellows in it but it wants a head – In fact heads are very much wanted all through the Service here & very badly.[15]

British Supply

The Commissariat

The supply and transport of the British army was divided between two separate organisations. The Commissariat Department was an entirely civilian organisation and a part of the Treasury. It handled the supply of food, forage, fuel and other 'non-warlike stores' to the army in the field. It was not responsible for the supply of winter clothing or campaign equipment such as camp kettles, tents or 'warlike stores' including weapons and ammunition as that was within the purview of the ancient Board of Ordnance.

Commissary General Sir William Filder was Raglan's long-suffering head of the commissariat. A civilian employee of the Treasury, he was a conscientious and hard-working staff officer. (*Library of Congress*)

The Commissary General was perhaps the most important officer in Raglan's army. Frustratingly for Raglan, the 64-year-old Commissary General Sir William Filder (1789–1861) was a civilian employee of the Treasury and did not come under Raglan's command. All Raglan could do was to make 'suggestions' and despite the numerous unfair claims of incompetence levelled at Filder, particularly by the domestic press, he was unable to sack him.[16]

The commissariat, part of the Treasury from 1816 to 1854, provided land transport and non-military supplies such as food and forage whilst in the field. The commissariat was not a permanent body and had no fixed structure and had to be organised for every campaign; by 1854 the commissariat had not been actively engaged on campaign for four years. Nor was there any training provided for commissariat officers, as it was the Board of Ordnance that was responsible for rations and supply for troops on home service; it was only when troops went on foreign service that the commissariat took on that role. Indeed, Lord Raglan believed that (peacetime) training would have been unnecessary as the only training school an officer needed was the hard knocks of active campaigning. One senior commissariat officer opined that, 'For all practical purposes we cannot be said to have any commissariat' and whilst the system 'worked perfectly in peacetime' it was a miserable failure on campaign. Immediately prior to the declaration of war, the entire number of active commissariat officers <u>globally</u> was only 178. With the declaration of war Filder had been called out of retirement and put in charge of the forty-four commissariat officers to be despatched to the Crimea. Many of these commissariat officers were entirely new to their job, having been swiftly recruited and with little or no experience and not having undergone any specific training. Filder complained he was hampered from 'an insufficient establishment both of officers and subordinate employees' and that his force was entirely 'unsatisfactory'. He estimated he needed at least double the number of officers under his command to make his force effective. Even Sir Charles Trevelyan, Superintendent of the Commissariat Department 1840–54 and thus Filder's superior, thought 'the officers have no experience or real practical knowledge of their duties'.[17]

It is no wonder, then, that many letters home complain about commissariat staff being beloved of red tape and the pedantic, minutely detailed regulations. Despite the transfer of the commissariat from the Treasury to the new War Department in 1854, the commissariat was still under civilian rather than army control. The system of petty accounting and disproportionate reliance on book work was unchanged. These men were guardians of the public exchequer and every penny had to be accounted for. As W.N. Funnell has described, 'there were too many responsibilities, too many accounts . . . [and] too many masters' and too few commissaries. The strict regulations did not tolerate, or encourage, the use of initiative and punished any errors severely with any discrepancies being made good by the storekeeper or commissary themself. Thus, it is not surprising that in the field these inexperienced

Commissariat Clerk Alfred Robert Thompson (1822–96) was one of the hard-pressed commissariat staff in the Crimea. He is seen here photographed here by Roger Fenton in spring 1855. (*Library of Congress*)

commissaries fell back upon what they knew best and could rely on: regulations. Whilst designed to prevent fraud and provide a paper trail for everything and anything, these complex procedures were not at all suited to the exigencies of campaign. Everything had to be taken down in triplicate, signed, countersigned and approved before any stores could be drawn. No wonder many referred to it as the 'Circumlocution Office' of Charles Dickens.[18]

The Ordnance Department

The Board of Ordnance can be traced to 1455, and between then and 1855 when the board was finally dissolved and absorbed into the new War Department the officers and men of the Royal Engineers, Royal Artillery, Royal Sappers and Miners had not been responsible to the Commander-in-Chief at Horse Guards but rather the Master General of the Ordnance. Because the ordnance troops were not a part of the army, they therefore had their own parallel medical and hospital departments as well as Field Train. The duties of the Ordnance Department were wide and diverse extending from national defences and barrack building to the manufacture of weapons and training of artillery and Engineer officers. Even though it was responsible for the production and supply of 'warlike stores' including cannon, muskets, sabres and bayonets, as well as gunpowder, it simply did not have the capacity to do so and had to rely on civilian gun-founders to produce muskets, or cannon. In 1855, for example, the ordnance contracted for 90,000 new rifles but the Birmingham gun-founders could only produce a maximum of 50,000. The ordnance therefore had to buy rifles from manufacturers in Belgium and the United States, but supply from the latter was slowed when it was found that the wrong pattern had been sent. There were not enough of the new Minié rifled muskets, meaning that the 4th Infantry Division was still armed with old smooth-bore muskets from 1842. The Ordnance Department was also responsible for the supply of greatcoats, water bottles, tents and other campaign impedimenta, which had to be drawn from the Ordnance Storekeeper rather than the commissariat. The creation of the War Department, which absorbed both the commissariat and the Ordnance Department, simplified things but only on paper.

The Contract System of the British Army

The British army was fed and clothed through contracts with civilian suppliers, and in order to avoid the expense of having to maintain a warehouse and large stores of garments or equipment, a 'just in time' system was in place which was designed to issue uniform and equipment once per year on 1 April. Prior to 1833 the 'Agents of Supply' had been responsible for ensuring that food and clothing delivered by these civilian contractors were of sufficient quality and quantity, but in that year they were abolished as a cost-cutting measure and the individual contractors became responsible for quality control.

Uniform and equipment worn in the Crimea was governed by *Royal Warrant and Regulations regarding Army Service*, dated 1 July 1848. This detailed the articles to be provided, how often, their official lifespan, who was to pay for them and the money allowed to each colonel for clothing known as 'off-reckonings'. Clothing was provided at the expense of the colonel when they were entitled to 'off-reckonings' and to the public purse when they were not. Articles of clothing had to 'be furnished in strict conformity to patterns deposited at the Office of Military Boards'.[19] Charles James, in *A New and Enlarged Military Dictionary*, defines 'off-reckonings' as: 'A specific account . . . which exists between government and the colonels . . . for the clothing of the

In spring 1855 Roger Fenton photographed men of the 68th (Durham) Light Infantry, smartly turned out in regulation uniform – but sporting the softer undress forage cap in lieu of the hated 'chimney pot' shako. (*Library of Congress*)

men. This account is divided into two parts, viz.: gross off-reckonings, and net off-reckonings.'[20] Gross off-reckonings consisted of 'all the pay of the non-commission officers and private men, above the subsistence'. Net off-reckonings were: 'The produce of the gross off-reckonings, reserved for the clothing of the men, after the warrant deductions of one shilling in the pound and one day's pay of the whole regiment for the Chelsea hospital; and also the deduction of 2d in the pound for the [regimental] agent, made at the pay-office.'[21] The *United Service Magazine* declared that 'the whole system is false, and always open to abuse'. Colonels could make a fortune, it opined, through falsifying their accounts and through 'favouritism' toward specific contractors. Regiments were run like businesses to make money.[22] The system of off-reckonings was abolished in 1855.

Clothing items such as dress coats, waistcoats, trousers and boots (two pairs for sergeants) were issued on an annual basis; in the Guards a bearskin cap was issued every six years and for the Line and Rifles a shako was meant to last two years. More expensive cavalry uniforms, such as the braided dolmens and pelisses of the Hussars, were issued every two years and the latter's busbies every four.[23]

Greatcoats, blankets, water canteens, haversacks, mess tins and camp kettles were within the purview of the Board of Ordnance and remained the property of the board. They were issued on a campaign basis and were, in theory, to be returned at the campaign's close. The Board of Ordnance was also responsible for supplying tents. Clothing was supplied 'ready made up' unless specified otherwise by the colonel and was 'furnished in various sizes, adapted to men of different stature' and for those men of 'extraordinary dimensions' clothing was to be altered as necessary, the cost of the alterations (1s.) be 'defrayed equally' between the colonel and the wearer. In the cavalry, the men were to purchase their own undress jackets.[24] 'Necessaries' such as shirts, forage caps, white linen trousers, braces, knapsack and straps, shaving kit and mess tins as well as all the impedimenta to feed and groom horses were provided at the expense of the soldier out of stoppages from their pay.[25]

Whilst this system worked well enough in peace time, it simply could not meet demand or wartime conditions as there were no magazines or stores of new or spare clothing to issue. Thus, when the Ordnance

Men of the 47th Regiment in 'Winter Dress', as photographed by Fenton. Supplied largely thanks to philanthropic efforts on the home front during winter 1854–5, such clothing arrived in the Crimea in spring 1855 when it was of little use.

Department placed an order in June 1854 for winter clothing, and this went down with the steamer *Prince* when it sank in Balaklava Harbour during the November storm, the loss was irreplaceable.

British Army Transport

The declaration of war revealed further shortcomings: there was no military transport and it was hoped that, as in the Peninsular War, local waggoners and their teams could be dragooned into service, but this was wildly optimistic. The Royal Waggon Train had served with distinction during the Peninsular War and at Waterloo but in 1833, as a cost-cutting measure by a penny-pinching Parliament, it was disbanded. This meant that the army had no means of moving its stores and supplies, either at home or in the field; during the Chobham Camp of 1853 the army had to hire civilian carters and all the rations and supplies were transported daily from London. Despite the praise lavished by the press and a confident announcement by the Duke of Newcastle that the commissariat arrangements made for the Crimean Expedition were 'thorough', these were very ambitious statements.[26]

Military transport was 'absolutely essential' for an army on campaign, and, in the opinion of Lord Raglan and Generals Airey, Brown and Estcourt, was the only area in which the British commissariat failed. Quite simply, the British army was crippled through lack of transport, and by comparison with the French, was 'perfectly helpless', 'incapable of moving'.[27]

It had been expected by the British that the Turks would have helped them with their transport needs, rather like the Portuguese had during the Peninsular War: the British commissariat was disappointed when little or no aid was forthcoming, leaving them stranded.[28] Furthermore, Commissary General Filder blamed the lack of transport on the French, whom he believed had requisitioned all the usable horses and waggons in Turkey and Bulgaria, 'selfishly' leaving none for the British.[29] Sidney Herbert suggested that the lack of transport animals was due to the commissariat officers not having the common sense or the forethought to purchase sufficient animals at the start of the war. He also suggested that they failed to stable them properly or send them somewhere warmer when winter set in, as the French did. He was also critical of the failure to provide any remounts.[30] General Estcourt bitterly remarked that the lack of transport was due to Commissary General Filder being incapable of organising a military

Despite its proud history of service in the Peninsula and at Waterloo, the Royal Waggon Train was disbanded in 1833 leaving the British army without any militarised form of transport. Lack of any form of transport became one of the biggest scandals of the Crimean War.

train, and furthermore, refusing to buy remounts or fodder for the horses he had because of the cost.[31]

Not only did the British lack any proper transport with which to move its stores and supplies, it also had no means of evacuating and transporting the wounded. Field ambulances had been introduced into the French army by Baron Dominique Larrey (1766–1843) in 1793, and his writings became the standard text on battlefield surgery. An 'Ambulance Corps' had been hastily organised when war broke out using cumbersome four-wheeled ambulances designed by Dr Andrew Smith. They presented a stark contrast to Larrey's light, two-wheel 'flying ambulances' of forty years earlier. These ambulances had been quickly designed by Dr Smith in February 1854 and went out to the Crimea with the army without any formal testing or trials. Contrary to the wishes of Dr Smith, they had been fitted with gun-carriage wheels not the light wheels he had intended, which did little to improve their mobility.[32] Smith's ambulances were large, heavy vehicles which became easily bogged down, and, crucially, needed at least four strong horses to pull them, something which the British army lacked.[33] Many commentators were universal in their condemnation of these large, heavy vehicles.[34] De Lacy Evans 'regretted they were sent out at all' and General Estcourt was of a similar opinion.[35]

To make matters worse, the hastily scraped together Hospital Conveyance Corps proved to be an abject failure.[36] One British officer wrote that the Ambulance Corps was 'much talked of' but had proved to be completely inadequate for want of arrangement and forethought.[37] In addition, each infantry battalion and cavalry regiment had its own tented field hospital, under the care of a surgeon, assistant surgeon and hospital sergeant, the latter being responsible for the transportation of the tent and medical supplies. To staff the hospital, orderlies were drawn from amongst the other ranks, who were thought to be 'ill adapted to their employment'. They were appointed with no previous experience and were: 'Men who volunteer for the occupation merely to avoid other duties, or who are inflicted upon the hospital establishment from their uselessness elsewhere.'[38] These orderlies were often too few in number, and matters were made worse as when the orderlies had developed some semblance of competency and training they were often sent back to their regiments or re-deployed elsewhere.[39] The Medical

Designed by Dr Andrew Smith for service in the Crimea, these were the British army's first ambulances. Compared with French designs, they were large and cumbersome and not a conspicuous success.

Baron Dominique Larrey introduced light, two-wheel ambulances like these into French army service during the Napoleonic Wars. They were an efficient design capable of transporting several wounded men from the battlefield.

Staff Corps, formed in late spring 1855, was one of the responses to the unfolding drama in the Crimea. Formed from eight companies, with HQ at Chatham, sadly it 'did not prove of the highest order'.[40]

Remounts and Replacements

The horse was the army's prime mover, and thousands were needed not just for the cavalry but for the artillery in order to pull the guns and caissons as well as for the commissariat stores. The British army, however, lacked any form of remount system or service until 1887. This meant that it was entirely reliant upon the civilian horse trade and the breed, and type, of horse available for the domestic market. There were no specialist horse breeders or dealers for animals for military service. Because it was totally reliant upon the civilian horse trade, this meant that cavalry and artillery horses were those suited to the domestic market rather than the rigours of campaign life. By 1850 the British cavalry was mounted on thoroughbred or thoroughbred-cross racehorses, hunters or roadsters. Whilst these were 'well bred' and looked very handsome and were large and showy on parade, they were not known for their hardiness on campaign and required high-quality feed and care, something lacking in the field. The minority of army reformers considered British cavalry and artillery horses completely unsuited to the rigours of campaign, but theirs were lone voices in the wilderness.[41]

Whilst this system worked well enough in times of peace, during times of war horse breeders and dealers could charge what they wanted. The same was also true of forage.[42] The British army, however, would only pay a maximum of £30 for a heavy cavalry or draught horse. This meant that during times of war, in the words of the reform-minded Captain Louis Edward Nolan (1818–54) who headed the British Remount Expedition, the British cavalry was mounted on: 'The refuse left by a nation of horsemen, horsefancyers [sic] and jockeys and indeed our cavalry is mounted on what no one else will buy for any purpose whatever, such horses alone become available for the low price of a remount horse.'[43]

During the first few weeks of the Crimean War the price of horses doubled over night, so that a 'good' horse which had sold for £35–40 before war was declared was by April selling for £80–100. As one cavalry officer wryly noted, it may have been possible to purchase a 'good' horse for £40, but it was more by luck than anything else. This meant that the quality of horses available to purchase by the army would have declined due to the army being unable and unwilling to pay a higher price for its horseflesh.[44] Out in the Crimea, General Estcourt urged the formation of a Government Stud (as the French had) for the breeding and training of cavalry and artillery horses. He condemned the current British practice of buying big, good-looking horses for show and described such animals as fit only for a parade in Hyde Park, an opinion shared by the radical press.[45]

Lack of a remount system meant that in order to replace the massive equine losses in the Crimea, every single regiment on home service had to be dismounted so that their horses could be sent to the front. In order to procure sufficient animals on the open market, the army relaxed its purchase requirements so that horses as young as 3 years of age 'so long as they were of sufficient height' were permitted. The usual practice was to take horses at about 5 years of age, as horses younger than that were still growing; using such young horses was unnecessarily cruel. Regulations for the riders, too, were eased with 1in being knocked off the minimum height of 5ft 2½in, and the enlistment bounty increased from £4 to £6.[46]

Captain Nolan's remount expedition to Syria was not as successful as the government had hoped. Louis was ordered to purchase 250 horses, at least 14hh., for £16 a head for cavalry purposes. He was hampered by the restriction on the price paid for remount horses, paying an average of £35 per animal, and managed to acquire 292 horses and 7 mules in Turkey. The animals he procured, however, were small in stature,

'Field Train Royal Horse Artillery', photographed by Fenton. The horse was the prime mover of military transport, but horses – especially those for transport purposes – were in short supply in the Crimea. (*Library of Congress*)

14hh. or less, so whilst usable as cavalry remounts would have been unsuitable for draught purposes; animals above that height sold for several thousand francs which the army simply could not afford.[47]

The other problem the army faced was actually transporting these horses to the Crimea, either from Syria and Bulgaria or all the way from Britain, during which time they were expected to lose condition and losses were also anticipated from deaths at sea. Nolan noted in his journal that even transporting horses and means of transport from Varna to the Crimea was fraught with difficulties, meaning that horses and carts collected for commissariat purposes in Bulgaria were left behind:

> Our means of transport was insufficient and the Carts & horses collected for the use of the Army . . . had to be left behind at Varna. No Officer was allowed except those in command of Regiments & their Majors, and the officers of the General Staff alone were allowed two chargers. No horses could be had for the use of the Medical Department & when we first landed there were no means of getting the Medical Panniers along.[48]

What transport the army had managed to cobble together comprised 350 farm carts 'drawn by horses oxen & Dromedaries' which had been captured by the Army in the Crimea.[49]

Chapter 2

The French Army

In direct contrast to the struggling British, the French army appeared to have a better working model. Admiration of the French army by reform-minded British army officers, supported by the various 'special correspondents' at the front, became important in the discussion of the failures of British army logistics in the Crimea. Complaints in the press were verified and given local colour by the officers and men at the front in their letters home to family and friends. This was especially true during the first winter (1854–5), the flurry of complaints reaching London resulting in a political crisis in the new year of 1855. Aided by the emotional response to the logistics crisis in the Crimea, rational study of French army logistics was all the more important as it provided, in the opinion of the reformers, a model on which to base British army reforms.

The French High Command

In command of the French army was *Maréchal* Jacques Leroy de Saint-Arnaud, a career soldier who had joined the army aged 19 in 1817. Often considered a political puppet due to his role in Napoléon III's *coup d'état*, Saint-Arnaud was an excellent leader of men, showed sound tactical sense and usefully was fluent in at least four languages. Saint-Arnaud's understudy, François Certain Canrobert (1809–95), commanding I Corps, was a far more cautious commander but was loved by his men and well respected by the British. One letter-writer described how 'He looks over everything himself and is always on the *qui vive* . . . The British soldiers run out and cheer him.' In direct contrast with their allies, these senior French officers were a generation younger than their British counterparts, and all of them had seen recent active

Above left: *Maréchal* Jacques Leroy de Saint-Arnaud commanded the 'French Army of the East'. A career soldier, he showed keen tactical sense and was a charismatic leader of men who was beloved by those who served under him.

Above right: *Général* François Certain Canrobert – nick-named 'Bob Can't' by *Punch Magazine* – assumed command of the French forces following the death of Saint-Arnaud. He was a conscientious commander but one who was 'scared of the body bags', but the right man at the right time to keep the French army together during the winter of 1854–5.

service in French North Africa. The volatile Pierre Bosquet (1810–61) led II Corps whilst in *Général de Division* Louis-Michel Morris (1803–67) the cavalry had one of the foremost cavalry commanders of the period at their head. Whilst British commentators dismiss the presence of Prince Joseph-Napoléon Bonaparte (1822–91) in command of the 3e Division as nepotism, Prince Napoléon was beloved by the men under his command. Whereas Raglan and others held their rank thanks to being sufficiently wealthy to purchase a commission (and perhaps pay a little extra for a fashionable regiment or the Guards), more than half of all French officers had been promoted from the ranks. Promotion was based on seniority (one-third) and merit (two-thirds). At the time of

Above left: The fiery Pierre Bosquet led the French II Corps d'Armée. He was a critic of both Canrobert and Raglan. As a witness to the Charge of the Light Brigade at the Battle of Balaklava, he uttered the famous lines: '*C'est magnifique, mais ce n'est pas la guerre: c'est de la folie*' – 'It's magnificent, but it is not war! It is madness.' (*Library of Congress*)

Above right: *Lieutenant Colonel* Jean-Pierre Vico was the epitome of the French *Officier d'État Major*. He was attached to Lord Raglan's staff as a liaison officer. Vico was one of the most fashionable officers in the French army and famous for his 24in waist. (*Library of Congress*)

the Crimean War, half of all French officers came from army families, compared with only 22 per cent in the British army; less than 5 per cent came from a 'noble' or aristocratic background, although the cavalry attracted the highest number of 'nobles' (16 per cent of all officers) compared with 13 per cent of British colonels being from the peerage and 25 per cent from the landed gentry. French officers tended to be robustly bourgeois, and certainly not the 'officer and gentleman' of the British military tradition.[1] Thus to many British commentators, French officers were 'self-made men' and were considered to be professionals who did not owe their position to family status or wealth, having earned their rank. To reformers the staff was the last bastion of the 'jobbing' aristocracy and Raglan's appointment of family members as his ADCs merely confirmed that opinion.² Lieutenant Colonel Henry Percy of the Grenadier Guards wrote:

> The [French] Generals are not effete officials and inactive ignoramuses, but active hawk-eyed soldiers. Their generals don't have attacks of nerves, and are <u>always thinking of their men</u> and not of their own comforts . . . Their [Officers] are not the product of nepotism. Their Generals are selected from experience, and not because they get round the ear of some woman – or worse than that – some man degenerated with women . . . The French Officer has . . . faults, but he is a soldier.³

French officers had to study at the *École Militaire* in Paris at St Cyr for two years; the top graduates of each class being considered for admission to the prestigious *École d'Application d'État Major* (Staff College) for a further two years before spending the next four years doing 'on the job training' as a regimental staff officer attached to an infantry regiment (two years) and then a cavalry regiment (two years) before joining the *Corps d'État Major* (Staff Corps) with the rank of captain. Unlike the British staff, which was hastily organised for a campaign, the *Corps d'État Major* was a permanent military formation. Whilst in theory meritocratic and open to all sufficiently well-qualified graduates of St Cyr, it meant entrance was restricted to those who had been able to afford the best education in France; poorer families missed out. Furthermore, being the product of the 'top minds' of each annual class of officers, the French staff quite naturally viewed itself as the elite of the French officer corps – and were hated for it. Similarly, cavalry officers had to have attended their own special *école*, so too the artillery and Engineers (just as they did in Britain). Although not as egalitarian and free from patronage as many reformers in Britain would have hoped, the *Corps d'État Major* was thought to present a better working model than their own, upon which the British staff should be re-modelled.⁴

French Commissariat: The *Intendance Militaire*

Whereas the British commissariat had to be organised virtually from scratch for every campaign in which it was engaged, the French commissariat was a permanent organisation with a 'peace' and 'wartime' establishment. The *Intendance Militaire* was a quasi-military organisation and was responsible for feeding and clothing the army, medical services (*Service de Santé Militaire*), veterinary services (*Corps de Veterinaires*), military justice (*Justice Militaire*) and transportation needs

(*Train des Équipages*). Supporting the *Intendance* were the administrative troops (*Troupes d'Administration*) which provided all the butchers, bakers, carpenters, cooks and nurses which the army required. One similarity shared with the British commissariat was that *Intendants* were civilians in uniform and as a result there existed a similar friction and resentment between the army and the *Intendance*.[5] Unlike Raglan who had no control over his Commissary General, the *Intendance* was under Saint-Arnaud's command. Despite being civilians in uniform, General Estcourt wrote to Sidney Herbert in London in the mistaken impression that:

> Their Commissary-General is a *Military Man*. His department is a military organised department. He can build magazines, ovens, workshops etc etc. He can repair as well as fabricate. He can bake all the bread for the troops, and does so. He has a train of wagons . . . and mules . . . all moving with regularity, and supplying the wants of the Army without doubt or uncertainty.[6]

Sir Charles Trevelyan asserted that the *Intendance* was superior in every respect to the British commissariat because it was a wholly military organisation rather than a mix of civilian and military under several different department heads.[7] Many other commissariat officers, such as Commissary Generals Smith and Adams, were of the same opinion: the British commissariat should be organised like the French *Intendance*, a single organisation with a fixed establishment in both peace and wartime, under the jurisdiction of the commander-in-chief rather than the civilian treasury.[8]

Whereas a British commissariat official had received no formal training for their role, to become an *intendant* a French officer had to have reached the rank of captain and have served on regimental staff or show aptitude for the position. Whilst Captain Strange Jocelyn of the Grenadier Guards thought French commissariat officers were 'bred to the thing, and understand it, and not fine gentlemen', French officers did not share this opinion, often viewing *intendants* as obstructive and beloved of red tape. *Général* Bosquet believed that nothing would go right with the army until *Général* Canrobert had placed 'two gibbets either side of his tent, one with the body of an *intendant* and the other an officer of administration'. Nevertheless, British army reformers considered the *Intendance* far superior to their own system because it was a fixed organisation, its personnel were better trained and more importantly more numerous and its militarised means of transport not only existed but was in working order.[9]

French Transport: *Train des Équipages*

Because the British had only the most rudimentary transport establishment, it is little wonder that General Estcourt described the 'efficient' French *Train des Équipages* as 'working like clockwork'. It was: 'The most perfect baggage train, and carry off all their stores and baggage to their camps the moment they land.'[10] The *Train des Équipages* had been formed by Napoléon I in 1806, in far-reaching reforms of French army transport and supply. Initially part of the artillery, at the

A private of the *Train des Équipages* drawn by Lalaisse. The *Train des Équipages* was described by British observers as 'the most perfect baggage train . . . working like clockwork'.

The French army was able to clear the battlefield of wounded men thanks to their wheeled ambulances and teams of stretcher-bearers (*brancardiers*) and *infirmiers* (nurses), who were distinguished by their white epaulettes.

suggestion of *Maréchal* Soult in 1842, it was united with the *Intendance* so that a single organisation was responsible for stores and supply. The *Train des Équipages* was responsible for moving the army's stores, supplies and wounded. Ammunition was transported by a separate organisation, the *Train d'Artillerie*, and the Engineers had their own specialist transport (*Train du Parc du Génie*). By the time of the Crimean War, the *Train des Équipages* consisted of six squadrons (*escadrons*) in peace time and eight in times of war. Each *escadron* was composed of four companies each, of which three were 'war' companies and the fourth was the depot. Each squadron also had its own *petit état major* which included the veterinary, farrier, etc., and a '*peloton hors rang*' (headquarters platoon) which contained all the clerks, orderlies, workmen and specialist craftsmen such as the master saddle-makers, boot-makers and harness-makers, meaning each *escadron* was a self-contained, self-supporting entity of 200–250 men and upwards of 350 horses. The first company was responsible for wheeled transport, and the other two for packhorses and ambulance mules. One squadron was attached to each division of the army, and in times of war each company was to be doubled providing the cadre for a *'compagnie bis'*. Where even these supplementary (*'bis'*) companies were insufficient, a *Train Auxiliaire* could be formed from hired civilian drivers and vehicles who were placed under military discipline. They were fed and paid by the army, commanded by regular army officers and NCOs. In order to build and maintain the vehicles and pack saddles, etc. there were five companies of specialist *Ouvriers-Constructeurs*, with no comparable organisation in the British army.[11]

The French system of pack mules and in particular ambulance mules was universally admired by their British allies; the ambulance mules carried two patients each on a folding, iron litter which hooked on to a pack saddle and in case of inclemency there was a waterproof tilt. Each ambulance mule also carried medical supplies and the patients were tended to by nurses (*infirmiers*) who displayed 'great kindness and gentleness' to the wounded. To British reformers, the *infirmiers* presented a stark contrast to the worn-out Chelsea Pensioners of the Hospital Conveyance Corps, or the boys and bandsmen who traditionally collected and carried the wounded. Indeed, many in Britain could not understand why the British army had not, and apparently could not, organise an Ambulance Corps similar to that in France. The lack of an effective British Ambulance Corps would later result in the French transporting British wounded.[12] Not all French army medical supplies were carried by mules: they also used four-wheeled supply waggons or *caissons* to move bulkier supplies such as hospital tents, cooking utensils and all the paraphernalia for kitting out a field hospital.[13]

Horses and Mules

In terms of remounts and replacements, again thanks to the reforms of Napoléon I, the French army had an efficient system of remount depots: by the outbreak of the Crimean War there were ten remount depots (reduced to six in June 1854 as a cost-cutting measure) and fourteen branch depots. In addition, there was the *École de Cavalerie* at Saumur and every French cavalry officer and NCO had to attend a course of instruction here, as well as farriers and veterinarians, the latter also having to have studied at their own *école*, of which there were three across France. At Saumur, too, was a breeding stud (or *harras*) for cavalry horses. At each of the remount depots there were stallions who were 'put' to mares in the local vicinity, and the foals thus produced were to be offered to the army, but the owner was under no compulsion to do so. But they could never supply horses in sufficient quantity, so the army resorted to a form of horse conscription. All the horses in each municipality between 4 and 7 years of age were registered and once a year these horses were inspected for their suitability for military service. The inspecting officers then wrote the name of each animal, as well as their valuation, on a slip of paper and those slips were placed in a bag and shaken up. The names thus drawn were completely random, and if the owner accepted the price for their horse, they were paid at once – usually the price offered by the army was higher than that in the domestic market to help encourage the sale of horses to the army. In times of crises the army could also turn to the domestic horse market and simply requisition horses as well. The remount depots were not only concerned with providing horses, but riders too. Each remount depot mustered 274 men, of whom 200 were trained cavalrymen waiting to be sent to a regiment. Three provisional companies of 'remount cavalrymen' (*cavaliers de remont*) were formed by Imperial Decree in August 1854. In all there was a pool of 1,600 trained cavalrymen and several thousand trained remount horses immediately available upon mobilisation, something which the British army conspicuously lacked.[14] *Général* d'Allonville led a French remount expedition to Turkey and Syria but these were for riding rather than draught horses, and rather like Nolan, d'Allonville found that there were very few horses to be had of sufficient size and strength for draught purposes, so *in extremis* the French had to use bullocks and dromedaries to haul their supply waggons.[15] Finally, whilst British observers were critical of French cavalry and artillery horses simply because they were not showy or good-looking, it was precisely because they were not thoroughbred or thoroughbred-cross hunters and racehorses that French horses were far hardier on campaign and better able to survive on sparse rations. Furthermore, whilst British cavalry and artillery horses spent most of their time indoors in stables, French horses were usually put out to grass.[16] All this meant that the French were in a far superior position than the British to be able make good the losses in horses and riders, and this helps to explain why the French *Train* managed to keep struggling on through the dreadful Crimean winter of 1854–5.

Contract and Supply

The French army was supplied with clothing, equipment and food through a system of contracts (as the British army was) but also through the establishment of *Ateliers National* (national workshops) and an efficient system of magazines and supply depots – a legacy of France having a domestic barrack-building programme – which meant that it had thousands of pairs of boots, pairs of trousers and greatcoats waiting to be issued. As with the British system, clothing was issued on an annual basis. Uniform articles such as headdress,

French soldiers photographed by Fenton. Three Line infantrymen in company with a Zouave: the are dressed in their habitual campaign wear of *bonnet de police à visère* (alias kepi) and iron-grey *capote*, which would see little change until 1915. (*Library of Congress*)

coats, undress jackets and trousers were classified a *'habillement'* and provided by the government, whilst *'petit equipment'*, including boots, shirts and gaiters, was paid for by the men out of stoppages. As part of its system of checks and balances on the public purse, the French army issued incredibly detailed regulations for army clothing, describing the specific types of cloth each item was to be made from, the number of stitches per centimetre, how buttonholes were to be made, how each item was to be constructed, and included scaled patterns and written descriptions. Regulations also specified the cost of every single individual item. Whereas in Britain the individual contractor was responsible for quality control, in the French army *intendants* were responsible for ensuring uniform and equipment was made correctly and to the required standard before issue. As with the British army, the supply of weapons and ammunition as well as campaign equipment was also the responsibility of the artillery.

Whilst the French army appeared to be far better organised, fed and equipped than the British army, underneath this popular and positive perception lay a bitter truth. In reality the French army was struggling to feed and shelter its troops. As early as May 1854 *Maréchal* de Saint-Arnaud had written to Napoléon III:

> It is with some regret that I tell Your Majesty that we are neither constituted, nor in a state to make war . . . We cannot make war without bread, without shoes, without camp kettles, without mess-tins . . . I beg Your Majesty's pardon for these details, but they prove to the Emperor the difficulties which beset an army thrown 600 leagues from its positive resources.

Saint-Arnaud's Chief of Staff (*Chef d'État Major*), *Général* Comte Édouard de Martimprey, agreed '[we] do not have the means of transportation. The train is insufficient, the same for carrying the wounded. Our magazines are also empty . . .'.[17] Despite Saint-Arnaud writing complaints to his political superiors in Paris, the French War Ministry kept repeating that he was merely 'wrongly informed'. This situation was made worse when the French armies' entire stockpile of bread, hard-tack biscuit and all but twenty-seven of its mobile bread ovens were destroyed in a catastrophic fire at the port of Varna in August 1854. Luckily, the French were able to cobble together an additional twenty ovens from spares and damaged parts, but it meant that their ability to supply fresh bread to the men at the front was severely compromised. Not only was bread and biscuit destroyed in the fire, but the entire stock of winter tents. These were irreplaceable losses, which would lead to a terrible rate of attrition amongst French soldiers, many of them dying from malnutrition and exposure, freezing to death without any shelter other than their tiny *tentes d'abris*. Yet, despite this calamity, thanks to British newspapermen's reports the British army, and public at home, were, to quote French historian Alain Gouttman, operating under the 'cruel disillusion, and in its effect disastrous . . .' that the French army was far better equipped and able to take to the field than the British. As the present writer has described, W.H. Russell was the best 'Public Relations Guru the French army couldn't afford'.[18] Despite this skewed perception, both armies were equally ill-prepared for a winter campaign, a winter campaign that had never been envisaged when the invasion of the Crimea had been launched.

Chapter 3

Supplying the Troops in the Crimea

As discussed in earlier chapters, British soldiers were supplied with rations, clothing and campaign equipment by separate organisations, the most important of which – the commissariat – was a part of the civilian Treasury until December 1854. The commissariat was organised from scratch before each campaign, ranks being rapidly filled with newly appointed officials. Crucially, unlike the French army or even Russian army, there was no military transport system, the British army being reliant upon hiring civilian drivers, carts and draught animals.

Thus, the British army had landed in the Crimea with a woefully inadequate system of transport and supply. In order to feed and supply an army of 25,000 men there were only 49 commissariat officers and clerks:

Commissary General	1 (William Filder)
Deputy Commissary Generals	4
Assistant Commissary Generals	6
Deputy Assistant Commissary Generals	21
Commissariat Clerks	6
Acting Commissariat Clerks	3
Bookkeeper	1
Storekeeper	1
Stationery Clerk	1
Temporary Clerks	6

In addition, there was 'a large number of temporary clerks and interpreters employed by Commissary-General Filder on-the-spot'.

The Commissariat Camp of the British Third Division, a far cry from the chaos that existed down at the port of Balaklava.

Filder also had the power to 'employ as many qualified persons as he thought necessary'.[1] Filder's initial transport estimate had been for 3,000 local waggons or *arabas* and 5,000 mules. An *araba*, or *aroba*, is a large four wheeled Turkish waggon or cart, usually unsprung and often covered. Via Lord Stretford de Redcliffe, the British Ambassador in Constantinople, Filder approached the Turkish government for the purchase of mules; additional mules and 200 carts were acquired from Malta, and 500 mules came from Spain. A local Board of Officers was established to discuss the transport situation at the end of June 1855. However, nothing started to be organised until 16 July when it was ordered that a 'Corps of Drivers' would be formed from 'brigades' of 50 drivers and 150 pack-animals under a 'superintendent'; wheeled transport was formed by brigades of 20 *arabas* drawn by a pair of bullocks or buffaloes under the charge of a 'superintendent'. The drivers were to be 'natives' and officers Europeans; the 'troops were ordered to treat the natives kindly and see that the animals were not overworked'.[2]

In order to form his 'Corps of Drivers' to meet the transport needs of the army, Filder eventually collected 5,659 mules and horses, together with 1,000 Turkish *arabas* which were on hire at the depot in Varna for a period of 2 months. The Turkish drivers and their *arabas*, however, were under no form of military discipline and lacked proper supervision. They were thought to be 'dirty' and did not take good care of their animals. They were also prone to desert and sentries had to be placed over them to prevent their absconding. Furthermore, Filder was faced with the problem of the desertion of 'many of the drivers . . . who have hitherto been faithful to us' but were 'afraid to embark for an enemy's country'. The use of hired hands and vehicles was also not conducive to the overall efficiency of the transport situation. Despite these setbacks, a confident Filder wrote to his superiors at the Treasury in London that the Commissariat Transport was organised as well as that under the Duke of Wellington forty years earlier and was in a high state of efficiency.[3]

Despite having over 5,000 animals and at least 1,000 heavy waggons in the depot at Varna, none of them were sent with the army to invade the Crimea. This was due to lack of forage to feed them and the physical means of transporting them. Thus, out of an estimated 14,000 transport animals needed to convey the commissariat stores, ammunition and baggage for 25,000 men and horses, there were only 1,203 ammunition horses and as few as 70 horses and carts for the commissariat stores. In addition were the regimentally owned *bât* horses for the transport of regimental baggage and also officers' personal *bât* ponies deposed as follows:

Bât horses	842
Regimental horse for carrying water bags	134
Horses for carrying reserve ammunition	1,203
Horses for miscellaneous duties	98
TOTAL	2,277[4]

Between them, the French and British armies were estimated to need 28,000 horses for transport purposes alone. Within several days of landing in the Crimea, the British had managed to acquire approximately 300 horses and mules for transport purposes; Filder notes that within a fortnight of landing in the Crimea he had: 'Imported into the Crimea 216 carts, with 216 Spanish or Maltese mules . . . and 266 pack animals . . . There were at that time, in addition, in the employment of the Commissariat, 193 hired country wagons.'[5]

In October, the Depot of transport animals at Varna was broken up. Filder believed that he had sufficient horses, mules and waggons 'adequate for our transport purposes' in the Crimea. He wrote to Raglan requesting instructions as to what to do with the 'excess' baggage animals. Whether they should be sold, in which case they would have represented a dead-loss to the Treasury of £4 10s. per horse as 'many of them are not worth the cost of their maintenance during the winter', or whether to send them to Constantinople. In reply, Raglan thought it 'most prudent' to send the commissariat horses and mules 'excess to our present wants' to Constantinople in case future operations of the army required them.[6]

Despite all of Filder's careful preparations, no plan of campaign ever survives contact with the enemy; in this case, the state of the roads and the rapid exhaustion of local supplies of forage for the transport horses. In a lengthy memorandum dated 8 October 1854 he admitted that the issue of rations to the men, despite the opinion of the newspapermen, whilst late never actually failed. Sadly, what did fail was the supply of corn and hay to the cavalry which due to local shortages had been 'irregularly issued'. Fresh meat had initially been obtained locally but this source was soon exhausted which meant that Filder would have to import cattle into the Crimea from the depot at Varna some 294 miles away. Similarly, the forage for horses was nearly exhausted and that too would have to be imported. The sailing transports used by the commissariat had hitherto been used to convey transport animals into the Crimea, but from now on would also need to be used to carry fresh rations. Hay would have to be imported all the way from Britain. A frustrated Filder also reported how rations and supplies had been left abandoned and later pillaged:

> Considerable losses of Commissariat stores have occurred. Whenever an araba laden with ammunition broke down, it was deemed expedient by the military authorities, in consequence of the limited supply on shore, to place the ammunition on the provision wagons, and to leave the provisions on the ground. Many of our own wagons . . . broke down, or the animals exhausted by fatigue. The supplies on these occasions were necessarily abandoned.[7]

On 12 October Raglan issued his first instructions to Filder to prepare for a winter campaign by laying in a stock of fuel at Scutari, and early

Faced with a lack of suitable draft horses, the British army had to resort to using mules and even dromedaries to pull a motley collection of supply carts and wagons.

in November sent an officer to the southern shores of the Black Sea to purchase timber for making huts for the entire army. Ships were also sent to the ports of Sinope, Samsoon and Trebizond. Following the failure of the initial bombardment of Sebastopol on 17 October, *Général* Canrobert was convinced that the French army would be in for a lengthy winter siege and ordered his army to prepare for a winter campaign. Additional rations of wine, bread, rice and biscuit were issued, with those men working in the trenches receiving an extra ration of brandy. Conscious of the hard work endured by the transport horses and mules, he also ordered their rations increased. Extra rations of firewood were issued from November, so too were thick, hooded overcoats with a shoulder cape, dubbed '*Criméenes*' by the French soldiers. Yet, it was only after the Battle of Inkerman (5 November 1855) that Raglan instructed Filder to prepare the British army for wintering in the Crimea. A few days later Filder wrote to his superior in London, Sir Charles Trevelyan, that he was 'full of apprehensions as to our power of keeping this army supplied during the coming winter'. The harbour of Balaklava was overcrowded and festering; he was only able to 'land sufficient supplies to keep pace with the daily consumption of the troops' and no more. Even worse:

Sketched by French war artist Henri Durand-Brager, British soldiers struggle to move their heavy artillery and stores wagons up to the heights. Exhausted horses collapsed and died where they fell.

> To add to our difficulties, the road from the harbour to the camp, not being a made one, is impassable after heavy rains; our obstacle in these respects will increase as the winter comes. We shall have many more stores to convey than we hitherto had – fuel, for instance. In short, I am full of anxiety and dread on the subject.[8]

Filder was deeply concerned about the transport and supply situation. The Crimean Peninsula had basically been stripped bare of anything edible by man or horse. He was now forced to import into the Crimea not only all the hay and forage for the cavalry and transport horses, but also salt meat to make good the lack of fresh meat available locally. It was impractical to send loose hay and straw for the horses by sea and so this would have to be collected locally until 'compressed hay', which was much easier to transport, could be sent out. Salt meat and hard-tack biscuit had to be sent from Britain, the resulting rations often being considered inedible. There was also nothing to burn to boil water or heat food as every single tree had been felled and root grubbed up. Filder noted that whilst his existing supply system for biscuit had been sufficient at the start of the campaign, the increase in the ration of biscuit to those men working in the trenches to 1½lb per man per day amounted to an additional 1 million pounds of biscuit per month which placed additional burden on the already creaking supply system. Furthermore, it was also the duty of the commissariat to provide rations for the sailors who were working in the trenches and batteries rather than the navy so Filder found himself with a system that had barely coped with feeding the British army and was now having to feed not only sailors and Royal Marines but also some 8,000 Turkish troops.[9]

Often blamed for the catastrophe in the Crimea during the winter of 1854–5, William Filder had been concerned about the prospect of a winter campaign back in the summer with the army in Bulgaria. He sent a memorandum to Lord Raglan on 1 August 1854 enquiring whether it was intended 'that the army or any part of it, is to winter in this country', noting that it would be desirable 'that arrangements for lodging and provisioning the troops should be commenced without delay'. Filder thought it was imperative that:

> To construct, convenient to the barracks, ovens capable of baking bread for the probable number of troops to be cantoned at each station . . . it would be requisite that slaughter-houses and sheds, for the public transport animals belonging to the Commissariat Transport Service, should also be constructed . . . The provision of fuel is a matter of great importance. I do not apprehend there will be any difficulty . . . but it would take time . . . It might also be desirable that proper persons be sent from the Tower [Armoury], to repair the tents and camp equipage.[10]

An over-confident Raglan replied that he would 'speak to Mr Filder' but no action appears to have been taken. Filder wrote to Raglan again on 13 September requesting any instructions as to wintering in the Crimea and preparations he should make in the case of such a scenario. A confident Raglan replied, 'I cannot give these orders at present.' An increasingly exasperated Filder wrote to Raglan on 8 October about preparations for a winter campaign, especially regarding collecting firewood and creating depots for stores; Raglan replied four days later that Filder should start collecting firewood but no other preparations for a winter campaign were made.[11] On 13 September 1854 Filder wrote to London requesting 2,000 tons of hay, which was eventually delivered eight months later.[12] As late as 8 November 1854 Filder was writing to London expressing concern that no provision had been made for the army wintering in the Crimea, and faced with a scarcity of hay and forage for the horses, requesting that large stockpiles of hay and corn be set aside for the army.[13] Despite the urgency of the memorandum of 8 November, the wheels of bureaucracy turn slowly and the Treasury minuted on 28 November that the Board of Admiralty had taken steps to supply 3 months of rations for 40,000 men comprising 225,000lb coffee, 394,000lb sugar and 450,000lb of rice. The Board of Admiralty also agreed to supply rum and spirits, equating to 40,000 gallons per month. Finally, 1,000 tons of hay was to be sent out from Britain. In the meantime, Filder turned to modern technology to help feed the army. He requested the requisition of two steamers, one to be employed in the 'collection of wheat and manufacturing of flour', whilst the second was to be fitted out as a floating bakery 'for making bread or biscuit by machinery', but these would not arrive until October 1855, after the fall of Sevastopol.[14] The slow-turning wheels of bureaucracy at Horse Guards and in the corridors of power in London meant that when on 28 November 1854 Filder sent in a requisition for 3,000 tents, 100 hospital marquees as well as other items including 6,000 nosebags for horses, they were still the subject of lengthy correspondence in Whitehall in April 1855. So much for urgency.[15]

Everything the British army needed had to pass through the confined port of Balaklava. There were two roads out of the port; the Woronzoff Post Road, the only metalled road, had been lost to the Russians following the Battle of Balaklava (25 October 1854) so that the only other road available was that out to Kadikoi. This was not a metalled road, and had been made from compacted clay and gravel. As one Russian historian has noted, 'While the weather was dry, the Crimean roads were tolerable, and allowed [one] to walk 88 miles a day. But the autumn rains began, and they deteriorated.' The Russians were well aware of the poor state of the roads in the Crimea. Surgeon Nikolay Pirogov (1810–81), who worked near Sevastopol, wrote that in November 1854 it took two days to travel from Sevastopol to Simferopol (about 44 miles), and in December it took two weeks![16] General Airey had written to Sir John Burgoyne concerning the state of the roads on 11 November and on the following day 'the attention of the army was called generally as to the state of the road' and it was ordered to reduce the loads carried on it as much as possible. Filder also drew Raglan's attention to the state of the road and on 14 November it was belatedly decided to put working parties together to work on the road

The French army too was suffering from transport problems: here French troops accompany a convoy of commandeered Turkish *arabas*. Faced with a lack of horses and mules to pull them, the French army instead used bullocks and buffaloes – originally intended to have been food – to haul their stores wagons.

using Turkish troops as the British army lacked sufficient manpower to spare as fatigue parties on road-building duties. Sadly, these men quickly became sick and unable to perform their duties. Hired labour was resorted to but these men also soon fell ill and died. Meanwhile, the French *Corps du Génie* had been busy building a metalled road from their port at Kamiesh to their HQ. Thanks to the writings of W.H. Russell in *The Times*, the Russian army in Sevastopol was well aware of the hardships endured by the British.[17]

Solving the Transport Crisis in the Crimea

Filder had never been happy with the ad hoc system of using a heterogeneous mix of hired drivers and vehicles to move the commissariat stores. He was correct in his assertion that 'the Transport Service is indeed of the greatest importance' to the army, and as such should be taken if not under army control, then the commissariat and placed under much stricter discipline than hitherto. Whilst the hired Turkish and Maltese drivers and mules had proved just about 'adequate', the drivers were not accustomed to military discipline or the rigours of the work involved. Thus, only a properly 'militarised' transport system with British personnel was the way forward. This was the first such organisation in the British army since the disbanding of the Royal Waggon Corps twenty-two years earlier.

Filder showed remarkable energy in organising from scratch a formal 'Corps of Drivers' for the commissariat service, and achieving this whilst on campaign and working remotely from his political chiefs in far off London. On 11 November Filder formally recommended 'that a Corps of 350 drivers be raised for the Commissariat Transport Service'. Potential recruits were to be aged between 18 and 30 and paid 2s. 6d. per day with free rations. He thought the best source of recruits would be from Ireland. There was to be one 'sub-superintendent' per twenty men and one 'superintendent' per fifty men. The uniform was to consist of 'plain, short frock-coat, double-breasted and made of good stout grey or blue cloth, with trowsers of a uniform colour, and a forage cap'. Filder emphasised that the men recruited for the new Transport Service should be 'young, active, hardy men who have been accustomed to the care of horses'. Raglan agreed to this suggestion and forwarded it to his superiors in London. The Duke of Newcastle and the Treasury concurred and official sanction was given to raising this corps of drivers. Commissary General Hewetson was instructed on 28 November to immediately proceed to Ireland, where he was to liaise with the Lords Lieutenant and Sir Duncan McGregor, 'inspector-general of the constabulary force', for their assistance in recruiting. Each driver was to be equipped with 'an outfit of warm clothing' consisting of:

1 fur cap
1 pea-jacket
1 pair stout trousers
2 flannel shirts
3 pairs worsted socks
1 pair stout boots
1 neck-comforter
2 pairs gloves

The final organisation consisted of one 'superintendent' per hundred drivers, paid 5s. per day and one 'sub-superintendent' per fifty drivers paid 3s. 6d. per day. Uniforms and other clothing were to be procured by Commissary General Hewetson from civilian 'wholesale establishments' which were used to dealing with such large orders at a single time.[18] Next to be organised were horses, mules and vehicles. The existing two-wheel Maltese carts had been found to be 'wholly unsuited', not least because the wooden axles frequently broke and it was thought desirable that these be replaced with an iron axle. As a result, between 22 and 28 November Filder ordered 220 new two-wheel carts with iron axles be made in Britain 'and sent out as soon as possible'. The commissariat also required larger vehicles. Filder next wrote to Sir Charles requesting the immediate provision of thirty 'fourgons or covered waggons' and twenty 'open waggons, of the kind known in the artillery service as of the Flanders pattern, with four horses each'. Filder also recommended a study be made of the French army transport service, and the adoption of the type of stores waggon then in use by the French. He further requested 350 horses, standing at least 15.3hh. and not less than 15.2hh., be despatched to the Crimea for Britain's transport purposes.[19] But the wheels of government turn slowly and it would be a month until Filder's request was dealt with by the Treasury. An approach was made to the French army for either one of their transport waggons, or copies of the technical drawings so that they could be built in Britain. These French army *caissons* were multi-use vehicles and were capable of carrying either 1,200 rations of bread or 13 wounded men or could be fitted up as a mobile forge. They were drawn by four horses or mules and accompanied by two *soldats du train*. Despite the praise heaped on French transport arrangements by the British press, *Maréchal* Vaillant, the French Minister of War, informed the British that experiences in the Crimea had shown these *caissons* were not up to the task. They had been found to be too heavy and needed four strong horses to pull them. The French were therefore busy re-designing them to make them lighter and thus requiring fewer horses to move them. The French had found that small, two-wheel Maltese carts, or light 'Marseilles waggons' drawn by two horses, were far more suitable. The Marseilles waggons were stronger and heavier than the Maltese carts and thus more durable on campaign, and a considerable number were built in Paris for use in the Crimea. Another problem faced by the British was that the Royal Carriage Department at the Woolwich Arsenal was 'already fully occupied' and unable to build the required waggons. Thus, Trevelyan at the Treasury recommended that the new waggons be built by private firms who supplied them to the likes of Pickford & Co. One of the firms selected was that of William Crosskill of Beverley (he is discussed in more detail later) and this firm eventually supplied 3,000 waggons and carts for the Crimea.[20] Crosskill's patent waggon had won first prize at the Exeter Agricultural Show. These vehicles had iron axles, weighed about 3 tons and could be drawn by two horses. They were 'made light and strong', fitted with an 'efficient' hand brake, and constructed from mass-produced, standardised components. He also offered a one-horse cart 'mounted upon patent wheels and axles and manufactured by machinery'. Both types were available immediately from stock.[21]

Of the 350 horses which Filder had asked for, 250 were embarked upon the steamer *Jason* at Constantinople on 26 November, but when the captain 'had shipped that number he found that his vessel could take a hundred more' but the commissariat officer in charge of the operation decided to 'despatch the steamer without waiting till more [horses] could be brought up from the depot'. *Jason* landed her precious cargo on 16 December. In order that more horses could be ferried from Turkey and Bulgaria to the Crimea, on 11 December all the 'sailing horse transports' were put at Filder's disposal 'to bring up transport animals'. A last-minute change of plan saw these 'sailing horse transports' being sent to carry wood for fuel rather than convey the much-needed draught horses meaning Filder would still be short of vital horses for transport purposes.[22] Despite all of Filder's careful planning, he would be overtaken by events in the Crimea with the Allied camps being wrecked by a hurricane on 14 November.

The French *caissons* were useful multi-purpose vehicles which could be used to transport stores and materiel, wounded and sick soldiers or even fitted up as a mobile forge. French experience of them in the Crimea found them too heavy and needing four horses to pull them – animals that were in short supply.

The 'Great Storm' and its Aftermath

At the start of the campaign, the politicians in London had informed Lord Raglan that the Crimean Peninsula enjoyed 'one of the mildest and finest climates in the world' and thus he should not be worried by the prospect of a winter campaign. This proved to be hopelessly inaccurate intelligence.[23] The weather had become cold and wet in late October. Rain had begun falling heavily in November, turning the ground into mud and the mood in the Allied camps sullen. The men, wrote Colonel Bell, were 'in the trenches twenty-four hours at a time soaked to the skin'. They had no change of clothes and no means of drying themselves before trying to sleep wrapped in a soggy blanket and greatcoat in their tents. There was 'hardly a twig to boil their bit

The Allied camps were wrecked by a 'Great Storm' on 14 November 1854: here French troops struggle to prevent their tents from taking flight.

of salt pork.'[24] Everything was cheerless. Then on 14 November it was as if the Crimean Peninsula itself had joined the forces of the Tsar to eject the Allies from Sevastopol. After a damp night, at about 6am on the morning of 14 November the Allied camps were wrecked by a 'great storm'. One officer wrote how 'everything went whizz bang in less time than I have to tell you'. One officer of the 21st (Royal North British Fusiliers) wrote to his sister in Wakefield that this tempest:

> Commenced suddenly at 6 o'clock in the morning and lasted til 12 o'clock. The wind blowing from the south directly on this bold and rugged shore. We had 16 vessels outside the harbour, some of the finest transports and steamers in our service, amongst them the 'Prince', quite a new vessel, she broke in half right in the centre, and sunk at once with 150 souls on board and a valuable cargo. The effect of this disaster is most serious to our proceedings, and it has thrown gloom over us all. Every vessel had stores and warm clothing for our poor but brave soldiers, so you may imagine how it will throw us all back. When the storm had moderated, I climbed to the top of a cliff, and from thence beheld one of the most awful sights ever witnessed by man (a sketch of witch [sic] I enclose). I counted 14 wrecks. Such a sea! The waves nearly equalled the height of the mountain on which I stood. You may guess the effect of this on the encampment. In a moment every tent was blown away: some were carried into the air like parachutes, those who indulged in sleep without their clothes were left in a state of nudity . . . The Colonel was carried inside his tent, down the side of the mountain; he was much injured, and was immediately taken to the hospital.[25]

It was not just the British camp that was wrecked, but the French camp too. The French army was unable to make good the loss of so many tents; their entire stock of tents had been destroyed in a catastrophic fire at Varna in August, which also claimed all but twenty-seven of their mobile bread ovens. All the bread and biscuit destined to feed the army was also ruined, a loss from which the French army never really recovered. This meant that French soldiers had to make do with their tiny and entirely unsuitable two-man *tentes d'abris*, which were designed for use in North Africa and in the summer campaign season, and certainly not in winter. Many French soldiers looked on jealously at the British soldiers in their bell tents. One French officer estimated that French battalions were losing as many as ten men a night from exposure. All morning the wind and rain raged, but at about 2pm its force slackened and emerging from their hiding places, British and French soldiers attempted to make good the wreck of their camp. Towards 5pm it began to hail, later changing to heavy snow.

Out at sea the story was just as tragic. The steamer *Prince*, which was carrying the vital cargo of 40,000 winter uniforms, was lost with all but 6 of her 150 crew. Joining her were 7 other vessels as well as the French battleship *Henri Quatre* and the steamer *Pluton*, which were also carrying food and winter clothing. These losses were irreplaceable because of the contract system of supply. As described earlier, the contract system used by the British army was geared up to supply one pair of boots or coat per man per year or one greatcoat per man every three years, with all clothing produced on a 'just in time' system. Thus, there were no stores of emergency clothing for the increasingly ragged British soldiers. Conversely, the French had magazines full of boots, trousers and greatcoats, churned out by the thousand by their *Ateliers National* or produced by private companies such as Godillot of Paris, and could, in time, make good these losses.

Wrecked camps could be repaired, and uniforms improvised but it was the loss of provisions and forage for the army that proved by far the biggest disaster for man and animal alike.

Following the storm, there was equal devastation out at sea, with the irreplaceable loss of food and in particular winter clothing for both armies.

British Supply Losses, 14 November 1854[26]

Vessel	Biscuit (lb)	Salt Meat (lb)	Live Cattle	Live Sheep	Rum (gallons)	Rice (lb)	Coffee (lb)	Forage Corn (lb)	Hay (lb)
Wild Wave	249,984				3,217		11,200		
Progress								63,300	800,000
Wanderer								856,360	
Il Malti		74,880			4,783	73,986		196,512	
Peltoma	109,760								
Rip van Winkle			157						
Kenilworth				645					
Totals	359,744	74,880	157	645	8,000	73,986	11,200	1,116,172	800,000

The loss of *Progress* and *Wanderer* represented the loss of forage and hay for the cavalry, artillery and transport horses for twenty-one days. The army as a whole needed 580 tons of hay per month. Filder immediately (15 November) requested a 'fast steamer' be despatched 'for the conveyance of supplies as the losses placed the army in a critical condition with respect to its supply of provisions and forage'. Filder hoped that other vessels could be despatched to Turkey to make good the losses in food but the loss of hay and fodder was 'irreplaceable' as 'none could be obtained in Turkey' and had to be sent out from Britain. He communicated as such to the Treasury on 18 November and contracts were placed for the provision of 50,000lb of sulla and 100,000lb of straw during November and December. He was informed by Treasury officials in London that every fourteen days a fast ship would be sent out from Britain carrying 40,000lb of compressed hay, but this would prove somewhat optimistic.[27] *In extremis*, Raglan authorised Filder to buy hay and straw for the horses 'from any place he could' on the shores of the Black Sea.

Stores of fodder for the horses were rapidly becoming exhausted and the horses had to go on short rations. Other problems began to overtake Filder. Commissariat staff and store keepers at Balaklava were falling sick and, as Filder noted on 14 November, the day of the 'great storm', with the change in weather the roads were becoming impassable. He wrote on 3 December:

> Up to a very recent period the troops have been abundantly supplied with provisions of excellent biscuit, fresh meat, rum, and rice, but latterly, owing to a continuation of bad weather, many of our transport animals, exposed without shelter to wet and cold, have, in common with the horses of the artillery and cavalry, died, and the roads . . . having become impassable to wheeled carriages, and nearly so for pack animals when loaded.[28]

Filder reported ten days later that the roads had deteriorated to the extent that 'a waggon of the Royal Artillery with 10 horses was unable to reach the camp, having a load of only 1,400lbs of forage corn'. Draught horses and mules were put to work as pack animals, but so weakened were they from malnutrition and struggling through the mud '[this] has diminished our transport by two-thirds, besides the losses by death from exposure and fatigue, and the animals, moreover, now take two days to do what they formerly performed in one'.[29] Raglan and Airey had been down to Balaklava to see what could be done about improving the transport and shipping situation. Filder was informed that it would take 1,000 men 2 months to build a metalled road from the port to the camps on the heights. These were men Raglan simply could not spare as he had probably less than 11,000 men who were able to bear arms. Turkish troops and hired labour were brought in to improve the road, and even the French were asked for aid.[30]

Without any means of transport to bring up shot, shell and rations from the port of Balaklava, Raglan ordered the remaining cavalry horses be pressed into commissariat service. The Light Brigade had lost 472 of its 643 horses during the Battle of Balaklava (25 October), whilst the Heavy Brigade had lost 250 horses since landing in the Crimea. The Inniskilling Dragoons and the 1st Royal Dragoons had lost nearly 200 horses between them before even having landed in the Crimea. At the end of October 1854 Lord Lucan, commanding the Cavalry Division, estimated he had 1,752 horses available to him. Then, on 12 December, Lucan announced to the astonished Lieutenant Colonel Hodge (4th Dragoon Guards) and the other cavalry commanding officers that 'we are to give 500 horses a day to carry the provisions of the infantry to the front. We are to be carriers for the Commissariat Department.'[31] Hodge, one of the most conscientious cavalry officers in the Crimea, raged that 'when all our men's things are destroyed, saddlery gone, and horses killed, they will tell us that we have neglected our regiments. It is too dreadful to think about.' The 4th Dragoon Guards were only able to muster 130 horses, of which 60 were on commissariat duties. Of the remaining horses and men, parties had to be sent down to Balaklava on a daily basis to carry the regiment's own forage and stores on a gruelling 14-mile round trip. In this the 4th Dragoons were lucky: the Scots Greys could only muster forty horses.[32] The veterinary surgeon of the Inniskillings wrote home how his horses were 'very short on provender, their food consisting of scant and <u>bad</u> hay, or barley straw'. Opthalmia (a condition of the eye which can cause blindness) was a major problem amongst the horses of the Heavy Brigade, 'every horse was more or less affected', the only remedy being to wash out the horses' eyes daily with as clean water as could be found. The awful weather conditions and lack of proper time to care for the horses lead to a high rate of laminitis and hoof rot amongst the Light Brigade in particular. Cold, wet weather also led to rheumatism in many of the cavalry and transport horses. The veterinary surgeons were over worked, lacked an adequate supply of medicines or even the ability to care for the well horses let alone those that were sick. Even worse was an outbreak of glanders and farcy amongst those horses in the regimental sick lines and in the 'horse hospital'. All of the affected horses had to be destroyed along with all their bedding, tack, saddles, etc. to prevent the disease from spreading.[33] But as Sir Charles Trevelyan noted: 'It is not the business of the commissariat or a cavalry officer to be acquainted with horses, except so far as they are in charge of a transport establishment or regiment, and a very rough knowledge is sufficient for that.' Furthermore, 'as to feeding horses, all that it is necessary that they should understand is, not horses, but forage'.[34]

What was even more galling was to see the mounted French cavalry 'pass in front of Balaklava and reconnoitre the enemy' and to have the 'old enemy' 'carry our sick and wounded and even carry our shot and shell . . . to the front' and help mend the road down to Balaklava. The French were more than willing to lend a hand and went about their tasks cheerfully, with only a soupçon of grumbling. Lieutenant Colonel Hodge of the 4th Dragoon Guards even had to borrow French soldiers to help build stables to protect his horses from the worst of the Crimean weather.[35] These horses had to make the 14-mile daily round trip from the British camp on the heights down to Balaklava and back:

> The roads in a terrible state. We have now been three days without hay, and we certainly shall not get any after this tremendous rain. Two more horses died last night . . . I begin

Faced with a shortage of transport animals, Lord Raglan ordered the remaining cavalry horses to be pressed into service carry rations and stores from Baklava up to the camps on the heights.

to despair of things now . . . Our arrangements are all so bad that we cannot get orders or information . . . Wood is getting terribly scarce . . . The roads so bad I could hardly struggle thro' the mud, I found several commissariat carts broken down upon the road, one had a barrel of rum in it, which had been tapped and drunken infantry soldiers were lying about in every direction.[36]

The cavalry horses were starving and overworked; by Christmas Day 1854 the Light Brigade had only 170 horses, most of which (122) were seconded on commissariat duties. The Heavy Brigade had 549, of which 381 were on commissariat duties. In the first fortnight of December alone, some 142 horses had perished. General Scarlett, commanding the Heavy Brigade, wrote to Lord Raglan that his loss was not sustainable: 'The daily deaths from four to five horses in the regiments in my brigade. The decrease of effective horses is so rapid, that some regiments will be unable to furnish the required number of pack-horses and draw their own forage . . . and give the picket.'[37] The veterinary surgeon of the Inniskillings wrote home how many of the horses were suffering from sore backs; the horses had lost condition, meaning that the saddles no longer fitted properly which lead to them rubbing and causing sores. The heavy weight of the commissariat stores exacerbated the problem. Saddle blankets were wet through and could not be dried. Everything was wet and rotting. Two or three horses per regiment were dying in the horse lines on a daily basis. The poor creatures were becoming 'debilitated, and partly paralysed, so as to be scarcely able to walk' struggling to their feet and then collapsing, 'being half smothered among liquid mud' in which they died.[38]

An indignant Filder wrote to Raglan on 4 January 1855 describing how the transport situation had completely broken down. The transport and supply issues were of such concern 'that there seems to be reason to fear' that if the road was not repaired then he would not be able to supply the troops at the front:

> The road in many places is impassable and everywhere is covered with dirt, so that soldiers and civilian drivers, waiting for loads with pack animals, due to the lack of necessary equipment for the quick transfer of supplies, have to stand for many hours in the cold and damp knee-deep in the mud. In my opinion, this circumstance, more than any other, should be attributed to the great mortality and morbidity that began among the superintendents of warehouses and workers on the pier, and it can be assumed that this should cause a corresponding morbidity among the soldiers.

He concluded asking 'why were not the roads built?' as soon as the siege began back in October 1854.

By mid-January 1855 Lucan had under his command only 500 horses: 60 per cent of the cavalry horses had perished since the start of December, and in a letter to Lord Raglan he expected to lose all his horses by the end of the month:

> The fearful consequence to the cavalry of having to continue in the discharge . . . of duties so totally foreign to their profession . . . Since the 12th December, no less than 426 horses have died . . . A cessation of these duties . . . might yet . . . save 400 or 500 more.

A lone British cavalryman leads his mount through the snow, carrying essential materials for building wooden barrack huts and stables. More British cavalry horses died performing these arduous duties than in battle.

Sadly, there was no respite for the over-worked and ever-diminishing numbers of cavalry horses. The horses were so weak that they could not even 'struggle up the hill with the sacks of corn. The condition of everything is awful.' The horses were standing knee-deep in mud and the men were not much better with hardly any time to sleep or wash, their uniforms reduced to 'mud stained rags'.[39] Lord Henry Hardinge, General Commanding-in-Chief at Horse Guards, wrote to Lucan on 9 February 1855, 'I don't expect you will have *any* horses of Cavalry fit for Service.'[40]

Something had to be done: the men in the trenches were freezing and starving to death from lack of proper shelter and food for want of the ability to carry rations and supplies to the front. There was a national outcry in the press, led by *The Times* of London, which reached a climax in January 1855 resulting in the appointment of the Roebuck Commission and the collapse of Lord Aberdeen's fragile coalition government. Having to be seen to be 'doing something', the new government sent out Sir John McNeill and Colonel Alexander

French and British soldiers sharing a scrap of food together in the trenches.

Tulloch to 'inquire into the whole arrangement and management of the Commissariat Department' and in February the government sent out a 'Sanitary Commission' to study the hospitals, medical services and health of the army. McNeill and Tulloch were to have 'authority to carry into execution immediately any change or arrangement they might think essential'. Finally, a Board of General Officers – later to be described as the 'white washing board' as it exonerated all concerned – was established so that 'justice be done to all parties'. The commissariat did not escape censure; McNeill and Tulloch thought it had been 'dilatory' and had made 'insufficient arrangements' and questioned the competency of Filder and Trevelyan. However, the lack of preparations for wintering in the Crimea, as discussed above, was something that Filder had been concerned about since August. The loss of clothing supplies and provisions during the 'Great Storm' was something that no one could have predicted but did reveal the shortcomings of the 'just in time' system of supply. Filder took the blame for the failure of the commissariat, yet he could not act without orders from Raglan, which, when they came, did not materialise until late in the campaign season.[41]

In London a commission was also formed to study 'Land Transport'; from Horse Guards Lord Hardinge wrote to General Richard Airey that he could not 'anticipate any improvements by the proposed changes unless Departments such as the Land Transport and Ambulances imitation [sic] the French'.⁴² More to the point, what the army needed was root and branch reform, as outlined by Lord Panmure (1801–74), the new Secretary of State for War:

1. A staff of competent General Officers.
2. A Staff Corps to train subordinate officers to the duties of the field.
3. Masses of troops to be provisioned, moved, and accustomed to life of camp, by which a combination of all arms may be secured.
4. A proper system for the conveyance of materiel and baggage.
5. The means of easy and immediate transport for sick and wounded.
6. Well-arranged means of communication between our Army abroad and the authorities at home.
7. An efficient Commissariat, which shall have a certain number of its officers employed in India with the large bodies of troops there, and where alone they can learn the science of collecting supplies of all sorts.
8. A well-appointed corps of artillery.
9. A siege-train suited to an army of 30,000 men, and which can be increased as occasion may require.
10. A good corps of Engineers.⁴³

Many of Panmure's suggestions were based on observation of the French *méthode*, including having a permanent staff corps which was responsible for training its subordinates, organising regular 'camps of instruction' and having commissaries who had previously served with the army and had gained direct experience in the field.⁴⁴ General Estcourt agreed: the British commissariat and transport should be modelled *exactly* on the French system; what was needed was a militarised system with 'mules and waggons organised into companies with captains, subs and sous-officers'.⁴⁵ In Estcourt's opinion, military transport: 'Should be taken entirely out of the hands of the Commissariat and given to the army, [it] should be organised after the manner of the French and have an active, intelligent officer at its head.'⁴⁶

So impressed were the British with the *Train des Équipages* that Lord Raglan had requested the French liaison officer at British HQ *Chef d'Escadron* Jean-Pierre Vico to prepare a report on French army transport in summer 1854, and Major General Knollys was sent to France to study the French *Intendance* and transport in 1855. A third report on French land transport and commissaries was requested from General Sir Hugh Rose, liaison at French HQ, by General Codrington in November 1855 which was published in January 1856. Yet none of these formal studies had any impact on the formation of the Land Transport Corps (Chapter 7) in December 1854. The Land Transport Corps was 'entirely new in the English service' and destined to 'undertake the whole of the transport for the Army, and will be carried out on a much greater scale than the Royal Waggon train was under the Duke of Wellington'.[47]

Whilst the Horse Guards made studies of the French army and wrote reports, the men at the front were dying. Lieutenant Thomas Bell wrote how British soldiers had to rely on the generosity of their Allies: 'Our own Government has managed everything in a very *bad* way indeed. The Commissariat is disgracefully conducted, and it was necessary to borrow . . . from the French. The French have managed everything perfectly well – and are a much effective force indeed . . . We carry all our necessaries on our backs.'[48]

Bridget France, wife of Private James France of the Durham Light Infantry, wrote home describing how:

> Our camp ground . . . [is in] a state resembling very much a ploughed field, and you cannot move a dozen yards without being up to the ankles in mud – this, of course, the men cannot help carrying with them into their tents, which besides, often admits the water, and then are we not in a nice pickle? Picture to yourself for your bed a mud floor with about two inches of soft mud, your bedding consisting of your ordinary clothing, and two blankets. The men, however, in this case, generally scrape the soft part off, which is but little improvement, as the ground is so damp that to sleep with any warmth is impossible, and thus you perceive what a deadly enemy we have in wet weather. We hear numerous reports and accounts of wooden houses to be sent for accommodation; but these, like a great many other things, will, I think, arrive too late to be of that service they would have been had they been thought of two months ago. They would have saved the lives of many hundreds who now lay cold in their graves . . . and where many more will surely rest if not better covering is provided than canvass.

Because the transport horses were dead and dying, and the roads impassable to wheeled transport, detachments from every regiment were sent down to Balaklava to manhandle rations and supplies from the port up to the tented lines on the Sapoune Heights. Robert Crawford (28th Foot) wrote to his mother in Wakefield, describing this exhausting experience:

> We are lying out in tents amidst frost and snow, and you would not be surprised to see six or seven dead in the morning. You are out of bed six nights out of the seven, and we are every second night on the trenches, and during the 12 hours we are on the trenches we have to lie on our bellies – if we did not do that we would be shot by the Russians; they are firing from their batteries all

Conditions in the trenches during the winter of 1854–5 were appalling; this sketch by Durand-Brager shows French soldiers wading through flooded trenches.

day and night. We have to go 10 miles to a place called Baliklava and 10 miles back for our rations, and the roads is so bad you would be up to your neck in muck. The men is dying like rotten sheep . . . We are very badly provided for as British soldiers out in the Crimea.[49]

In stark contrast were the French who seemed well-provisioned, cheerful and who made gifts of bread and wine to the Allies and often shared their meals with British soldiers. The French also supplied their allies with tins of *'buillon de boeuf'* (the canning process had been invented in 1810 but the tin-opener only in 1855!), which was transliterated by British soldiers as 'Bully Beef'. Malnutrition, exposure and over work soon led to a debilitating rate of sickness, putting massive strain on the medical services.

With the British army in crisis, the famous railway contractor (and richest man in England) Sir Samuel Morton Peto MP approached the Duke of Newcastle with the idea of building a railway from Balaklava to the camps on the heights.

Chapter 4

The Military and Railways

By the outbreak of the Crimean War in spring 1854, Britain's railway network covered some 6,621 miles and transported an estimated 100 million passengers each year. The railways of France had a much

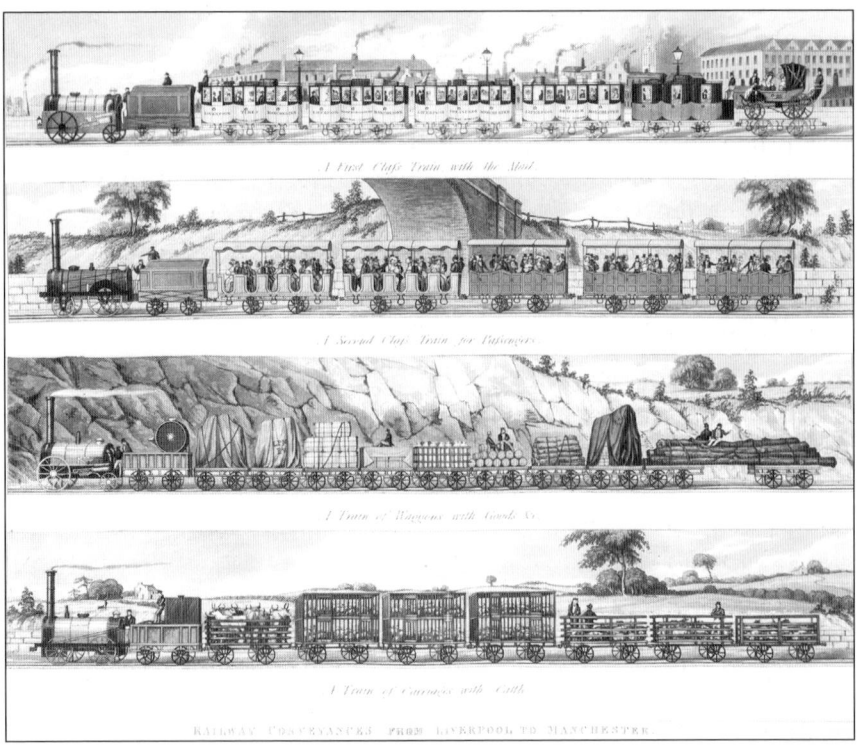

The Liverpool & Manchester Railway had opened on 15 September 1830 as the first, modern, main-line railway. As such it was also the first railway to carry troops in 1832.

slower start largely due to the political situation which existed before 1830. During the reign of Louis-Phillipe (1773–1850, r. 1830–48), thanks to the policies of French politicians such as François *'enrichez-vous'* Guizot (1787–1874) and Adolphe Thiers (1797–1877), the system rapidly expanded. This was especially true under Napoléon III, who, it was said during his reign, never visited a city, town or village without opening a railway station. By 1852 the French network had grown rapidly to 2,400 miles.[1] Whereas the British railway network consisted of dozens of competing companies, in France all the various smaller companies were united within six 'great' companies in 1855;[2] this presaged a similar event in Britain during the 1920s with the formation of the 'Big Four' (LNER, LMS, GWR, Southern). Whilst the British railway system had grown somewhat haphazardly and with little regulation or central planning, in France the role of the government was to identify key strategic routes, and then invite companies to compete for a concession to build and operate that line. This meant that the French system was more compact, had less duplication of routes and was far more geared toward not just economic but also military interest. Playing catch up in terms of railway development, Russia had a mere 310 miles of railway by 1850. In what would be an industrial war, Britain was able to produce 3,119 metric tons of pig iron per year, France 771 tons and Russia just 213. In the technological conflict that was to come, the Allies clearly had a decisive advantage clearly capable of out-producing Russia.[3]

The British Army and Railways

Whilst the Duke of Wellington is popularly considered to have opposed railways, as Master General of the Ordnance he was in favour of the construction of railways in Canada in 1819. He wrote that: 'the object of a military communication can be insured by the assistance of railways for the necessary portages' both as a means of defence, but also improving internal communications.[4] His later objections to the early public railways was perhaps not only because he disliked the idea of the masses moving about, but also from having witnessed the fatal accident to William Huskisson MP at the opening of the Liverpool & Manchester Railway on 15 September 1830. Yet, as early as 30 October 1830 the L&M board agreed to carry soldiers for 2*s*. 6*d*. each, the journey between Liverpool and Manchester taking 2 hours instead of two days marching to cover the 30 miles between the two towns. The government thought this charge excessive, however, and the rate was lowered to

2s. 2d. whilst the rate for officers was 6s. – first-class, of course. Of the 'women belonging to the regiment' – of whom ten were allowed for every hundred men – up to a total of ten travelled for free. The railway refused to carry gunpowder, but regimental baggage was carried at 8s. per ton. The first 600 soldiers were carried by train from Warrington to Liverpool in June 1832. A War Office circular issued in 1841 reduced fares to just over 2d. and 1d. for officers and men and officers were granted 2cwt of luggage free of charge. Military horses were carried at 4d. per mile.[5] Increasingly railways came to be seen as part of the 'forces of order' enabling large groups of soldiers to be moved around the country to help put down Chartist agitations and the 'Plug Riots' of the 1840s. General Sir Charles Napier recognised the value of the railways in rapidly moving large quantities of soldiers to centres of public disorder, and recommended housing troops close to railway stations to help facilitate this. The Regulation of Railways Act of 1842 compelled the various railway companies to carry soldiers at fixed charges to facilitate this. In 1844 Sir James Willoughby Gordon, the Quartermaster General, estimated a battalion of 900 men could be sent from London to Manchester in case of emergency in 9 hours instead of several days' forced marches. Thus, the railways added 'immeasurably' to the power which could be exerted by the government. A lesson quickly learned in Continental Europe. The usefulness of railways for 'home defence'

Troops departing from Euston to help put down civil unrest in Birmingham and the 'northern manufacturing districts', August 1842.

was also noted by the Duke of Wellington, who in 1845 stated that rail connections were of 'pivotal importance' in case of invasion. Indeed, the duke was one of several officers, including Sir John Burgoyne, who believed the railways had a vital function in transporting troops, munitions and materiel in case of invasion, or upon mobilisation. Burgoyne argued for a 'mobile reserve' to be maintained, which could be quickly rushed by train to any invasion point on the southern coast. Whilst Burgoyne thought it was cost-effective to transport infantry and even artillery by rail, cavalry was a different matter entirely. Similarly, the use of railways to transport men and materiel was received favourably by the Board of Ordnance. Thus, by the time of the Crimean War, Britain's military authorities had long seen the advantage of using railways to move large numbers of men and munitions in case of emergency.[6]

The French Army and Railways

At the same time in France the military was investigating the possibilities of transporting troops by rail. Whereas the railways of Britain had grown organically without governmental control, the French railways were subject to far closer scrutiny with routes of strategic importance – particularly those toward the eastern frontier and major garrisons such as Lille, Metz, Strasbourg and Lyon – being identified and then awarded concessions to build them under the supervision of the Minister of Bridges and Roads and its engineers (*Ingénieurs des Ponts et Chaussées*). The first French soldiers had been transported by rail on the *Chemin de Fer de Paris à Versailles* in 1837, and during October 1840 an entire regiment of infantry (1,500 men) was moved by train from Paris to Versailles to take part in a review. The 12-mile journey was accomplished in 29 minutes and the soldiers returned to barracks on the same afternoon.[7] To achieve this thirty-six carriages and two locomotives were required.[8] Indeed, by the law of 20 March 1835 the French government had reserved the right to 'direct troops and military materiel' by railway which in time of war was to be immediately put to government use; the law of 1842 which established a national rail network for France compelled all railway companies to carry soldiers at rates determined by the government.

The Napoleonic veteran *Maréchal* Soult (1769–1851), as French Minister of War, appreciated the strategic value of moving troops quickly by rail both in the case of mobilisation and civil unrest: in Britain troops had been sent by train to Birmingham in 1842 to quell

Railways became a symbol of and force of order and reinforced existing societal mores. This splendid re-enactment of travel by train in France *c.* 1860 clearly emphasises the difference between first-, second- and third-class travel.

the Birmingham Riots and other disturbances in the 'manufacturing districts'. Whilst it caused public outrage at the time, the lesson was quickly learned, especially by observers in France who saw the railways as a means of preventing revolution.[9] As early as 1843 *Général* Jean-Jacques Pelet (1777–1858), head of the French *Corps d'État Major*, outlined a plan for mobilisation which utilised the railways and the railway telegraph. This was followed a few years later by *Capitaine* Raymond de Coynart (1806–80), a staff officer serving as part of the central *Depot de la Guerre* (the French army's central think-tank), producing several forward-thinking studies during the mid-1840s on moving soldiers by rail. This included troop-carrying capacity and loading times, all supported by practical tests. This was largely in response to a German essay published in 1842 and translated into French in 1844 which showed that Germany's rail network far outstripped that of France at the time and thus Prussia could send troops to the front line faster than France.[10] Despite dire warnings of the effect of a fire on the train, of a boiler explosion, and of artillery fire on a locomotive, Coynart's 1846 study was a perceptive piece of staff work. Coynart concluded that a division of 20,000 men together with its artillery and cavalry could be rapidly moved to where it was needed by rail, being able to cover 200 miles in 24 hours – hitherto soldiers could march up to 15 miles per day. Furthermore, stores and supplies could be moved with the same ease. An infantry battalion of 800 men needed 20 passenger carriages, 4 horseboxes and 4 waggons for the baggage. Practical tests showed that a battery of 6 6-pdr guns required 36 waggons divided into 3 trains to move it, whilst a battery of 12-pdrs required the same number of waggons but broken down into 4 trains. Cavalry could also be effectively transported but at considerable extra cost and there were doubts over the well-being of the horses being cooped up for so long. An experiment was made in February 1847 when a squadron of the *7e Lanciers* (134 other ranks and 125 horses) was moved by the *Chemin de Fer du Nord* from Paris to Valenciennes on the Belgian border in a train of 32 vehicles pulled by 2 locomotives: 4 third-class carriages for the other ranks, 1 first-class carriage for the officers, 20 cattle waggons for the horses of the other ranks, 2 horseboxes for the officers' horses and 5 baggage cars. The horses arrived fresh and 'in the best condition' and had thus avoided a fatiguing 131-mile trek. It was concluded that the 'problem [of moving cavalry by rail] is completely resolved'. But yet in March 1847 a commission was established, presided over by *Colonel* Michel Louis Ney (1804–54), Duc d'Elchingen – the eldest son of Napoleonic hero *Maréchal* Michel Ney (1769–1815) – to 'examine the problem of transport cavalry by railway'. It reported in May 1847 noting the success of the February experiment, but did add that whilst the cattle waggons used by the *Nord* were acceptable for light cavalry horses, they were too small and cramped for heavy cavalry and artillery horses and recommended a new larger pattern be made. The railway companies preferred the easier, and cheaper, solution of carrying fewer heavy cavalry horses per waggon, and running either longer or more trains. The French army now accepted that cavalry could be moved as easily as infantry and artillery by rail, and the movement of French soldiers by rail became a key part of any mobilisation strategy or dealing with periods of civil unrest.[11] At the same time, there was considerable debate in the *Journal des Chemins de Fer* about the role to be played by the railways in any future war, and also the use of soldiers to actually build the French railways. Soldiers had been used to build the Paris–St Germain line and on road and bridge building in the mid-1830s largely as a means of bypassing labour disputes, but by the 1840s thoughts were turning to making the army 'useful to the public good' and the national interest.[12] Railways were seen in France as an instrument of nationalism and building up the state by bringing it closer together with improved transportation links. The railways were also increasingly viewed as a means for maintaining order, the railways coming to the fore during the 1848 revolutions in Paris and Berlin. The use of railways to transport troops grew in the later 1840s; the Prussians were the first to use railways to transport soldiers and materiel in a time of war during the Prussian-Danish War of 1848–51, and the Austrians moved 75,000 men, 8,000 horses and 1,000 vehicles by train to the Silesian frontier in the winter of 1850.[13] The Prussian general staff was the first in Europe to develop written instructions for the use of railways for military purposes during the same year.

Despite her tiny railway network, Russia had not been idle. The first Russian troops were moved by rail in July 1848. Following the opening of the St Petersburg–Kolpio section of the St Petersburg–Moscow Railway, 250 recruits were transported to St Petersburg. This having proved successful, in August three regiments of the 1st Grenadier Division numbering 7,500 men were moved by rail from St Petersburg to Kolpio. The Russians watched developments in Prussia and the Austro-Hungarian Empire closely and between 1852 and 1856 the Russian army moved over 800,000 men, 58,000 horses and 11,000 stores waggons, etc. by rail.[14]

Railways and Mobilisation

Thus, by the time of the Crimean War, the railways had come to assume a significance in maintaining public order. Furthermore, the railways were becoming a part of any mobilisation plan. Indeed, during the Crimean War the railways came to prominence in transporting troops to their point of embarkation, with troop trains being run in Britain and France. In March 1854, in order to avoid an arduous sea voyage, with foresight the French government proposed transporting the British Cavalry Division across France from its northern ports to Marseilles by rail via the newly opened *Chemin de Fer de Paris à Lyons et à la Meditérannée*. This novel idea of Napoléon III came as something of a surprise to the *Chemin de Fer du Nord* upon which the Cavalry Division would make its initial journey from the Channel ports to Paris, as it did not possess sufficient horseboxes or cattle waggons. Eventually a thousand such vehicles were collected in and around Calais, and trains were to be despatched carrying 150 men and horses 'day and night' to Paris and thence Marseilles. The ambitious project failed to come to fruition due to 'difficulties over transport' and worries over the reception of English troops in some rural parts of France. It was, however, a very bold and forward-thinking move and had it been successful it would have saved the lives of 204 British cavalry horses that died on the sea voyage.[15] The French railways played a major role in transporting troops and materiel to Marseilles for the Crimean Expedition, and to Calais and Boulogne for the Baltic Campaign. The *Chemin de Fer du Nord* carried an estimated 40,000 troops to the Camp of Boulogne in only five weeks in summer 1854. Special drills were held to expedite the loading of such troop trains: a 1,000-strong infantry battalion being able to board a waiting train in just 12 minutes whilst a squadron of cavalry took upwards of half an hour.[16] In just a quarter of a century following the inception of the first main-line railway in September 1830, and despite initial mistrust, the military authorities across Europe had embraced the railway as a rapid means of moving troops and materiel during times of peace, internal strife and war. But, so far, a railway had yet to be built in a war zone itself. That was to change with the Grand Crimean Central Railway.

Chapter 5

Building the Balaklava Railway

The idea of using a railway to transport military stores and materiel was not new when it was made by Sir Joseph Paxton (1803–65) of Crystal Palace fame in May 1854. Paxton had suggested the formation of a 'Civil Engineering Corps' to build a railway in the Crimea; Brunel famously quipped in 1855 that he and a team of navvies could have taken Sebastopol far quicker, and with considerably less loss of life, than the army. This was an idea quickly taken up by others including the influential newspaper *The Times*. Through organisations such as the 'Administrative Reform Association', many members of the middle class believed the country – and the army – would be much better managed if they were run on the lines of business. *The Times* newspaper, which best represented this growing class, had been outraged at the appointment of Lord Raglan to command in the Crimea as well as the selection of his personal staff from family members. In the opinion of these largely middle-class commentators and reformers, the army was perceived to be the last bastion of 'the jobbing aristocracy' and that it would be much better organised and managed by 'men of business'. The national public outcry following the publication of the harrowing dispatches of newspapermen like W.H. Russell (*The Times*) or Lawrence Godkin (*Daily News*), who of course were writing with a reform-minded agenda, added a sense of outraged urgency to the demands of army reform. Thus the suggestion by Paxton and later by Peto, Brassey and Betts to build, at cost, a railway in the Crimea in order to solve the muddle the 'aristocratic' army had got itself into was part of this clamour for reform.[1]

In order to extract the army from this mess, on Thursday, 23 November 1854, only one day after returning from Denmark to discuss a railway contract, Peto met with his business partners Thomas Brassey and

Edward Betts to discuss his 'great idea' of building a railway, at cost, in the Crimea. In fact, his was not the only proposal to build a railway or tramway in the Crimea; the Governor of Malta, Sir William Reid, also put forward the idea of constructing a railway to solve the transport crisis. Nor would it be the only railway built to serve the British army during the Crimean War as a short railway was built to serve Brunel's iron hospital at Renkioi.[2] At the Woolwich Arsenal, the Royal Engineers were also studying the portable railway system developed by William Crosskill (1800–88), a Beverley ironfounder, in December 1854. His system was intended for agricultural use and consisted of pre-fabricated narrow gauge (2ft 6in) panels of track using set geometry for curves and

Sir Samuel Morton Peto MP, the richest man in England and progenitor of the Balaklava Railway, which he and his business partners built at cost.

points (rather like model railway track) in track panels 12ft long. He also supplied ¾-ton capacity waggons. It was first advertised in 1847 and Crosskill demonstrated it at the Great Exhibition of 1851 where 3ft-gauge track and 2-ton capacity waggons were on show. Crosskill defined the concept of the portable railway – a set of cheap, factory made, standard components including points, turntables, straight and curved sections of track which could be easily assembled to meet a temporary transport need, then dismantled and re-used elsewhere, time and time again:

> The railway is laid down in lengths of two or three yards. The rails are fastened to longitudinal sleepers, which again are held in place by transverse ones. At one end of each of these 'lengths' is a socket of iron, into which the end of the next sleeper fits, and is fastened by means of a bolt; the rails are in the usual form, but rather lighter in their make.[3]

The waggons could be pushed by hand or drawn by horses, which walked at the side of the rails, a train of four fully loaded waggons being managed by a single horse or two men. Crosskill's railway proved popular for agricultural uses, one writer stating that, 'In ten years' time farm railways will be in use upon our best farms.' It was also predicted that the Crosskill system would be in use in the colonies competing with 'the twenty-oxen Cape Waggon' and that light railways, built to narrow gauge, would 'cobwed the surface of the country'.[4]

With an eye toward future military needs, in May 1854 Crosskill introduced a double-track version of his railway system 'by which army carriages, parks of artillery, &c., might be transported'. The contemporary press described Crosskill's portable railway as being adapted for both 'common road carriages, with common wheels, as well as for railway carriages' suggesting a form of combined plate- and edge-rail. The track could be easily laid on 'very irregular ground, presenting sharp curves and steep inclines'. The cost of laying a railway using the Crosskill system was estimated to be 21s. per yard, and a mile could be laid in a day costing around £1,000.[5]

Captain Collinson RE, superintendent of works at the Woolwich Arsenal, wrote to William Monsall at the Ordnance Office 'expressing his approbation of Mr Crosskill's portable railway' for use in the Crimea. Collinwood believed it to be the 'most efficient and expeditious thing' of its kind. In turn, Monsall forwarded this letter to the Duke of Newcastle (Secretary of State for War and the Colonies) for his perusal.

Officers and Personnel of the Balaklava Railway. From left to right: Albert Swann (Assistant Engineer), J. Cadell (Assistant Surgeon), H.B. Middleton (Assistant Cashier), Albert Howes (Surgeon) and J.R. Kellock (Assistant Engineer). (*Library of Congress*)

An enthusiastic Crosskill, 'acting under the advice of Capt. Collinson of Woolwich', sent Newcastle a proposal 'respecting his portable railway', stating that it could be of use in the Crimea. He further commented that the main benefits of the 'portable railway' were the ease with which it could be transported and laid down and that it could be laid where a traditional railway could not. It was hoped a meeting could be arranged between Crosskill and the duke. But there the matter appears to have ended, and instead of a narrow gauge (2ft 6in or 3ft) railway being laid with Crosskill's portable railway system, a less radical option, that of a traditional heavily engineered standard gauge railway was adopted, built by Peto, Brassy and Betts, one of the leading firms of civil engineering contractors in the country.[6]

Furious activity by Peto and James Beatty resulted in a lengthy memorandum on the construction of the 7-mile railway and formation of a 'Civil Engineer Corps' dated Monday, 27 November. A meeting with the Duke of Newcastle was arranged for Wednesday, 29 November 1854 and the formal proposition by Peto, Brassey and Betts was made a day later.[7] The Duke of Newcastle presented the scheme to the Prime Minister, Lord Aberdeen, who was:

> Deeply impressed by the scope of your plan and even more by the terms in which you expressed it. It does you and your colleagues, sir, great credit. I and my Cabinet are happy to accept your proposal in its entirety, and I want you to know, my dear Peto, that I consider your offer a most handsome, patriotic gesture.[8]

The fine details were described in a lengthy memorandum from Horse Guards. Peto, Brassey and Betts were to carry out the undertaking 'without any contract of personal advantage whatsoever, to superintend and manage the details both of the preparation and maintenance of a Civil Engineering Corps' which was to be solely employed 'putting down a line, or lines of rails, from Balaklava to the Heights'. Peto, Brassey and Betts were, via a certified agent, to superintend the work and workmen but not to pay any of the salaries or wages. They were also able to 'purchase and provide all necessary tools, engines and material and stock of every kind for the purpose' including accommodation and shelter for making the railway.[9] Peto, Brassey and Betts were to build the railway, 'without any intention of receiving individual profit or hope of gain or return to themselves', the estimated cost of building the railway being £45,000 with transport at an estimated £55,000, but this figure would prove optimistic and the final cost of transport was £135,000.[10] Trevelyan was to ensure that Commissary General Filder 'provide and issue free rations of provisions to each and every of the persons so to be employed' on the railway. Filder was also responsible for paying the navvies and engineers.[11]

Edward Betts was the partner who was most concerned with the Balaklava Railway.[12] He wrote from his London office on Great George Street to the Duke of Newcastle on 30 November with his 'suggestions for a Civil Engineering Corps' for the Crimea. The personnel would include:

200–250 Navvies and miners with 10 gangers (foremen)
20 Masons, bricklayers and foreman

80 Carpenters with 3 foremen

20 Blacksmiths and foreman

10 Enginemen and fitters.

4 'Timekeepers or Under Clerks'

1 'Chief Clerk'

1 Draughtsman

2 Assistant Engineers

1 Chief Engineer 'to be a thoroughly practical Civil Engineer who understands the Management of Men and personal conducting works generally'[13]

To 'prevent any difficulty in the Civilians working with Military Engineers' the 'Civil Engineering Corps' was to 'act entirely under the Direct Superintendence of the Engineer' who whilst not under the orders of Sir John Burgoyne, the Senior Royal Engineer in the Crimea, was to be 'in direct communication' and to accept his 'suggestions'.[14] Betts also laid out the pay of the Civil Engineering Corps:

Navvies and Labourers	5s per day & rations
Miners	6s per day
Carpenters	7s to 8s per day
Smiths	7s to 8s per day
Masons	7s to 8s per day
Engineers	8s to 10s per day
Timekeeper	£150 a year & rations
Clerk	£350 a year & rations
Draughtsman	£300 a year & rations
Assistant Engineer	£500 a year & rations
Chief Engineer	£1,500 a year & rations
Firemen and Inspectors	£10s to 15s per day each[15]

The navvies sent out to build the railway would be entirely civilians; James Beatty was to be appointed Chief Engineer on a salary of £1,500 per year and Donald Campbell as his assistant. Beatty had been born in Enniskillen in 1820 and joined Peto, Brassey and Betts in 1842. He was a well-respected civil engineer; he had surveyed railways in New Brunswick and Nova Scotia during 1852–4 which gave him considerable experience of developing a railway in somewhat inhospitable terrain.[16]

The other twenty-six salaried staff, included his two assistants, Donald Campbell and John Kellock:

Donald Campbell	Assistant Engineer	£500
John Kellock	Assistant Engineer	£500
Edgar Swan	Assistant Engineer	£500
Charles Camidge	Chief Cashier	£500
Henry Stone	Draughtsman	£300
R. Shaw	Timekeeper	£150
George Raymond	Medical Superintendent	£500
Albert Howse	Surgeon	£500
Thomas Fayes	Missionary	£182
John Parker	Horsemaster	£300
William Cole	Storekeeper	£300
Richard Brasier	Medical Storekeeper	£300

Sir Charles Trevelyan at the Treasury approved the 'employment of a Civil Engineer Corps in the Crimea' and that the Treasury was 'prepared to authorize payment . . . on account of expenses actually incurred or disbursed'. A copy of the rates of pay and rations was forwarded to Filder in the Crimea.[17] The Duke of Newcastle wrote to Raglan urging him to give every 'cooperation and assistance' to the 'Civil Engineering Corps', including providing labour 'as may be necessary' and hoped

Navvies in their 'Full Rig' for the Crimea, as depicted by the *Illustrated London News*. There was considerable outcry that these civilians were better clothed, equipped and fed than the fighting soldiers.

that the railway would 'materially contribute to the success of any . . . operation which the Allied Army may undertake'.[18]

Donald Campbell was sent out to the Crimea with a team of surveyors to undertake the initial survey of the railway and make preparations for the arrival of the navvies and all the heavy equipment, which Betts had outlined to the Duke of Newcastle: 'Tools of every kind . . . Barrows, Planks, Picks, Bars, Shovels, Drills, Patentee Fuzee, Forges, Anvils, Vices, Iron and other Stores, Stationary, Instruments, Camp Equipages and Clothing.'[19]

The heavy plant included: '4 Portable Steam Engines with [winding] Drums and Machinery; 2 Lathes and a Drill with sets of circular saws and benches; Cranes, Crabs, Jacks etc.; 3 miles of Wire Rope or Chains; and 6 capstans "to be had from the Dockyard at Woolwich".'[20]

Finally, the railway components including 1,500 tons of rails and chairs with spikes and sleepers, 'switch bars with connecting rods, crossings, for 60 sets of points' and 20 large and strong trucks 'capable of carrying 6 or 8 tons each; 100 iron wagons with brakes and 20 sets of spare wheels, axles, and pedestals'.[21]

The rails and fastenings were supplied by the Eastern Counties Railway, and were 'shipped for the Crimea' from the company's works at Stratford during the week before Christmas 1854. Wooden sleepers for the railway were produced by Messrs Reed & Co. of Monkwearmouth; 'about 20,800 are now about ready', reported the *Carlisle Journal*, 22 December 1854, and were transported to the docks at Newcastle by the North Eastern Railway free of charge. Messrs Butler of Stanningley in Yorkshire supplied 6,020 cast-iron chairs weighing 21 tons 10cwt which were despatched in two batches: the first on 13 December 1854 to Leeds thence Birkenhead; the second on 19 December to Sunderland, transported gratis by the NER.[22] These must have been joint chairs, since photographs taken by Roger Fenton show the flat-bottomed rails spiked directly to the sleepers, and only chairs being used at rail joints rather than fishplates.

A proud *Stamford Mercury* reported that the stationary steam engines were supplied by Clayton & Shuttleworth of Lincoln:

> The Portable Steam Engines required in the formation of the railway from Balaclava to the heights near Sevastopol, have been ordered from Clayton, Shuttleworth & Co., Lincoln who engaged to deliver them within ten days of the date of the order. Four engines are ordered: two are to be of ten-horse power, and two of fourteen horse power each.[23]

One of the engines was tested on the docks at Balaklava on 10 February and it astonished the Turks by 'making great puffs of steam from its iron lungs, and by sundry shrieks and screams'.[24]

'Seven Miles in Seven Weeks'

It was one thing having proposed to build the first railway in a combat theatre, but an entirely different proposition to build it. First and foremost, men had to be recruited. Food and clothing were provided by the company. Prospective employees had to sign a contract agreeing to work for Messrs Peto, Brassey and Betts for a period of six months, under the authority of James Beatty. The *Daily News* announced:

> The railway . . . constructed by Mr Peto and his partners . . . as contractors, are to complete it with their own men; and that when it is completed they are to hand it over to the army at the exact net cost, refusing to accept a single shilling for their labour, management, or the use of their capital.

A recruiting office for navvies for the Civil Engineering Corps was opened in London. More than 500 men were needed, twice the original estimate. And not only navvies, as a chaplain, a barber and four female nurses were also on the payroll. They received higher pay than ordinary soldiers and were not subject to military discipline. Furthermore, unlike the ill-shod and ragged soldiers at the front line, the navvies

Crimean navvies collecting their 'travelling kit' before preparing to embark for the Crimea in London, spring 1855.

were lavishly equipped which drew much criticism from the army and especially from the men at the front:

1 painted canvas bag (waterproof)	1 blue worsted cravat
1 painted canvas suit (waterproof)	1 pair leggings
3 coloured cotton shirts	1 pair boots
1 red flannel shirt	1 rug and blanket
1 white flannel shirt	1 pair of blankets
1 flannel cholera belt	1 woollen overcoat
1 moleskin vest	1 pair grey wool stockings
1 'fearnought' slop	1 pair mittens
1 pair long fishermen's boots	1 pair Lindsay drawers
1 pair fishermen's boots	

Ten prefabricated wooden huts were sent out as accommodation, each hut housing forty men in comfort. There was a portable cooking stove for every ten men, 'which will cook, bake and fry in open air'. 'An ample stock of medical stores' and a 'selection of books' were sent from London and every man was equipped with one of Dean & Adams' revolvers. One newspaper added:

> It is stated the navvies, plate-layers &c. are to be armed with a short carbine, and a pair of short pistols, and a cutlass each man; the pouch and frog for the cutlass will be suspended from a waist belt, which will be worn underneath the frock or gaberdine. By the arming of the workmen it is not intended that they shall act on the offensive, but the arms are solely for their own defence should they be surprised by the enemy whilst at work.[25]

The first '52 stout navvies' left from London by train for Liverpool on 13 December 1854. They sailed from Liverpool in the week before Christmas 1854 onboard the 457-ton *Wildfire*, which Peto had purchased:

> On Thursday, the ship Wildfire, Captain Downward, left the Mersey with 52 stout navvies and materials for constructing the railway at Balaclava ... The Mohwak, Captain Barclay, is intended to be shortly despatched with stores, provisions, &c., intended for the expedition. The men are in excellent spirits, and were provided with everything that would conduce to their comfort. On Saturday last, about 150 navvies ... left London by a special train for North Shields.[26]

Navvies for the Crimea making their farewells as London's Euston Station, January 1855.

It was not all plain sailing for *Wildfire* as when she reached Malta on 20 January some of her crew mutinied, the first mate 'having shot Captain Downand'. He was immediately 'landed and taken into custody'. On arrival in the Crimea, *Wildfire* was to be re-purposed as a Hospital Ship.[27]

Next to sail was *Hesperus,* out of London. *Hesperus* (800 tons) was a newly built iron-hulled screw-driven steamer, and in addition to her compliment of eighty navvies ('nearly all of them young men') carried 800 tons of rails, chairs and sleepers. She was seen off by huge crowds of well-wishers, with speeches and toasts.[28] Her captain, Captain Andrews, addressed his ship's company and the navvies:

> They were going to the aid of their brave countrymen, who had to fight the Russians as well as work in the trenches, and the success of the siege operations in the Crimea might be said to depend in good measure upon them. They must expect some hardships and privations; there would be no public houses to go to, but plenty of good, substantial refreshments would be provided for them . . . they were volunteers, perfectly free to go or stay, and they would have good clothing, good food, a good ship, a good captain, and a good cause.[29]

Crimean navvies on board the *Hersperus* being addressed by Lord Henry Clinton prior to their sailing.

Lord Henry Clinton, deputising for the Duke of Newcastle, also spoke, describing the Crimean Railway as 'magnificent enterprise, beyond all praise', which would 'triumph over every obstacle'. Speeches and toasts over, *Hesperus* 'then steamed down the river amidst the congratulations of all present'. The *Daily News* further reported that:

> The Admiralty is engaging all the available screw colliers to take out stores to the Crimea. They are stout vessels, made to encounter rough weather, and are well suited to the purpose. Three powerful new iron screw vessels, built on the Tyne, have just been secured by the Government to take out plant belonging to Messrs Peto and

Brassey for making the railway from Balaclava to the English lines. These ships are fitting out to take 120 navvies.[30]

Next to sail were the *Prince of Wales* and the *Earl of Durham*, carrying eighty and fifty navvies each. It was quite the armada that carried the navvies and their equipment to the Crimea:

Lady Alice Lambton (511 tons)
Great Northern (578 tons)
Earl of Durham (554 tons)
Baron von Huboldt (420 tons)
Prince of Wales (627 tons)
Levant (694 tons) (paddle steamer)
Mohawk (850) (clipper)

There was trouble when Peto's fleet steamed into the harbour at Constantinople. The navvies were not allowed ashore, resulting in a near riot:

> They insisted on going ashore, and when told that they could not go, as the place did not belong to the Queen, they explained it ought belong to her, and that it soon should, if they had their

The *Wildfire* sailed from Birkenhead carrying the first contingent to the Crimea.

way . . . Grumblings and growlings, more or less uproarious, which they have had amongst each other since their arrival, seem to have begot fears among the military authorities that there may be serious disturbance. But those who know the idiosyncrasy of the navvy think nothing of these little manifestations, and regard occasional phlebotomy, in the manner prescribed in one of the luxuries essential to the unanimity of the 'roughs', which they will indulge in, matter at what alarm to the nerves of disciplinarians, whether in black coats or red.[31]

Fanny Duberly, wife of the paymaster of the 8th Hussars, noted in her journal on 12 January that 'they are taking the levels for our railroad from Balaclava to the Front, which will be a great saving of horse life'. The roads were 'sickening to ride along' due to the number of dead and dying horses. She notes the first 'cargo of navvies' landed on 24 January, making a 'great sensation'. As soon as several of them got ashore they 'set out for a walk to see if they could see ee'er a – Rooshian'.[32]

Construction Gets Underway

Donald Campbell had arrived at Balaklava at the end of December 1854 to carry out the preliminary survey, and to clear a path for the railway at Balaklava Harbour.[33] The railway's first objective was to be Kadikoi. Campbell reported home on 29 December 1854: the wrecked house he was living in at Balaklava lacked both windows and doors 'long since been broken to pieces . . . for firewood' but the roof proved watertight. He had 'neither chairs nor table' other than his heavy portmanteau. In order to reach the camps on the heights, the railway would have to ascend 500 or 600ft and did so by climbing along the side of the valley 'in which Kadi Koi is situated to a height of 570 feet in 2 miles and 60 chains' via an inclined plane. It than ran along 'a sort of table land broken by a series of undulations'. Whilst Lord Raglan had informed Campbell that the railway would 'be of immediate service . . . if it can only be laid down and got to work speedily', he could expect no help from the army.[34]

William Govett Romaine, the Judge Advocate General, would serve on the Railway Board as its Honorary Secretary. He dined with Raglan on the evening of 19 January, the same day that Beatty arrived in the Crimea. The conversation naturally turned to the proposed railway. The assembled company seemed to think 'that it [the railway] would help them in moving heavy shot and shells &c' whilst the opinion of

Commissary General Filder was the opposite: 'it would not help him' in the least.[35]

The first handful of navvies arrived toward the end of January, but they lacked numbers and more importantly tools. Beatty wrote to Raglan from onboard the *Australian* on 21 January 1855 requesting that 'A Wharf or Yard at Balaklava be surrendered to him.' He also requested a fatigue party of 200 men 'be supplied immediately' to help break ground on the railway, permission to 'make use of any old walls or buildings on the Line of railway' and permission to camp his men 'anywhere along the Line of Railway' that he deemed suitable. Richard Airey, the Quartermaster General, replied that part of the wharfs at Balaklava were to be given over to Beatty for railway purposes and granted him permission to use or demolish old buildings and walls in Balaklava but the 200-strong fatigue party was the remit of James Estcourt, the Adjutant General, and as such he did not have power to make it so.[36]

The cramped confines of Balaklava Harbour can be seen from the mass of tightly packed shipping. Many of the buildings of the town had been demolished by the British army and more would follow to create a route for the railway. (*Library of Congress*)

The port of Balaklava that greeted Beatty and his navvies was a festering hellhole. Fanny Duberly described it thus:

> If anybody should ever wish to erect a 'Model Balaklava' in England, I will tell them the ingredients necessary. Take a village of ruined houses and hovels in the extremest state of all imaginable dirt; allow the rain to pour into and outside them, until the whole place is a swamp of filth . . . catch about 1,000 sick Turks with the plague and cram them into houses indiscriminately; kill about 100 a day and bury them so as to be scarcely covered with earth . . . collect all the bat ponies, dying bullocks and wornout camels and leave them to die of starvation . . . Collect together from the water of the harbour all the offal of the animals slaughtered . . . together with the occasional floating human body, whole or in parts, and drift wood.[37]

Captain Earle was confident that the mess at Balaklava was the fault of General Airey and his deputy, Colonel the Hon. Alexander Hamilton-Gordon, the son of the prime minister, described by Colonel Lacey Yea of the Fusiliers as a 'red tapist of the worst description'. Airey was 'indolent' and 'incompetent'; Earle complained how:

> Everyone could plainly see that when clothing, food, hutting, and a thousand etceteras were daily being disembarked at Balaklava, some place, some store, would be required . . . and that for this purpose the houses of the town would be eminently useful; for the business of transporting them . . . a clear space & uncrowded streets would be necessary . . . a clear, authoritative business-like Head would be absolutely essential. Instead . . . Turks, sutlers, paymasters, quartermasters & all the followers of the army . . . occupy the best houses . . . We build no quay, whereon vessels could be speedily disembarked . . . Lastly, to crown all, we place an old worn out Colonel at the head of this Babel, for the simple reason he is an Old Colonel and is unfit for regimental duty . . . All the difficulties [at] Balaklava arose from the thickheadedness (if I may use the expression) of the Quarter Master General and his immediate inferior, the late Prime Minister's son [Alexander Hamilton-Gordon].[38]

First things first, the harbour had to be cleared up and put into some semblance of order. The tiny harbour was very congested with ships competing for the limited wharfage. In charge of this mess was the eccentric Admiral Edward Boxer (1784–1855) who had controlled shipping arrangements at Constantinople and was made Superintendent of Balaklava. In the opinion of many he was 'quite incapable of reducing the muddle'; even Raglan thought that 'No man can make him a man of arrangement.' Everything was in disarray. Despite his reputation for muddle and confusion, one Merchant Marine officer wrote of Boxer that he:

> Did his duty well! What kind of a place would Balaklava have been but for him. The wharves he had built round the harbour for loading stores, roads made under his directions, mooring of ships; the rules and regulations that he made, given to each ship that enters the port, they are all excellent and prevent confusion. The police boats he had to ply up and down the harbour night and day, (the men have proper uniforms), to quell all disturbances that might occur on board the ships, and numerous other duties devolve upon them, in various ways. I was told by the best authority that the admiral got up at all hours of the night in winter, with scarcely any clothes on his back, in an open boat, looking after the safety of the shipping. If a fire broke out afloat or ashore, you would find the old man first there. He was an early riser, by four or five in the morning, and in his boat pulling up and down in the harbour, hailing ships, and giving orders &c.; sometimes would be in a burning hot sun, afterwards in a drenching rain with little or nothing to protect him from the weather. He generally retired to bed early. Believe me, that man never passed any idle moments: his sole aim seemed to be intent upon doing everything to the best advantage.[39]

Despite this hard work, Julian Portch, the 'Special Correspondent' and war artist of the *Illustrated Times*, wrote in May 1855, 'It is very amusing to the see the horrible hovels which are dignified by the titles of post-office, police station, main-guard, &c., and the mud huts.' The streets of the town were filthy and muddy, and the roads in such a state 'nobody I am sure can have any conception of the mud'. He also reported that in order to improve discipline in the little harbour, a 'Water Police' had been inaugurated by Admiral Boxer who daily rowed about the harbour 'seeing all things were right' and shouting at everyone through a speaking trumpet.[40]

In charge of Balaklava Harbour was old Admiral Boxer who instituted his 'Harbour Police' to improve discipline and make order out of chaos.

In order to liaise between the civilian 'Civil Engineering Corps' and the Army, a Board was convened comprising:[41]

President: Major-General Sir Colin Campbell KCB, commanding the garrison of Balaklava

Secretary: William Govett Romaine, Deputy Judge-Advocate

Members: Lieutenant-Colonel the Hon. Alexander Gordon, Assistant Quartermaster General
　　Lieutenant-Colonel Anthony Sterling, Assistant Adjutant General, Highland Division
　　Captain George Robert Barker, Royal Artillery
　　Lieutenant Howard Crauford Elphinstone, Royal Engineers
　　Captain Leopold George Heath, Royal Navy, commanding the Port of Balaklava
　　Deputy Commissary-General William Henry Drake

Drake remarked in a letter to his wife Louisa: 'Lord Raglan has just selected me by name expressly to be one of a Board to enquire into the feasibility of the Railway here, His words were, '"Tell Mr. Filder

I request he will nominate Mr. Drake" ahem – you see my grandeur will become rather troublesome however I don't care for the work.'[42]

The army was initially sceptical of the railway, and there was much friction between the military men and the civilians because it 'show[ed] the Army that there are other and better means of transport . . . they may yet derive some assistance from the skill and science of civilians . . .'.[43] Raglan's Chief Engineer, Sir John Burgoyne, wrote:

> These Civil Engineers do great things, chiefly, however, by an unlimited expenditure; still they do great things, and make great improvements, which we shall be too happy to copy whenever the need requires it: but I think the Duke of Newcastle etc. are somewhat too quick in adopting their proposition for us, on their own enthusiastic views that what does so well in the midst of the civilization of Great Britain will answer under the circumstances in which we are placed here.[44]

Lest Burgoyne be thought of as a stick-in-the-mud, he wrote in February 1855, 'I have done all I can do to encourage the Railway, and I now hope we may begin to benefit from it.'[45] Beatty sent a lengthy memorandum to Lord Raglan on 22 January 1855 containing numerous requests for men, equipment and horses. He proposed that the railway would:

> Commence from the Post Office in Balaklava where there is at present a considerable space of vacant ground . . . convenient as regards access from both land and water side . . . From thence the Line will proceed almost direct to Kadi Koi with a branch from the Diamond Wharf on the west side of Balaklava Harbour.
>
> From Kadi Koi it will proceed as the ground will admit inside the entrenchment to the summit of the hill at the flagstaff near the Turkish Camp. From thence I have not had time to examine the country . . . The principal matter being to get the line completed up to that point first.
>
> It is not intended at first to make it very high finished, the principal object now being to construct such a line as will be immediately available for the transport of provisions, shot, shell, etc., to the front and to complete it perfectly afterwards which completing will however not interfere with the working of it for the Army when the Rails are once laid down.[46]

Amongst Beatty's requests to Lord Raglan was for a fatigue party of 200 men 'to be increased to 500 men as soon as possible'; 1,000 to 2,000 faggots 5 to 12ft long which Beatty thought could be had from Turkey, and 'a supply of at least 30 horses'.[47] Romaine replied to Beatty on behalf of Raglan enquiring as to the use of stationary engines or capstans and ropes to work the inclined planes, whether there was any possibility of using locomotives in order to save on men and horses, the time taken to send ten carriages from Balaklava to the camps on the heights and how long Beatty would require the 500 soldiers on fatigue detail for. With no tools for the navvies to work with, Beatty requested the use of 'barrows, planks, pickaxes, shovels, and hammers' from the Royal Engineers.[48]

In order to discuss these requests, the Railway Board held its first meeting on 25 January 1855. At this meeting Beatty proposed 'to take the line through the centre street of the town [Balaklava], and engages to widen the line [sic, street?] so as to leave eighteen feet clear in all places . . . so as to enable [road] traffic to go on while the line is being laid down'. In terms of motive power, Beatty stated to the board that it was 'not possible to work a locomotive Engine up the hills' and instead proposed to work the line from Ordnance Wharf to Kadikoi using horses and then, unless water could be obtained for steam engines, up the first incline of 1 in 15 using ropes and capstans. The remainder of the line was to be worked by horses, including the second incline of 1 in 20 and that it was 'not advisable that it should be worked with a stationary Engine' due to the lack of water for its boiler.[49]

The railway waggons weighed 1½ tons and could carry a load of approximately 4 tons, but due to the worn-out and enfeebled state of the army horses they were only able to 'draw a ton weight on the rail', meaning that more or new horses were required; Deputy Commissary General Drake stated that the 'average supplies including clothing, hutting and commissariat stores' exclusive of ammunition which could be moved daily was about 150 tons. In order to do so, 'The Board was of opinion that 250 horses of this country would be required'. Transport horses in the Crimea were tentatively put to work on the railway, with harness being supplied by Captain Heath RN 'which may be used by four horses working in a line one before the other'. The board 'strongly recommended' 250 sets of harness be made immediately.[50]

Finally, the board agreed to a single line of railway being laid from Balaklava to Kadikoi and that it be doubled as soon as possible. Beatty was given permission to pull down any old houses and walls in Balaklava town which were in his way, but there were problems

The Railway Yard at Balaklava. The tarpaulins on the roof of one of the wooden huts carry the legend 'Eastern Counties Railway'. Note the piles of rail and crude half-round wooden sleepers. (*Library of Congress*)

regarding manpower and tools. The navvies had not arrived and Beatty requested a daily fatigue party of 200 men and Major Hall RE was asked to supply, temporarily, all the tools needed.[51] The principal depot was established opposite the semi-derelict post office in Balaklava – where Campbell had set up his quarters – the 'Railway Yard' was to be established; one letter-writer described the depot as a 'horrible, squalid space in the rear of the post office'. The post-office building had originally boasted a wooden veranda, had been neatly whitewashed and kept scrupulously clean, with a neat little garden. But by spring 1855 doors, window frames, veranda and furniture had been stripped and burned by British troops for firewood.[52]

Colonel Anthony Sterling was opposed to the railway not only because of the manpower required to build it, but because when it was finished – and more importantly – it could only be used by railway vehicles, whereas the same amount of labour could have built a properly macadamised road, which could be used by any wheeled

The post office at Balaklava where Beatty made his HQ was one of the few buildings to survive the war. The railway passes just feet from the front door. Also note the pile of flat-bottomed rail which was simply spiked to the sleepers.

vehicle. He requested that his opposition be recorded, which it was in the minutes of the Railway Board.[53] Colonel Sterling wrote in his diary for 29 January 1855:

> I have been one of a board to receive the statements of the head railway man about a proposed Balaklava railway. The first thing he said was, that he should want labour and horses – 500 men, and I know not how many horses! Really, now, is it not provoking? If we had had labour, we could have made a good road without him; and if we had horses, we could even now send up our stores without a railway. They do not bring any locomotives with them, only wagons – weight, one-and-a half tons – to be drawn along a tramroad by our miserable ponies. The navvies are not come. If they had sent the latter with spades and sledge-hammers, to make a good Macadamised road, that would have been far more sensible in my opinion. The labour and expense of making railway would

have made a grand road indeed, upon which, every sort of cart, pony-chaise or truck, could have been drawn. However, we are in the hands of the philistines.[54]

Although initially advocating stationary engines ('could be used without difficulty'), Beatty had instead proposed to use 'Capstans and ropes in place of steam engines' due to the difficulties of finding water for their boilers. Lord Raglan was not happy with this change, and wished Beatty 'to state in writing the reasons for such change of plan'. Raglan also wanted to know how many waggons could be pulled up the incline by capstan compared to winding engine and, conscious of the lack of horses, whether there was 'any intention of using Locomotive Engines to move the Carriages . . . or is the line when laid down to be worked by horse entirely'.

Major Hall, the assistant Chief Engineer, prepared a memorandum the following day (26 January) outlining points raised in the meeting including the 'demand upon the Naval and Military Departments' to aid construction of the railway and the 'manner in which the construction of the works will affect the communications and supply'. The matter of locomotive power was also raised. Firstly, it was resolved that a steam vessel was required to fetch timber and faggots which Beatty had requested from Sciope in Turkey. The steamer *Gothenburg* was duly placed at Beatty's disposal and dispatched to Turkey to collect 'tramway materials'. She was ready to leave on 28 January, but the order was rescinded the same day.[55] Regarding horsepower and manpower, Major Hall recommended that sixty strong artillery draught horses be 'attached to and taken charge of by the Railway Department'. This, however, deprived the Royal Artillery of ten gun or waggon teams as the artillery had no spare horses or remounts left alive. Stables were ordered to be built for them at Kadikoi. The working party of 200 men was approved but on a temporary measure until further navvies had come out to the Crimea.[56] Hall also provided an estimate of the materiel which could be carried to the front by the railway. The waggons were 20ft long, weighed about 1½ tons and could each carry 4 tons. It was hoped that the railway could carry 150 tons every day to the camp on the heights. If the railway was to be worked by horsepower alone, then it would require 250 horses which the army simply did not have. Thus, the use of stationary engines was deemed absolutely essential. In order to alleviate the horsepower situation, Peto, Brassey and Betts purchased and sent out to the Crimea fifty heavy draught horses, with forty-five of them arriving on 3 February 1855. However, there was no forage for them, the railway having to rely on forage imported from Britain as none could be acquired locally.[57]

The Railway Board approved construction of the railway and use of stationary steam engines: 'Agreeing that one set of rails with several sidings connected with the railway except along the steep incline near the French Camp, where there are to be two sets with a Stationary Engine.'[58] The railway was to be laid at a gauge of 4ft 8½in (1,435mm) and there were to be two inclined planes. The first of 1 in 15 about 300yd above Kadikoi worked by stationary engine, and the second of 1 in 25 which raised the line to the top of the heights. It was not proposed to work the second incline by steam due to lack of water for the boilers, and instead horses were to be used to haul up the waggons. In order to meet the anticipated 150 tons per day, Lieutenant Elphinstone estimated that because of working the second incline by animal power, and the heavy weight of the waggons sent out, the railway would require 450 to 500 horses – twice the number the board had thought necessary! Elphinstone therefore proposed that instead of using the heavy railway waggons, lighter and 'more easily moved . . . commissariat wagons and French Carts . . . or Artillery Wagons to which small iron or even wooden flanges could easily and speedily be attached and answer quite as well'. It's not clear whether this idea was taken seriously. Like Colonel Sterling, he thought the railway:

> A very crude and ill-digested matter. A light train way and trucks easily drawn when loaded by one horse such as are employed in constructing Railway Cutting embankments etc. should instead have been sent out. At present we have neither the horses nor the harness required for the Line. I believe a suggestion was made some time ago of a plank 'tramway' [which] would have been preferable in every respect. Every description of carriage would have gone along it, it would been completed long ere this and at a trifling expense in comparison.[59]

The suggestion of building a 'plank road' had been made by Sir Francis Bond Head in December 1854, based on his experiences in Canada. In a letter to the Duke of Newcastle which was published by *The Times*, he criticised the use of a 'cast iron railway' as being costly and too specialised. Instead, he recommended the construction of a 'plank road' which would be far cheaper, quicker and required less specialist equipment and labourers. Such a road could be built first by levelling and tamping the roadbed by a gang of unskilled men with 'spades and rammers'. Next 'four or five rows of strong beams', laid longitudinally, were put in place securely packed with ballast. On top were then laid transverse planks. Finally, the surface was dressed with a thin layer of sand. Unlike a railway which required specialist rolling stock, 'Waggons of all descriptions and horsemen of all ages walk, trot, canter, and gallop, over it.' Sir Francis noted such a 'plank road' had a life expectancy of about twelve years if well-maintained and several miles could be laid very quickly. It was an ideal solution for the Crimean roads, but was not taken up.[60]

The matter of motive power was discussed in an optimistic memorandum sent by Beatty on 8 February:

> As regards Engine Power
> It is intended to erect a stationary Engine at the top of the 1. in 15. incline from Kadikoi to the French Camp as I do not doubt we shall get water to work it.
> The other inclined of 1. in 25. from the French Camp to the Flagstaff must for the present be worked by horses – there will be no difficulty in doing this.
> The 1. in 15. incline is the only one we can at present work with Engine Power.
> As regards the time required to go from Balaklava to the top of the Hill at the Flagstaff – two hours will be quite sufficient . . . for taking a train of ten carriages.
> No locomotive Engines are provided, a further supply of horse power in addition to our own will be provided . . . I am quite of the opinion that 100 horses and drivers in addition to our own . . . will be sufficient to work the Line – which will be done by skilled men we have brought out.

In order to build his railway, Beatty had asked for 500 labourers. Colonel Sterling again lodged a protest about building the railway and using regular soldiers to do so:

> I made a protest alone against employing the labour in this way, because making a Macadamised road between the rails, which, when made, would only be available for the railway wagons and horses, whereas a good ordinary Macadamised road would have been available to all sorts of carts, mules etc.; and such a road requiring immense extra labour.[61]

Despite this opposition, Beatty was lent 200 men from the 39th (Dorsetshire) Regiment and could begin construction. The men were engaged to work on the railway for only a few days, however, from 27 January to 6 February. Their withdrawal 'retarded . . . progress very much'. Some 400 Croats were hired by Beatty on 1 February, who were paid 3*d*. per day, as well as an interpreter who could speak English, French and Turkish, paid 4*s*. 6*d*. per day. Most of the Croats, with the exception of about fifty, however, were found 'utterly unfit for railway work' and Beatty considered them useless to him. Captain Foster was put in charge of them and 'furnished with 4 interpreters. There are also 2 attachés to them', who had accompanied the labourers from Constantinople. General Airey proposed breaking down the existing work gangs of fifty men into squads of ten men with their own 'chief', that they be given their own huts and some understanding be shown of their cultural practices, such as letting them cook for themselves and that 'the hours of meals must depend on national customs which of course should be respected'. With a 'little time and patience' they would be 'extremely useful'.[62] There were other problems with the Croats, however, concerning pay and the bounty that was claimed by one Osman Aga who had 'collected the body of Croats or Bosnians' to the number of 1,043 and had 'entered into an agreement with the British Embassy at Constantinople . . . by which he was to receive 3 shillings a day for every labourer he procured'. Osman Aga had also promised the labourers 3*s*. per day (rather than the 3*d*. they were actually paid) and quite naturally they refused to accept the lower rates of pay and showed great discontentment toward Osman Aga. There were also difficulties with exchange rates and the problems that represented in terms of pay. A board was convened to resolve this dispute and to consider the claims by the labourers for the pay they had been promised. The board ordered that Osman Aga be sent home immediately, that each Croat 'receive his pay of 3*s*. a day in the presence of some English official' and that Captain Foster (above) 'select such men as he requires' as sub-officers; and that those Croats who 'do not chose to work' be dismissed. To improve discipline ten men were to be detailed from the Royal Sappers and Miners who were 'not fit for work in the trenches' and put under Captain Foster's orders 'at the rate of one sapper to 100 Croats to keep their names, and act as timekeepers'.[63] W.H. Russell was full of admiration for the Croats who 'astonish all who see them by the enormous loads they carry'. They had: 'Great physical strength and endurance. Broad-chested, flat-backed men, round-shouldered, with long arms, lean flanks, thick muscular thighs . . . living simply, and living quietly and temperately'.[64]

Much hard work was done by hired Croat labourers, such as this group photographed by Roger Fenton. (*Library of Congress*)

Colonel Sterling, despite his misgivings about the railway, was impressed with the clearing up of Balaklava:

> The shop-keepers in Balaklava have received orders to move out of the village, and to erect huts for themselves near Kadikoi. This will clear the streets in Balaklava. No one will go there any longer

to drink, and the houses given up by the shop-keepers will become available for stores or for hospitals: the folly was ever letting any shop-keeper in. War cannot be made upon amiable principles; it is a stern reality. I believe they thought that all the inhabitants were to remain peaceably in their houses, that no grapes were to be pulled, no fowls seized; in fact placing 50,000 men between starvation and stealing and fondly imagining they would prefer the first. Now the village is entirely stripped; there is not a tree, nor a bush, nor an inhabitant remaining.[65]

One officer serving on board HMS *Royal Albert* wrote home on 30 January 1855:

Navvies have arrived at Balaklava, and have commenced the railway, which will be the greatest possible benefit to the troops; for at present the road from the Camp to Balaklava is so bad that horses cannot perform the journey there and back in a day – 15 miles! I believe, with respect to the railway, there is one great difficulty to overcome, which is no less than the want of water. It is intended to have a stationary engine on some elevated position; but I believe, from the nature of the geology of this place, water cannot be procured. Be that as it may, I dare say the difficulty will be overcome: and I can only say, that if the idea of having a railway originated with Sir Joseph Paxton, he is worthy of all praise. Doubtless the Russians will make an unexpected dash during its construction; and should it be completed, the whole line will have to be defended.[66]

Despite the prodigious quantity of work they could do, the navvies were frequently in trouble with the military authorities. They were in the 'habit of getting desperately drunk and neglecting work'.[67] The *Illustrated London News* remarked:

The Navvies have commenced work clearing a space for their rails and sleepers. They are ruddy in health and astonish everyone by the labour which they are able to get through . . . There is great discontent among them on account of the lack to them of an indispensable element of existence. The navvies want their beer. Beer however there is none and each fresh complaint has been met by an additional supply of rum . . . they receive no less than four rations of rum per day, and this so far from satisfying the men appears to have led to some very mutinous proceedings.

One of the first tasks of the navvies was to build their own accommodation, laying out straight streets (named after Peto, Brassey and Betts) and their wooden huts. This was in stark contrast to the ragged tents of the soldiers camped on the heights.

Captain Henry Clifford of the Rifle Brigade was also unimpressed with the behaviour of the navvies, whilst W.H. Russell noted how: 'The navvies are hard at work picking and growling and fighting amongst themselves. There was a regular battle on board one of their ships last night and the Provost Marshal will have to give a few of them a taste of his quality ere they are brought to a sense of their responsibility.'

One of these quarrelsome navvies got his comeuppance at the hands of the Provost Marshal, as Colonel Sterling relates: 'One of the navvies has passed through [the Provost Marshal's] hands, and the rest of the fraternity appeared to be much amused by it. He roared like a bull, and I fear afterwards had the philosophy to remark, that he had been flogged for the honour of his country. They grumble considerably.'[68]

Work got underway in earnest with the first rails being laid on 8 February. Russell of *The Times* remarked:

> The only great type of life and motion visible to me in the early part of February was the navvy's barrow . . . The navvies worked

heartily, pulling down the rickety houses and fragments of houses near the post-office at Balaklava, so as form the terminus of the first bit of the Grand Crimean Central Railway (with branch line to Sevastopol). They have landed a large quantity of barrows, beams, rails, spades, shovels, picks and other materials.

Staff Officer Somerset Calthorpe was sceptical about the railway. He fumed in his journal about the delays in getting work under way:

I suppose the railroad will now be commenced. Considering that the Duke of Newcastle said that the Navvies would be here by the 20th of December last, and three weeks from that date construct the tramway that would carry all the requirements for the siege and army up to the plateau – and that up to this day nearly six weeks have elapsed.[69]

An equally sceptical Captain Clifford, however, was astonished by the progress of the work: the navvies looked 'unutterable things' but 'in spite of the absence of beefstakes and "Berkely and Perkins Entire" work famously and . . . do more work in a day than a regiment of English soldiers do in a week'.[70] French Staff Officer Émile Vanson (1825–1900) – who would be the first Director of the French National Army Museum – wrote how the *'terrassiers anglais'* would walk through the French camp of an evening, their jackets slung over their shoulders. The sound of their pickaxes, the waggons rolling on the railway and the 'bells which sound the hour' gave 'a completely different aspect to this corner of the allied camps'.[71]

One navvy wrote home on 13 February 1855 that Lord Raglan had, in order to show official approval of the railway, visited the navvies at Balaklava. He thanked them for their effort and said 'how pleased he was to see so fine a body of Englishmen so actively engaged upon a work of so great importance'. He gave the head ganger a sovereign with which to 'drink his [Raglan's] health'.[72] *The Globe*, in its edition of 5 March 1855, reported that the 'Navvies at work on the railway are still cheerful and satisfactory.' The progress on the railway had outstripped expectations founded on the first hasty survey, as had the 'progressive cheerfulness and contentedness of all engaged upon it'.[73] The *Daily News* was full of admiration:

10th February. The Railway is making very respectable progress. It has wound itself up the greater part of the main street of Balaklava;

and the engine has been astonishing the Turks by great puffs of steam from its iron lungs, and by sundry shrieks and screams as it has been put in play by the Engineers outside the Post-Office-yard in order to see if its constitution had suffered by the sea voyage. The railroad is simply constructed – the wooden sleepers are laid over a bed of stones and the road and rails are fastened down over them . . . About fifty yards of rails have been laid down in the main street but the road is in many places in a state of forwardness and will soon be ready to receive the rails.

16th February. A mile of the road was laid . . . the Chief Surveyor expected to get up to Kadikoi on the 17th. At that place is the first dêpot, and there commences the first incline, which is to be worked by engine power . . . The surveyor, his staff, and workmen, had to rely, in a great measure, upon their own unaided energies. Lord Raglan is said to take a great interest in the line, and Sir John Burgoyne was doing his best to promote it: but owing to the condition of the army no assistance could be had from it. The Navvies in general worked pretty well. Some black sheep there were; and the facility with which rum could be obtained at Balaklava rendered it difficult to keep some of them in hand. The greatest problem was the want of transport. The worn-out horses supplied by the artillery were of no use.

19th February. The progress of the railway is extraordinary. It is already completed out to Kadikoi, to-morrow it will have passed through it on its way out to the plateau and on Wednesday [21 February] it will in all probability be used for the transport of a cargo of shot and shell.

One letter-writer described how:

The navvy, his barrow and pick-axe, are in possession and he is 'master of the situation.' The noise of the 'blasts' in the rock, the ring of hammers, the roll of train, the varying din of labour, sound all round the harbour. The railway has crept up the hill, about three miles outside the town, and two engines have been dragged to the top of the greatest elevation which the engineers will have to surmount, and will speedily be at work moving the dram to drag up the heavy trains laden with shot, and shell, and other provisions.[74]

The navvies worked in two 12-hour shifts, enabling the railway to be laid at a rate of 'a quarter of a mile per day'. One Royal Artillery officer wrote:

> The progress which this tramway is making is perfectly marvellous. It is now progressing at a quarter of a mile per day, including all the delays which arise from bridging small streams, levelling and filling up . . . Half the men are employed on laying down the rails and sleepers during the day, and the remainder work at night boxing up with earth and stones the spaces left between each sleeper. As an instance of the rapidity with which the work proceeds, a pile-driving machine was landed one evening, and carried piece meal up to where it was necessary to sink piles for a stout wooden bridge across a small stream . . . which runs into the harbour. The machine was erected early the following morning, and before that evening the piles were all driven, the machine removed, the bridge finished, and the rails laid down for the space of 100 yards beyond.[75]

The line was built firmly but simply. A roadbed was built from ballast quarried from the demolished buildings in Balaklava. This was tamped

Work on the railway took place night and day: here the artist of the *Illustrated London News* tries to capture something of the frenetic pace of construction with flaming braziers illuminating the scene.

down and the sleepers laid on top. The rails were fastened directly to the sleepers with dog spikes; chairs were only used where each rail met – 'Joint Chairs' – rather than fishplates. Somewhat crude, but effective. Beatty reported:

> Stones from the several old buildings and walls . . . were placed on the site of the railway, to form a base for the rails . . . with a sprinkling of ballast over them . . . We have been fortunate to find a large bed of tolerable ballast close to the town which has been of great service in making the road . . . over the soft valley as far as Kadikoi . . . where had had not sufficient stones to form a base.

Photographs by Roger Fenton show sleepers and rails laid directly on the old road surface in Balaklava. The first mile-and-a-half of the line to Kadikoi 'was nearly level' but from there to the foot of the first incline was on a rising gradient of 1 in 60. Beyond Kadikoi, however, 'there is no ballast' other than that which was excavated from the cuttings through the sandstone. Unfortunately, this lack of ballast hindered rail operations on the heights themselves as the soil turned into a 'tenacious and deep mud' under the hooves of the horses. Not only was there a lack of ballast but also lime. Beatty wrote to Romaine at the start of February about how a constant supply of fresh lime was 'very important' not only for the railway but for general building purposes. He had spotted an old disused lime kiln near Diamond Wharf where the artillery unloaded their guns, shot, shell and powder. He sought permission to use this lime kiln, but due to its very close proximity to a powder magazine it was therefore dangerous to use. He also lacked the coal with which to fuel the kiln. But by March lime-burning had commenced in kilns in quarries 'in front of the Third Division' where the 'volumes of smoke' attracted the attention of Russian gunners who began 'shelling the spot at intervals ever since' much to the annoyance of Major General Barnard commanding the Third Division as a Russian shell had 'burst amongst his temporary establishment of cocks, hens, and sheep' and had injured several. Another problem was a shortage of blasting powder, with two barrels having to be requisitioned from the Royal Engineers.[76]

The army was unable to supply any draught horses or mules, so the horses to work the railway had to be imported from Britain, enduring an arduous sea voyage. The railway had 100 draught horses and some 20 commissariat mules to work the line. In February 1855 25 draught horses and 20 drivers together with other railway materials were dispatched on board the *Candidate*. She also had on board 25 joiners sent to erect wooden hospital huts.[77] A shipment of 68 horses and 50 navvies arrived in April conveyed by the SS *Earl of Norwich*. Sadly, 12 of the horses died en route. The horses and their harness cost a staggering £10,662.[78] Lieutenant Colonel E. Bruce Hamley RA admired the 'huge, fat dray-horses, suggestive of ale and stout'. The 'magnificent cart horses' excited 'great admiration', and, no doubt, a certain amount of jealousy.

The route out to Kadikoi was relatively simple to build: Private William Baines (20th Regiment) wrote to his family how, 'The Railway is going on betwixt Balaklava and the camp here; the navvies are working away like fun, [but] there are many laid up with frost bit feet and diarrhoea.'[79] The 1½ miles from the Ordnance Wharf to Kadikoi was completed in a matter of weeks; the first train of commissariat stores was run on 23 February 1855, just fifteen days after the first track had been laid. A Highlander wrote to his family in Glasgow from camp at Kadikoi:

Feb. 24
Three days ago, the provisions for this regiment were sent up by the railway. It has now progressed far beyond this, and in a week our poor fellows before Sebastopol will have benefit of it also. The division of the French near us also avail themselves of it, and so we are fair able to pay them back for all their kind acts to us . . . One more word about the railway. I read in a late newspaper 'that it was likely impediments would be thrown in its way.' Far from it, let me assure you, every one, from Field Marshal down, have evinced the greatest anxiety for its success, and I believe we may now look forward with confidence to its speedy termination.[80]

From Kadikoi the line had reached the foot of the heights by the beginning of March. The branch to Diamond Wharf was begun on 2 March 1855, by which date Beatty was able to report to Romaine that he was taking 'a considerable tonnage in the shape of Commissariat Huts and Shot' up to Kadikoi on a daily basis. He was, however, struggling for want of horses. The horses he did have were all employed 'drawing rails and materials for constructing the line' and the 'few we had from the artillery' for draught purposes were all 'sick and half condemned already' when they were seconded to the railway. They were 'of little use' and were so worn out by the work that they were 'withdrawn and we are left entirely to our own resources'. Beatty hoped that the army could supply him with '12 good horses . . . especially appointed for Railway Service'. They would soon get accustomed to the work and walking over the railway sleepers. Without them, Beatty thought he would be unable to operate the railway at all. General Airey was of the same opinion and agreed to send '20 of the stoutest and best mules' for railway service. There were still problems with proper harness for the railway horses and Airey hoped that this problem could be solved also.[81]

The depot established at Kadikoi for the reception of artillery and pyrotechnic stores was not large enough, so men from the Highland Brigade were detailed to carry shot and shell, by hand, from Kadikoi a further 3 miles to the main Camp Depot. Colonel Sterling remarked on 1 March:

> Our Highlanders are ordered to carry up shot to the siege; but I am glad to say that the rail road will help them a little, that is, as far as Kadikoi. The line runs right into the Ordnance Wharf at Balaklava, and the thirty-two pound will be placed in empty sand bags, and then a wagon drawn by the railway horses to Kadikoi; where the men will parade, and shoulder their load of cold iron. We did hope that this shot-carrying was over. It is the proper business of the Artillery, and is imposed upon the Infantry as consequence of the non-competence of the Artillery to do their own work.[82]

A few days later Sterling was a bit more optimistic, noting that, 'The railway is beginning to be very useful as far as Kadikoi. It saves the fatigue-men a good deal of time as well as labour. But the men at the siege are worked very hard.'[83]

Not everything went smoothly, of course. The waggons were a motley collection, largely ex-contractors' stock supplied by Peto, Brassey and Betts and there was great variation in the heights of the buffers which presented a perpetual nuisance when forming trains of waggons. Only those waggons with the same buffer height and spacing could be run together, effectively reducing the availability and turn-round time of the rolling stock.[84] Photographs taken by Roger Fenton in 1855 show the waggons to have been mostly side-tipping contractors' waggons, which whilst ideal for building the line would have been of little use for carrying stores and supplies to the front.

Two men were killed in an accident on 10 March. One of the Spanish muleteers, Raimondo Martinez, and John Giles, a brakesman, were killed and another man seriously injured. The accident took place on the incline down from the French Camp. Two waggons under the control of brakesmen Jacob Stephens and George Morris had 'started from the top of the incline at

The Balaklava Railway was laid simply and quickly using flat-bottomed rail simply spiked to half-round sleepers. Chairs were only used at rail joints. Here navvies are loading up a waggon to take more rails to a track-laying gang further up the line.

the French camp'. This pair of waggons was 'almost immediately followed by two others in charge of John Giles and Joseph Cole, on which were riding the two Spanish muleteers. Running too close behind, Giles lost control of his waggon' and 'in consequence the wagons acquired a great velocity and ran into the first two; the hindermost of the last two wagons mounted the first and went off the rails, instantaneously killing one of the muleteers and inflicting wounds on Giles'. Both Stephens and Morris were dazed and confused as a result of the accident, but on recovering 'their first attention was directed to their mate, Giles'. The commotion of the accident had drawn observers and several French soldiers helped move Raimondo's body. One of the platelayers (H. Gibson) had witnessed the accident. Giles was placed on a stretcher and carried down to Balaklava, where he died three days later. Raimondo's body was 'placed in a wagon and accompanied down to Kadikoi'. In the meantime, however, the second Spanish muleteer had vanished and had not been seen since. An inquiry into the death was held, chaired by Romaine. It transpired that Raimondo had had upon his person £100 tucked in a leather money-belt around his waist but between the accident and his body being found he had been robbed. Donald Campbell informed Romaine that the money and leather belt had been found and 'that the robber was the wounded muleteer, the companion of the dead man' who had disappeared immediately after the accident, and had not been seen since.[85]

Sadly, as Russell of *The Times* reported, there was still friction between the railway and Commissary General Filder. Filder did not think that the railway was in a state of completeness or readiness to receive commissariat stores – although it was carrying artillery stores to Kadikoi with some 2,000 shot being transported – and was of the opinion that 'such a partial use of it would impede the formation of the rail, derange his own Commissariat Transport and produce endless confusion'. That said, however, the Commissariat Staff of the 2nd Division was allowed to use the railway between 6am and 8am, and had managed to move 500 tons of stores and provisions to the front by that means in only a few days.[86] James Beatty wrote to Romaine seeking clarification over the formation of a Forage Depot for the Cavalry Division. He reported how Captain Keane had been ordered to erect nine huts at the top of the incline in order to establish the Forage Depot. In Beatty's opinion this was not a sensible move as it was 'not quite as convenient' as Kadikoi was for the cavalry camp and furthermore, it meant hauling all the forage 'up by the Engine where movements will be necessarily slow – and will thus occupy that portion of the line unnecessarily I conceive'. In addition, because the engine-worked incline was being used to carry materials for 'continuing the line ahead' Beatty thought it desirable that it be relieved of as much traffic as possible so as not to slow progress on building the railway. Lord Raglan agreed with Beatty's sentiment and ordered a depot established at Kadikoi for 'the wants of Cavalry, Highland Brigade etc'.[87] Distrust of the railway, and indeed Colonel William McMurdo (1819–94) of the Land Transport Corps (see Chapter 7) appears to have pervaded the commissariat. W.H. Drake wrote:

> The Quarter Mast: Generals is the very worst & most inefficient in the whole Service – They are the regular laughing Stock of the whole Army & yet have had more promotion that any other – Mr. Filder is in a regular quandary about Colonel McMurdo's business, it certainly will interfere very much with us & I think impair the working & efficiency of the Dept. as to expense it will be a most extraordinarily heavy affair altogether.[88]

Romaine hoped that, 'The Railway [will] turn out famously & be of capital consequence to our operations.' It had already proved 'most useful' and he estimated that in another fortnight, 'will I hope have surmounted the dreadful hill'.[89] In order to ascend that 'dreadful hill', an inclined plane of 1 in 15, worked by steam winding engine, presumably by both of the 14hp engines supplied by Clayton & Shuttleworth, was required. Before the engines came into use, the waggons were hauled up the incline by horses and capstans. The first engine was erected at the summit of 'Frenchman's Hill'; W.H. Russell reported that the 'wire ropes and rollers' for the winding engine had been 'laid down' by 16 March, the anticipated completion date. The track on the incline was laid with two parallel lines: one for hauling trains up, and the other down. Despite teething troubles with the first engine, the first train of waggons was hauled up 'Frenchman's Hill' on 23 March. The 'Special Correspondent' from the *Illustrated London News* watched the operation:

> The stationary engine for drawing goods up the incline . . . [is] not adequate to the fulfilment of the task imposed on it. On the 23rd ult. twenty-four French waggons were loaded with materiel before half-past eleven o'clock, but the engines had not worked

At the top of 'Frenchman's Hill' was the 'engine station'. Here were erected one, later two, stationary engines to work the inclined plain. Also note the artesian well to provide water for the boilers.

them to the top of the incline at four o'clock. Perhaps it will be more advisable to give it a more moderate draught. An overtasked engine is as bad an economy as an overworked man.[90]

The French were fascinated by the railway that ran through their camp. *Lieutenant* Charles Minart (*27e Régiment de Ligne*) wrote home to his mother:

> 1st March 1855. The English, for their part, have a sign of life, their railway which links their camp to Balaklava is almost finished; the route and the rails are completed. It passes between both of our battalions. The locomotives [*sic*, stationary engines] are installed in our camp to draw the wagons up an inclined plane. Only the English would think of a job like this!
>
> The railway renders immense services to them, because they have all the ills of the world to transport their materiel from Balaklava to their camp. Before this, we have had to do it all for them, on an un-paved road, and all their projectiles were carried by us, on the backs of our men, to their camp.[91]

Serving alongside Charles was his younger brother, *Sous Lieutenant* Alfred, who noted: 'The English railway is finished. The station is in the middle of our camp. It is a great boon.' Charles wrote again at the end of March, noting how French soldiers were detailed to protect the working parties on the railway:

> 27th March. We are also out of camp to protect the workers on the railway. Its construction continues perfectly. We built a village of huts for the workmen, and there is even a clock to call them to work. They represent for us the clock at a railway station. Also, every time it is rung, we hear the men employed on the railway shout out 'Balaklava! Everyone descend.'[92]

Chapter 6

The Railway Starts Work

By the middle of March 1855 the railway had been completed as far as the French camp and it had begun to carry stores and supplies as far as Kadikoi and even up to the French camp. An enthusiastic Beatty informed Romaine on 16 March that he was therefore in a position to 'take up all the Commissariat Stores, Huts etc for the Army'. The line out to Kadikoi had 'been in operation some time' and despite some earlier friction with Filder, 'a depot is found there'. The depot at Kadikoi could be 'increased to any extent' and in order to alleviate pressure on facilities at Balaklava, Beatty recommended that the 'Commissariat issue to be removed out of Balaklava altogether to Kai Koi [sic] or some equally convenient place', pending the approval of Filder, of course. The branch line down to Diamond Wharf on the opposite side of the harbour was also in operation. Three days later Beatty had an interview with Mr Bailey of the Commissariat Department regarding the carriage of commissariat stores on the railway, which would begin on Tuesday, 20 March. However, for this to take place an additional siding would need to be laid at Balaklava and Beatty would have to employ additional manpower both to lay the siding and also to act as porters to load and unload the railway waggons. This done, the railway first carried commissariat stores on 23 March and shot and shell three days later.[1] This was to prove difficult as there was a shortage of manpower. Already there were 200 Croatian labourers at work under the orders of Captain Forster, but none of them could be spared to help load and unload the railway waggons which meant that McMurdo of the LTC had been forced to use fatigue parties of soldiers to do this work for him. McMurdo therefore requested 300 Croatian labourers to work as railway porters, Captain Forster being unable spare any men from the 200 Croats under his orders, and in fact had 'repeated applications for more hands'.[2]

As soon as the line had been built as far as Kadikoi, it began carrying hutting material forward for the troops camped on the heights, accompanied by a fatigue party to unload at the other end.

One newspaper correspondent gushed how 'the public will learn with satisfaction' that the railway was in operation from Balaklava to the French Camp, 'at the top of the steep incline, hitherto [worked] by horses . . . but the stationary engine has now begun'. The branch to Diamond Wharf where the Artillery and Engineers had established themselves was available for moving heavy guns, shot and shell to the front. The Commissariat Depot at Kadikoi, 'with requisite sheds and conveniences', was under the superintendence of Mr James Bailey of the commissariat who 'gladly acknowledge[d] the assistance he receives' from the railway in forwarding up to 1,000 sacks of barley to the troops at the front.[3] A second stores depot was established at 'The Col de Balaklava', and by the last week of March twenty to thirty waggons per day, carrying upwards of 50 tons of ammunition, were making the journey from Balaklava. One letter writer reported how, 'The Railway is now complete for two miles and fast progressing.' A timber building acted as Balaklava Station and still carried the legend 'Eastern Counties Railway'. 'Every morning at eight o'clock the train starts laden with commissariat stores, and at present dragged by horses.'[4] Romaine reported in a letter dated 29 March that, 'The Railway has reached the top of the hill so that we will be able to keep the batteries supplied, as long as the stores at Balaclava hold out.' By May he was able to write that, 'The Railway has been wonderfully successful & seems now so much a matter of course that the days of muddy roads seem as far distant as those before the Flood.'[5] The Special Correspondent of the *Morning Herald* on 29 March reported:

> The business of getting up the filled and empty shells goes on rapidly. Each day for the last three days 82 railway trucks, filled with 10-inch and 13-inch shell have been forwarded to the front. Each truck holds 32 shells, so nearly 8,000 have been sent up since the 26th . . . the Railway now takes its traffic close to the rear of our lines, and beyond Karani, about a third of a mile from head-quarters. It is expected it will be entirely completed . . . in the course of two or three days more. Mr Beattie [sic] certainly deserves the very highest credit for the admirable manner in which he conducted all the minute details connected with this tramway.[6]

Loads of ammunition was standardised according to the calibre being transported, the nominal loading being approximately 3 tons: 35 x 13in shells, or 78 x 10in shells, or 164 x 8in shells. They were all transported empty.[7]

The railway did not have the monopoly of transport on shot, shell and ammunition to the front as during the same period (9–26 March), 500 filled 8in shells and 32-pounder shells had been sent up by mule and 500 empty 10in shells were taken up daily by artillery waggons by road.[8]

Beatty then set about extending the line up the final incline, via 'The Col' to HQ on the Chersonese Plateau, this final section opening by 2 April 1855. Lord Raglan wrote on 31 March that the railway had been completed as far as 'The Col' and advantage immediately taken to 'bring up large quantities of ammunition and stores'. The railway had an almost immediate positive effect on the living conditions of the men at the front. One soldier wrote to his parents in Hereford that:

> We are pretty well off here now. We have wooden houses to live in, with a good stove in the centre of it; plenty to eat and drink, also plenty of work to do. We have plenty of good warming clothing

sent out to us from Old England . . . There was as great talk out here a little since of peace being made, but it appears we are far off as ever; we were all in good spirits thinking we would soon get home . . . I forgot to tell you, I have been working as a carpenter building our wooden houses, and it helps to keep my hand in practice. You would smile to see us now; you would not imagine us as soldiers by our dress; we have all the colours of the rainbow about us; and everyone dressed after his own fancy . . . we have great hairy caps each of us, and coats lined with fur, made after the Turkish fashion, sheepskin lined with fur; then we have a blue Pilot great coat . . . good flannel shirts, vests, and drawers and socks; we also have long red boots which reach half-way up to the thigh, and good warm comforts for the neck, leather gloves lined with fur, also knitted woollen ones.[9]

The men were able to supplement their rations by making purchases from sutlers at Balaklava or Kadikoi but often at greatly inflated prices:

We get coffee in the evening and a little salt meat for dinner, either pork or beef; perhaps fresh meat once or twice a week; the pork or beef we seldom eat, it is so very salty. We get tea in the evening, this is the meal we like best through the day, but no bread, all biscuits . . . However, I manage sometimes to get a little bread at a very dear rate; I manage to get about a pound and a half for a shilling; butter 2s per pound; English cheese from 2s 6d to 3s per pound.[10]

William Shardlowe of the 50th Foot wrote home to his parents in Derby that the railway was a great boon: 'We have quite surprised the Russians now for we have got a Railway running from Sebastopol. They neither see horses nor engine, but the train running like lightning. It has eased us of many heavy fatigues. We cannot complain of our rations now.'[11] The *Norfolk News* described the 'rapidity and comfort by which their baggage was carried up by the railway'. Formerly it had taken 'three or four days' to take up to the camps the baggage of a single regiment, yet, thanks to the railway all the baggage and arms belonging to the 48th Foot, 2nd Battalion of the Royals and the 10th Hussars could be transported from Balaklava to camps in a matter of hours.[12]

Not everyone was so impressed. A sceptical *Leeds Intelligencer* thundered:

The Balaclava railway, which is just beginning to be formed when the provisions and clothing of the army have found other means of conveyance to the camp, when the heavy guns and ammunition have been got up to the lines before Sevastopol, when even the huts have been moved to where they were wanted, and, above all, when the remnant of the army is changing its position to the vicinity of the port, – this railway which, under such circumstances promises to be the most useless job on a large scale of the whole expedition.[13]

The railway was too little, too late and the human tragedy that unfolded in the Crimea during the winter of 1854–5 was a result of a failed 'system' which had 'every precaution against . . . expenditure' and thus 'rendered prompt action impossible'.[14]

Yet, for many of the troops in the Crimea the railway was undoubtedly of service and did much to alleviate the suffering of man and animal. Since January 1855 the *Mulets d'Ambulance* of the *Train des Équipages* – which carried two patients in a folding iron litter on either side of a pack saddle – had been carrying the sick and wounded down to Balaklava. Each of the mules was attended by a trained nurse, called an *infirmier*. So successful were the French mules, that Raglan ordered

For most of its existence the Balaklava Railway was worked by horse. Here a train heads out toward Kadikoi, passing through the sutler's camp (dubbed 'Dorneybrook Fair') at Kamara.

1,000 French-style iron litters be made to carry the British wounded. On 2 April, Russell reported that an experiment had been made, carrying the wounded via the railway:

> The first human cargo – one of sickness and suffering was sent down to Balaklava to-day. Four wagons, filled with sick and wounded soldiers, ran from Headquarters to the town in less than half-an-hour. The men were propped up on their knapsacks and seemed very comfortable. What a change from the ghastly processions one met with some weeks ago, formed of dead and dying men, hanging from half-starved horses . . . or French mule-litters.[15]

Colonel William McMurdo of the Land Transport Corps (see Chapter 7) notes that during April some ten waggons were available on a daily basis for the conveyance of the sick down to Balaklava, the sad little train leaving 'The Col' at 12-noon each day.[16] It was not just the sick who were transported by rail, the *United Service Gazette* on 21 April 1855 reporting how 450 men of the Brigade of Guards returned from the trenches to Balaklava 'by rail'. Unfortunately, the carriage of the sick and wounded down to Balaklava by rail had a knock-on effect on the transport of essential stores and ammunition up the line to 'The Col'. McMurdo wrote to Airey in June 1855 that the 'traffic of the line was completely thrown out' by the 12-noon train of sick and wounded. The line was only single track and whilst it operated bi-directionally, the steepest incline up to 'The Col' could only be worked by one train at once. Furthermore, there were very few passing places or sidings allowing trains working in opposite directions to pass each other. This meant that traffic was essentially at a stand-still until the train of sick and injured had wound its way from the heights down to Balaklava. In consequence of this Airey ordered that 'the Sick should be conveyed down to Balaklava in Ambulances drawn by artillery horses' rather than going by rail. Experimental though this was, this had been the first ambulance train in the world.[17]

The railway began its vital task of transporting supplies to the front at the start of April, the earliest cargo transported up to 'The Col' consisting of wooden huts for the Quartermaster General's Department, and two complete hospital huts for the hospital of the 3rd Division.[18] With the railway beginning to come into use priority was to be given to transporting the sick and getting the men under proper cover. Lord Raglan was 'very anxious to make a commencement, as far as possible,

THE RAILWAY STARTS WORK

The efficient French *Train des Équipages* had been carrying the British sick and wounded down to Balaklava for many months when the Balaklava Railway carried its first trainload of sick in April 1855.

of carrying up the hospital huts' to the heights so as to establish a hutted hospital as the first priority. The second was the transport of huts and hutting materials to provide better shelter for the men. Finally, were 'the Stores, Provisions &c. &c. to be carried'. Captain Gerald Goodlake VC (1832–90) of the Coldstream Guards and Captain Keane were to be assigned to superintend the erection of the hospital huts at a site near the Monastery of St George. McMurdo replied that this could be done, and that Beatty had given over six of his waggons per day to carry the hutting materials, 'without effecting the present Distribution of the Railway and other Departments'. These waggons were able to transport about 12 tons of hutting material daily. McMurdo agreed to establish a depot at the 'head of the rail' for the reception of hutting materials. They were unloaded at the depot 'at the head of the railway' near HQ. Lieutenant Powell was to superintend this and was also to 'receive and act upon any Requisitions from the Quarter Master General for the Conveyance of these huts by carts' from the 'head of rail' to where they were needed.[19] Despite Raglan's and McMurdo's best efforts, it transpired that none of the ships that had arrived at Balaklava Harbour carrying hutting materials had any components for making hospital huts on board. Everything 'coming out from England' was sent in 'great disorder'. McMurdo also noted how thirty sets of draught-horse harness had been sent out 'without the traces or back bands' meaning they were useless. A furious Lord Raglan ordered the establishment of a

The hutted commissariat stores of the Fourth Division; note the large piles of timber for building barrack huts.

'Commission & Board to inquire into the mismanagement' of the stores being sent from Britain and the loading of supply ships.[20]

By the middle of April 1855, the railway began carrying commissariat stores and almost immediately came under censure from Filder. He wrote a strongly worded memorandum to General Airey on 17 April that: 'The quantity of fuel conveyed by Railway to the "Col" up to the 15th instant did not suffice for one day's supply . . . whilst that of hay not half a day, and of corn about half a day's issue has been carried up'.[21] As a result, Filder sent out orders to divisional commissariat staff to issue the absolute minimum of stores and recommended that a 'great number of [railway] cars . . . be appointed for this service'. Unless this was carried out, Filder opined that fuel and forage would have to be issued at the bottom of the hill at Kadikoi rather than 'The Col'.[22] In reply, McMurdo believed there had been 'a grievous miscalculation by Filder'. He 'made a Commissariat officer on the spot give his own estimate of the quantity' delivered to 'The Col' which was calculated to be 40 tons. McMurdo stated that his railway waggons were each capable of carrying 30 tons which equated to 22,600 rations of fuel which could be carried to 'The Col', about 5,000 rations of hay and about 4,000 rations of corn. Rations of charcoal were also sent up 'on top of shot waggons' which was 'beyond my calculation'. A furious Beatty penned his own reply, noting that thirty-two waggons were at the disposal of the commissariat, each train sent up to 'The Col' carrying 96 tons of supplies.[23] McMurdo informed Airey that the railway was able to supply the following stores to the depot at 'The Col' on a daily basis:

Estimated Stores to be Carried on a Daily Basis		
Supply	Quantity	Weight
Corn	500 bags (150lb each)	75,000lb
Hay	120 bales (150lb each)*	18,000lb
Fuel, wood and charcoal		45,000lb
Total		138,000lb

* The hay bales are recorded as weighing more than 150lb, 'it is 200lbs and sometimes 230lbs', suggesting a higher tonnage was in fact carried to the front.

Beatty Reports Home

Beatty reported to Peto at the beginning of May 1855, stating that 'the line commences at both sides of the harbour, and proceeds direct up the valley to Kadikoi'. From there it 'turned sharp to the west', round the foot of a hill and then through the French camp and 'thence along the side of the hill to the flagstaff at the top of the plateau', approximately half a mile from British HQ. Branches were built to serve each of the four infantry divisions and the siege train.[24]

```
Memorandum – Daily supply of provisions for the front:-
Biscuit                  300 bags, 112lb each        33,600lb
Salt meat                100 casks, 450lb each       45,000lb
Corn                     500 bags, 150lb each        75,000lb
Hay                      120 bales, 150lb            18,000lb
Fuel-wood and charcoal   45,000lb
Total                                               246,000lb
                                            112 tons per day
```
[25]

He added: 'Up to last night the railway has taken up, as nearly as can be, a thousand tons of shell and shot, 300 tons of small arms, 3,600 tons of Commissariat stores . . . besides upwards of 1,000 tons of miscellaneous – viz. Guns, Platforms, huts, Quartermaster-General's Stores, &c.'[26]

Not everyone was impressed by the railway and indeed the commissariat would prove to be consistently antagonistic. One officer wrote home to family in Manchester opining that instead of the railway a 'properly organised wagon train' was wanted instead:

> Everything has been done too late; had the railway been contemplated and carried out a month or two earlier it would have saved the lives of thousands. It will even now be most useful, and is daily proving itself a most valuable adjunct to the siege. I am one who thinks railways and sieges should never go together. They may tend to much inconvenience; an army should be complete in itself . . . If you have assistance of tramways, where hundreds of tons may be carried miles in a day, you throw over your legitimate mode of transport [to the railway], and when you come to advance, you cannot carry the rail with you, and your other means of transport being too feeble, you are placed hors de combat. What is wanted . . . is a <u>properly organised waggon train</u>.[27]

Despite all the naysayers and sceptics, Beatty believed the railway was a success:

> It has relieved the artillery horses the killing journey uphill from Balaklava to the Camp . . . It has . . . been the means of cleaning up Balaklava . . . and has shown the army how to work . . . It will show the army that there are other and better means of transport than ordinary roads; that, without infringing on the prerogative of military men, they may yet derive some assistance from the skill and science of civilians; that a railway – one of the most improved means of transport – can be laid over an ordinary country as easily and quickly as a common road; that an immense amount of tonnage can be removed in one-fifth of the time required on common roads.[28]

There was still friction with the military authorities. Beatty wanted to run trains on the hour, every hour from 7am until 7pm from Balaklava to the incline at Frenchman's Hill, but there was still considerable antipathy between Commissary General Filder and the Railway Board:

> The biscuit, salt-meat, and groceries, Commissary-General Filder has not made any arrangements about issuing it . . . The Commissariat have now at their disposal every day 30 wagons or

THE RAILWAY STARTS WORK

more, and these might be filled on average twice a day, sufficient to take up everything in the shape of stores; but the Commissariat Men will not work before 8 in the morning nor after half-past 5 in the evening, and the Commissary-General does not seem disposed to take any steps . . . in fact he will not put himself out of the way one step to forward the comfort of the army as far as the railway is concerned.[29]

Beatty's censure of Filder caused considerable consternation both in London and at HQ in the Crimea. Lord Panmure forwarded a copy to

The railway immediately proved a boon to the men at the front – it saved them the gruelling task of carrying up their own rations and hutting material from Balaklava. A soldier of the Royal Artillery has a rapt audience as he reads aloud from a newspaper.

Raglan, asking for 'an explanation of Mr Beatty's report'. If a satisfactory answer was not forthcoming, 'Lord Raglan was to relieve him of his duties.' Romaine interviewed both Beatty and an irate Filder, both of whom were to provide a written explanation to Lord Raglan, which appears to have defused the matter.

Despite friction amongst the higher-ups, to the men at the front the railway was a godsend. Farrier Sergeant W.H. Elam of the 17th Lancers wrote home to his family in Huddersfield that:

> We have got a railway that starts from the shipping in Balaclava and goes now half-way to Sebastopol, and they will very soon complete it. They carry shot, shell, and provisions to the troops that are in the trenches – poor fellows, they have suffered a great deal of hardships this winter, and not a bit better off than you saw it printed in the papers. Suppose a ploughed field in England situated on marshy ground, and that it had been raining for a week in succession, you would not like to walk across there in that state. Such has been the state of the ground here for miles and miles where the camp was, but thanks be to God the weather has been very fine this last week or ten days, and the ground is getting beautiful and dry. We have now got very good clothing and wooden houses to live in, but we have not had them long.[30]

Chapter 7

A Transport Revolution

It was always understood that as soon as the railway was completed it would be handed over to the army for operation under the orders of Colonel McMurdo of the Land Transport Corps, and this promised to bring about a transport revolution.

The experienced Lieutenant Colonel William McMurdo was appointed Director General of the Land Transport Corps in January 1855. He grappled with the twin task of both forming the LTC in the field as well as supplying the army's land transport.

The Land Transport Corps

The reportage of the various 'Special Correspondents' of the newspapers, given local colour and verification by the thousands of letters home describing the unfolding human drama in the Crimea, stung the politicians in London into action. What had been described as the 'finest army ever to leave these shores' was reduced to rags, wading through mud, living in tattered tents, and starving. Despite the best efforts of William Filder, the transport system had broken down under the strain, horses and mules ensnared in sticky mud on the road to the camps from Balaklava. *The Times* had been critical of the transport and commissariat arrangements from the beginning. W.H. Russell fumed:

> Who was the wise man who warned us in times of peace that we should pay dearly for shutting our eyes to the possibility of war, and who preached to us in vain about our want of baggage and pontoon trains and our locomotive deficiencies? No outlay, however prodigal, can atone for the effects of a gripping parsimoniousness.[1]

In this observation, Russell was to be proved cruelly correct. It wasn't just the newspapermen but politicians, too, who were critical of the transport – or lack thereof – of Lord Raglan's army. Lord Ellenborough had asked searching questions in Parliament. Quoting Sir Charles Napier, he estimated the army needed one horse per man, plus 30 per cent 'for contingencies', but because the commissariat was part of the Treasury, it paid no heed to either the sage advice of Napier or Ellenborough. Raglan and Estcourt both appreciated the lack of land transport whilst in Bulgaria: the army's 'principal want' was land transport. Indeed, Commissary General Sir Charles Maclean wrote a lengthy memorandum to Sir Charles Trevelyan at the Treasury on the merits of a militarised transport service but no action was taken. As noted in Chapter 1, the major shortcomings of the British transport system was all the more galling due to the perceived success of the French *Intendance* and *Train des Équipages*.[2] On 12 December 1854 the radical MP A.H. Layard, who had been out to the Crimea and whose brother was serving as an officer, gave a damning speech in the House attacking the government's mismanagement of the war. The road from Balaklava was 'in a dreadful state. The mules &c are overworked and underfed . . . the Commissariat could not get our rations or our forage'. The ambulance service was 'worse than useless' and the British had had to invite the 'old enemy', the French, to carry their sick down

French staff officer Emile Vanson's watercolour sketch of a member of the Land Transport Corps showing his dark-blue uniform; natural leather equipment; and red facings indicating he is a member of the 2nd LTC Division. He appears to be wearing a farrier's badge (a horse shoe) on his upper right sleeve. (*Yves Martin, Private Collection*)

to the ships at Balaklava.³ The shaky coalition government of Lord Aberdeen had to be seen to be 'doing something' and even suggested recalling Airey, Estcourt and Filder. This would have 'drawn the sting' of many of the press complaints, but importantly also meant that if any further calumnies befell the army in the Crimea, the government was able to say it had done its best in sending out new staff.⁴ The Duke of Newcastle was spurred into a flurry of activity. In January Major General Knollys and Commissary General Sir Charles Maclean were sent to Paris to study the *Intendance*. Their report of 5 March 1855 was a detailed investigation into the administration of the French army, upon which it reported favourably. Before waiting for this report to be published, however, Newcastle set about organising a means of transport 'quite new to the English service'. He informed Lord Palmerston of his intention on 9 January and eleven days later wrote a lengthy memoranda to Lord Raglan that a Royal Warrant was being immediately obtained for the formation of the Land Transport Corps (hereafter LTC). Because the politicians urgently needed to be seen to be taking action, he was 'unable to take Raglan's counsel and advice'. Nor did Newcastle take – or have – the time to seek the advice of the Commissariat or Quartermaster General's Departments, both of which he was convinced would 'dislike it as an innovation upon the practice and as an infringement of their functions'. Meanwhile, Colonel William McMurdo, who had come to prominence under Sir Charles Napier in India, and who had proposed the formation of Corps of Muleteers back in June 1854, was asked to draw up a detailed plan for the organisation of the new corps, to which he was later appointed to command. Thus, the establishment of the LTC was formed without any reference to the Commander-in-Chief in the Crimea, or any meaningful study of land transport either at home or abroad. The creation of the LTC was 'based less upon battlefield necessity' but more on the 'precarious position of the government at home'. Thus, it is hardly surprising that the LTC did not live up to the high expectations placed upon it, but it is still remarkable it managed to achieve so much of what it did.⁵

McMurdo was a Scot from Kirkcudbrightshire, having been commissioned into the 8th Foot in 1837. He served in India under Sir Charles Napier, and eventually married Napier's daughter. It should come as no surprise, therefore, that McMurdo chose his brother-in-law Lieutenant Colonel William Napier (1818–1903) as his second in command. Lord Hardinge, the Commander-in-Chief at Horse Guards, wrote to General Airey on 5 January 1855, 'McMurdo is ready to take charge of the Baggage animals or baggage & seems a ready resolute officer . . . He seems most energetic & intelligent & will not spare trouble.' Lieutenant Frederick C. Herbert RN was appointed as McMurdo's assistant, 'with the rank, pay and allowances of Captain'.[6]

The formation of the LTC was one of the last acts of Aberdeen's government which fell on 23 January following the radical Sheffield MP John Roebuck giving notice of a motion for a select committee on the conduct of the war. The LTC received its Royal Warrant the following day, but it wasn't until a month later (24 February) that its paper organisation was approved. McMurdo was authorised to raise a force of 2,275 British drivers, 5,789 'native drivers' and 17,000 mules.[7] The Royal Warrant stated that:

> The Land Transport Corps shall be established as part of her Majesty's regular armed forces, which shall be charged with the Transport of all stores, supplies and necessaries at all times required by her Majesty's army in the field, it is hereby publicly notified, that the objects of this corps are: The general organization, as a military body, of the entire land transport service, with a view to the more effectual supply of the army in the field with all that is essential to its convenience, its rapid movement and its efficiency . . . to undertake the whole of the transport for the Army, and will be carried out on a much greater scale than the Royal Waggon Train was under the Duke of Wellington.

Drivers were to be recruited from men aged between 20 and 40 years old and over 5ft 2in in height: 'Second Class Drivers' were to be paid 2s. 6d. per day, 'First Class Drivers' (ranking as corporal) 3s. per day, 'Sub-Superintendents' (ranking as sergeant) 4s. per day and 'Superintendents' (ranking as sergeant major) 5s. per day. 'Drovers and men accustomed to the care of animals will be preferred.' Also preferred were police constables and members of the Irish Constabulary, who were usually mounted and therefore used to caring for horses. Indeed, adverts for 'Third-Class Drivers' were printed in Irish newspapers offering an enlistment bounty of '£5 in cash and Necessaries' and offering the 'high pay' of 1s. 3d. per day. Enlistment was to be for ten years for men aged over 35 and twelve years for younger men. Irish papers also reported how a 'large body' of the Irish constabulary were 'daily joining the Land Transport Corps'.[8]

These rates of pay were far higher than for the Line, and there was much disgust directed toward the men of the LTC – who remained civilian auxiliaries – from those at the front. To encourage men to enlist, a bounty of £5 was offered and 'Free Rations', in other words not paid for out of stoppages from the men's pay.

Promotion was by merit and not by purchase, as in the other technical arms, the Royal Artillery and the Royal Engineers. Whilst a few officers appear to have appointed from cavalry NCOs, the majority were appointed from the Royal Artillery and Royal Sappers and Miners; the *London Gazette* of January 1855 noted, for example: 'To be Cornets: Sergeant George Hall, from Royal Artillery; Sergeant James Petherew from Royal Artillery; Colour-Sergeant J. Faulkner, from Royal Sappers and Miners; Sergeant H. Macleod, from Royal Artillery; Sergeant W. McIntosh, from Royal Artillery; Sergeant Henry Adams, from Royal Artillery.' These NCOs from the Artillery and Sappers and Miners would have experience of working with horses and rolling stock. Higher ranking officers were recruited from volunteers from the cavalry, artillery and the forces of the Honourable East India Company. Unfortunately, many of the cavalry officers were 'full of airs and graces' and the whole corps 'savoured too strongly of Cavalry'. Their uniform was a 'blue tunic, with two rows of buttons', 'blue trowsers, glazed cap and boots' with an additional free issue of 'warm clothing of fur cap, sheepskin coat, woollen drawers (two pairs), socks and mittens'.[9] Not all of the recruits sent out to the Crimea for the LTC were either fully kitted or even supplied with uniforms. McMurdo fumed in a letter to General James Simpson at HQ that many of his men had only been supplied with greatcoats, 'were without tunics and, it appears never supplied with clothing'. Major Ireland who had command of the Depot at Horfield Barracks in Bristol reported to McMurdo that a recent draft of 1,190 men was sent out to the Crimea without any uniform other than their greatcoats.[10] McMurdo complained how the men had been sent out without uniforms or camp equipage, only to be informed the uniforms would be sent out separately from Britain at a later date. Whilst officers sent out from Britain did have uniforms, the majority of his officers who had been seconded to the LTC or promoted from the ranks serving in the Crimea had no uniform, and moreover were expected to purchase their own which they could not do. No one seemed to know to which formation they belonged or what their exact authority was. Luckier was the detachment sent out on board the steam transport *Germania*. They landed in the Crimea on 11 July 1855 armed with 320 carbines for the drivers, 25 swords for the sergeants and 356 pistols. The drivers were equipped with a dress jacket (but no undress jacket), two flannel waistcoats, overalls, field hats and watering caps, and cavalry cloaks.

The NCOs were similarly attired but they also had boots and spurs suggesting that they were mounted.[11]

The LTC would eventually reach a strength of 3,478 British and 4,700 native drivers, and 12,000 horses and mules. It was organised in a 'double echelon' system, each wing intended for duty on alternate days:

> This corps will be divided into two wings, each under the orders of separate chiefs, also of high military rank. These two wings will next be subdivided to correspond with the divisions of the army which they accompany – each division to be under the command of a commissioned officer, and distinguished as far as possible from each other by different [facing] colours pervading their clothing, equipments, and vehicles. Again, each division will consist of two brigades, command of which will be given to quartermasters.[12]

Personnel of the Land Transport Corp, as depicted by the *Illustrated London News*. The uniform was dark blue, with brown-leather equipment and each battalion had its own facing colours, which were also carried on its vehicles.

Each of the brigades were organised from companies, 'sections' and 'sub-sections':

> The brigades will be divided into two companies or division, each under the command of a sergeant-major. These companies will be broken up into two subdivisions, of two sections, under the command of a corporal. Each of these sections will comprise – 1 corporal, 9 British drivers, 1 native superintendent, 30 native drivers. Each of these sections will be made into four squads – each squad to consist of 1 British driver, 3 native drivers, 10 mules.[13]

Each 'native driver' had care of three mules, meaning that there was one spare animal, so that animals could be rested in rotation. The 'native drivers' were under the supervision of the British drivers. The 'native drivers', locally recruited from Tatar peasants and paid 2s. 6d. per day, were entrusted with 'the conveyance of mule loads, each of 200 pounds weight'. Unlike the British drivers, they were not armed because until 'the character of the Tartar peasant has become more thoroughly understood, it may not be prudent entrust the native drivers with arms'.[14] British drivers were armed with a carbine, bayonet and a revolver for *defence* only: the LTC was not a combat force. Some of the native drivers were eventually armed with revolvers for their own safety, but in October 1855 Major Cook in command of the left wing received an irate letter that a provost sergeant had dis-armed a native officer, the provost claiming that there was no 'authority' to allow the arming of natives, either drivers or officers. Cook was to write to the Provost Marshall or even the Judge Advocate General (Romaine) about the case.[15] Some of the native drivers had taken to arming themselves by nefarious means and a carbine and six naval cutlasses were found in the tents of a group of native drivers, which McMurdo presumed they must have stolen from the Naval Brigade. The matter was handed over to the Adjutant General.[16] The LTC was to be organised in two 'wings', each one set out as follows:

4 Squadrons	=	1 Section
2 Sections	=	1 Company
2 Companies	=	1 Brigade
2 Brigades	=	1 Division
6 Divisions	=	1 Wing

Each of the six divisions was commanded by a 'Captain of Division' and each division was to be attached to each division of the army it served and the facing colours and vehicles of each division were to be of a distinctive colour:

1st Division	=	light blue
2nd Division	=	red
3rd Division	=	yellow
4th Division	=	white
5th Division	=	grey
6th Division	=	green

In other words, the organisation of the LTC was similar to the French *Train*; in the French system each *escadron* of three 'active' companies was attached to each division of the army. Initially there were twenty-six companies of the *Train des Équipages* serving in the Crimea, but they proved insufficient, and eventually thirty-six *Train* companies were on active service. In addition, were the '*bis*', or 'provisional', companies and eventually seventeen '*auxiliaire*' companies, most of which remained in Bulgaria, were formed from 'natives'. These *auxiliaire* companies used both horses, mules, buffaloes and bullocks to pull their somewhat mixed bag of waggons which included Maltese carts and native *arabas*.

Whereas the LTC was united in a single tented camp and horse lines, the French *Train* remained concentrated at their main supply base at Kamiesch (8 companies) and at the French Head Quarters (*Grand Quartier General*) near Kadikoi (eighteen companies). A further nine companies were on detached duties. This type of organisation meant that the French *Train* was close to its point of supply and did not, unlike the British LTC, have to carry its own supplies and stores to its camp in addition to those of the troops which it was supplying. The LTC was effectively performing double duties in having to transport its own stores, which placed twice the strain on the men, materiel and horses than was placed on the French *Train*.

In the field the LTC was to be responsible for the transport of all 'warlike stores', provisions and the movement of the sick and wounded. These duties were outlined as being:

1. To carry out such arrangements as may be necessary for the operations of the army generally.
2. The providing of transport for the baggage of the army.
3. The carriage of ammunition.
4. The transport of provisions.
5. The conveyance of the sick.

The first will bring the chief officer of this service communication with the department of the Commander of the Forces; the second will lead him into close communication with the Quartermaster General; the third will enforce an alliance with the Engineers' and Ordnance departments; the fourth involves a junction of interests with the Commissariat; while the fifth will bring upon the Land Transport Service the stern, implacable requirements of the department of the Inspector General of Hospitals.[17]

This was a far broader remit than the *Train des Équipages*, the main duties of which, in times of war, were:

1. Transport the sick and wounded.
2. Transport medical supplies; camp equipage; and clothing.
3. Carry rations and supplies.
4. Transport material belonging to the treasury and postal service.
5. Carry the archives of the *État Major* and *Intendance Militaire*.

This meant that the LTC was not only expected to perform the same duties as the French *Train* but, in carrying ammunition and suchlike, the additional functions of the French *Train d'Artillerie*, which carried ammunition, shot and shell, and the specialist *Train du Génie*, which moved supplies for the *sapeurs*. Again, this meant that the LTC was expected to carry out a far broader range of duties, with fewer personnel and animals, than the French *Train* and furthermore carry out those duties which the French had given to more specialist units (*Train d'Artillerie, Train du Génie*).

Forming the LTC

Whilst the LTC now existed on paper, it was down to McMurdo and Napier to organise this new force. McMurdo left for the Crimea on 12 February 1855 with the first detachment of 257 officers and men, leaving Napier in charge of the depot and recruitment in Britain. Lord Panmure, the new Secretary of State for War, was optimistic about the LTC. Despite wishing McMurdo success and hoping that 'as quickly as possible his officers and men will rally round him', it rapidly became obvious that the LTC existed on paper only. In Parliament, the under-secretary of state for war announced that this new force would amount to 8,000 drivers and an undisclosed number of horses, which were to be purchased locally in the Crimea and Turkey using agents and local contracts, a system that was open to much abuse and immediate doubt was cast upon the success of acquiring sufficient animals. The LTC also needed experienced personnel and waggons, both of which would take time to amass; it wasn't until May that plans for a depot in Bristol at Horfield Barracks was noted.[18]

Upon landing at Constantinople, McMurdo 'at once began to purchase mules' from as far afield as Baghdad, Aleppo, Damascus and Samsoon which began to be delivered in March.[19] He landed in the Crimea on 12 March, but with no real command.[20] By the end of April 1855 400 men had been recruited from the London area and the first detachment sent out to the front. The last batch of recruits for the LTC was from London and was inspected by Queen Victoria and Prince Albert outside Buckingham Palace before boarding a specially chartered GWR train at Paddington for Bristol. Amongst the earliest recruits for the LTC was Benjamin Strange of Norwich. Almost immediately promoted to the rank of 'corporal or first-class driver', Strange wrote home how:

> We sailed from Plymouth on board the troop-ship 'Northfleet', No. 35, April 19, and landed here in Balaklava on the 18th of May . . . encamped for a few days at Kadekoi. . . . Our duties, which are as follows: at the sound of the gong we turn out at 3 o'clock in the morning to feed the mules, after which we get a pint of coffee and biscuit for breakfast. As soon as this is over we take the mules to

An officer and other ranks of the Land Transport Corps manning a water cart, which were used to take water to the parched men in the trenches. They are wearing the short-lived 1855 pattern double-breasted tunic.

water, each man taking three, and immediately after watering the mules are saddled and off we go to the stores at Balaklava, to load the mules with rum, barley &c, having charge of three mules in each file, as well as looking after natives who are taken into English pay. We often form a string of a quarter of a mile in extent, and then off we go to the front . . . where we unload and then return to our tents quite tired out and glad to stretch ourselves upon the ground and fall asleep. The only meal a man is sure of is his breakfast. No doubt things will go on better here bye and bye, but we certainly have had to bear the brunt of the work.

John Wallace and his cousin joined the LTC in spring 1855, John having previously been a 'servant in the Police Barrack of Boyle' in Roscommon. They sailed from Queenstown having had a 'very pleasant voyage' arriving in the Crimea on 2 March. He wrote home twenty days later presenting a stark contrast to the experience of Benjamin Strange:

My cousin and I are, I am happy to say, very comfortably situated, and feel quite at home here, plenty of good provisions – Rum and Clothing supplied us gratis with no more than three hours' work to perform daily. There are three companies of us stationed together on the side of a pleasant hill commanding a fine view of the surrounding country and the harbour . . . We are employed at loading Waggons, at other times in bringing provisions to the front . . . We have never to clean or look after our own mules; we have only to hand them to the Turks (who are kept at work here same as slaves), and they must tackle and load them for us.[21]

On 16 March 1854 Raglan's Adjutant General, General James Estcourt, ordered that all 'public animals' attached to the commissariat or regiments be immediately placed under the aegis of the LTC; all forms of wheeled transport were also to come under its control. Also transferred were 'all the artificers, carriage-makers, harness, and stores' so that all the means of transport – and its day-to-day maintenance – was under a single organisation, emulating the French system. These 'public animals' amounted to 2,170 horses and mules, of which 886 were 'unserviceable' and had to be euthanised, just over 100 buffaloes and 112 carts. As a first step to getting his new organisation rolling, McMurdo appointed to each division one sergeant as a transport superintendent and a second as quartermaster sergeant, and one driver was appointed to every three animals, 'under a steady corporal'.[22] In the French system one driver

The tented camp and horse lines of the Land Transport Corps; sadly, due to over work and lack of specialist staff, the LTC had one of the highest rates of sickness and mortality (human and equine) of the British army.

looked after two horses, meaning there was a far higher ratio of drivers to animals suggesting that French animals were probably better cared for.

McMurdo had the onerous responsibility of not only forming the LTC whilst out in the Crimea, but also moving the army's supplies and sick at the same time. It was an uphill struggle as he was short of pretty much everything, from officers to blankets and waggons. The task never seems to have been fully completed. As Sweetman has indicated, the LTC under McMurdo had never been fully realised and its organisation was found faulty. It had been hastily organised primarily to meet a domestic political crisis and was described in London as 'a complete failure' requiring a 'more military organisation'.[23]

One of the first tasks assigned to McMurdo in the Crimea was to assess the transport requirements of the British army, both for its present strength and a theoretical maximum establishment of 40 infantry battalions. He wrote to Lord Raglan on 9 May noting that he then had 2,291 mules and horses, 143 buffaloes, 12 American waggons, 9 'smalls arms ammunition waggons' and 337 Maltese carts with a mix of wooden (112) and iron (225) axles. He was also expecting 70 *arabas* from Constantinople as well as a further 44 buffaloes and 50 waggons from Sinope.[24] In addition, he stated that whilst he had sufficient transport available for a 'forward movement' of the army, he had 'no means of transport available for the Conveyance of Provisions and Medical Stores; no Carriages for the sick'. For a force of 40 battalions, a cavalry division and engineers and artillery it would require 3,860 horses and mules but he was unable to meet this, being deficient of 1,560 horses and mules. In order to meet the transport needs of the army as it then stood in the Crimea he required 2,794 draught animals, so again he was short of horses and mules but only by 494.[25] In a confidential report to General Airey, he noted that to supply an army of 30,000 men he required 15,142 pack animals, 4,305 draught horses and 1,088 waggons and carts. Furthermore, he needed an additional 4,400 draught horses and 2,000 waggons and carts 'for the transport of grain and forage' for the transport animals. McMurdo thought that some reductions could be made by using 'animals of greater power such as Camels or Buffalos' but in general he was not hopeful of being able to supply the army's transport needs, especially if it took to the field.[26] On 1 May 1855 McMurdo notes that the LTC consisted of 372 'European' drivers and 879 'native', total 1,251, the effective strength – after deducting officers, 'European' NCOs, orderlies and clerks and those men sick – being 847. There were 400 carts and waggons in service, leaving 447 drivers to manage the pack animals, or 1 driver per 5 mules, a ratio that McMurdo quite rightly thought was too high.[27] On the same date, there were 2,294 transport animals of which only 1,568 were serviceable. Thanks to the sending out of remounts and replacements, by June this figure more than doubled to 5,028, of which 4,424 were serviceable.[28]

Given the high proportion of 'native drivers' in the LTC, it was apparent that translators would be needed. The first Turkish and Spanish porters and drivers had arrived in May but had no translator with them. As late as August 1855 the LTC had none or very few. Major Evans wrote to HQ requesting that three 3rd Class Interpreters, later four 2nd Class Interpreters, who spoke French and Turkish be attached to the LTC. One interpreter, 3rd Class Interpreter John Kolsovski, was reported to General Airey for being found dead drunk and was 'extremely insolent' to another officer. Several of the Turkish drivers were 'in such a state of discontent and mutiny as to require the intervention of the Provost Marshall' over the matter of their pay because the 'excitable' Kolsovski had informed them they would be paid 2s. 6d. instead of the 1s. 8d. which they would receive.[29]

The personnel of the Land Transport Corps were recruited not just from Britain but from across Europe and in the Near East. Here a party of Spanish muleteers are on their way to the Crimea.

McMurdo was chronically short of officers. By August 1855 out of the 43 he ought to have had on duty, only 27 were present, of whom 5 were absent, sick. He reported to HQ that: 'There is at present an entire Division of the Corps, consisting of two Brigades and remembering 718 men and 1077 animals without an Officer to pay, or take charge of them.'[30] McMurdo requested 2 captains and 10 subaltern officers be attached temporarily to the LTC – which General Simpson at HQ agreed – but also that the establishment of the LTC be increased to include an additional captain in each division.[31]

By October 1855 McMurdo noted he was still short of buglers, in fact fifty-six of them. McMurdo wrote to General Simpson at HQ that: 'In a service such as the Transport where the duties are required to be correctly timed in order that the requisition, of the army should be duly complied with, it is absolutely necessary that means should exist for turning the men out at the appointed hour.' Whilst McMurdo was 'perfectly aware' that it was impossible to solve this problem immediately, it meant that he was labouring with the problem 'of turning the men out of bed without the means of general and recognised signals'. This also affected the day-to-day routine of the LTC in watering and feeding the mules 'and in carrying out the interior economy . . . of this Corps'. The officers and NCOs were attentive in their duties but were impeded in their management and command of their men. He also noted about the most recent batch of 302 recruits sent out from Britain, '63 of whom are blessed with the most civilised Clap that the ladies of Bristol could bestow'.[32]

McMurdo was also short of carpenters and blacksmiths, which would be a perennial problem. In July he wrote requesting permission to second men with the suitable experience who were serving in the Crimea to the LTC, with increased pay (4s. per day) and free rations. McMurdo was also requesting wheelwrights and harness-makers.[33] Not only was McMurdo short of skilled artificers but their tools and equipment as well, noting in April he was short of farriers' tools and that none of the farriers sent out in a recent draft to the Crimea had any. By 28 May some 150 Turkish porters, 100 drivers and mules had arrived. There were also nineteen Spanish muleteers and their mules. However, they had landed 'all without shelter'. He urgently requested fifty bell tents.[34] It later transpired that one of the Spanish muleteers, Miguel Mormeneu, was in fact a deserter from the Spanish army. He was arrested and dealt with accordingly by the military authorities.[35] Against this background, Lord Palmerston's claim that the LTC was 'in a state of complete efficiency' is highly misleading. Estcourt's June summation that the LTC was 'forming itself by degrees', but that it was still 'uphill work' is closer to the truth.[36]

It's little wonder when faced with these problems that the LTC may not have lived up to expectations, especially those of the gentlemen of the press. The 'Special Correspondent' from the *Illustrated Times* sketched out the situation and reported that in his opinion the LTC was 'useless':

> Among the various army improvements that our Crimean disasters have given rise to, one that was thought likely to be of much benefit was the institution of a Land Transport Corps, that should relieve the soldier from a good deal of harassing labour . . . They are a newly-instituted corps . . . though to a certain extent they have been useless here. They are very unpopular amongst the troops; and although they go about armed to the teeth, and carry as great a weight as any man in the army . . . yet they are called a lazy, useless set.[37]

Equally unimpressed was the man from *The Times*, W.H. Russell. He thought them 'ruffians' who did know how to care for their horses: 'Yesterday I saw a ruffian beating a horse across the loins with a heavy billet of wood used to cog the wheels of the trucks to a halt. The navvies understood how to use their horses; the men of the Land Transport Corps . . . seem to do their best to kill them.'

An anonymous NCO of the LTC agreed with the sentiments of the press. He wrote to a friend in Glasgow that:

> This Corps is a complete failure; one Native is worth two Europeans; the natives work more, and cost the country less. We have a lot of young men who joined this corps that the belief that they were to be gents., such as clerks, shop-boys, and so on; but such men are for no use here, only an encumbrance. A good hard-working man is the person required here. He has to drive three mules, with pack-saddles on, and do other work besides; and to drive mules is no joke, for they are as stubborn as the 'Old Boy' himself.[38]

The men of the LTC were too few in number, and as a result overworked and filthy. Our anonymous NCO continues:

Shoeing a somewhat reluctant LTC mule. The mule has been 'hobbled' by a group of 'native' drivers whilst the LTC farrier attends to its feet.

We are up in the morning at quarter to three, when we feed our mules, then parade with our arms and accoutrements at a quarter to four; then water the mules, take breakfast, saddle three mules per man, and off they set with their loads towards Sebastopol, returning to camp in the evening, take dinner and supper together; turn into bed with every stitch of clothes on, the only thing we take off is our boots.³⁹

One Aberdonian officer wrote home to his family explaining how 'service in the Land Transport Corps is no sinecure':

The Land Transport Corps . . . have to convey the provisions, the forage, and all supplies to the camp, and have frequently to carry shot and shell to the batteries the greater part of the night. These fatiguing duties and the troublesome class of men who form the corps of drivers is an unpleasant contrast to the luxurious life of an officer of the Hon. East India Company, to which I have hitherto been accustomed!⁴⁰

In Sickness and Health

The LTC suffered from a debilitating rate of sickness during its first few months in the Crimea, largely the result of over-work, 'Crimean fever' and because its new recruits were not sufficiently acclimatised to the rigours of not only active service, but the local climate. Part of this problem was due to a lack of tents, blankets and even uniforms. McMurdo fumed about 'when the Land Transport Corps was formed, the necessity of supplying it with Camp Equipage' from Britain as there was none to be had in the Crimea. All well and good, but such camp equipage was slow coming out to the Crimea. Some of the officers had arrived with their own tents, and with uniforms, but many of the ORs had landed in the Crimea in just their greatcoats and civilian clothes and had no tents or blankets. Only forty bell tents had been issued for the LTC, and those were in use by the men of the Commissariat Transport Corps.⁴¹ In terms of uniform, there was confusion as to the exact status of the LTC and whether it was able to draw Ordnance Stores, which included greatcoats, mess tins and so forth, as well as clothing whilst in the Crimea. In May McMurdo wrote to General Airey requesting 'an extra allowing of clothing' from the 'stores of the army' including greatcoats and boots. There was a problem, however, with the exact status of the LTC as it was thought they were civilian auxiliaries and thus not able to draw 'public' stores. McMurdo settled the matter by quoting the Royal Warrant of January 1855 which stated the LTC was a 'part of the Regular Land Forces' and that the men were 'all enlisted as regular soldiers' and thus able to draw on 'public stores' including boots, mess tins and greatcoats which were supplied by the Ordnance.[42] Red tape duly untangled, McMurdo requisitioned the following stores for the LTC:

2,000 Capotes or Greatcoats
3,000 Blankets
9,000 Boots
1,000 Haversacks
10,000 Canteens
1,800 Camp Kettles
Hatchets 'in the usual proportion'

This was to ensure that each man would receive a greatcoat, blanket, two pairs of boots, haversack and canteen.[43] Without tents, blankets or greatcoats its little wonder many men soon fell sick. McMurdo reported to HQ on 1 June 1855 that cholera had broken out amongst his men, and that up to 31 May, eight had died.[44] Benjamin Strange wrote of his life in camp:

> Tent life is a very curious one – 16 men in a bell tent lying all round with their greatcoats under them and covered over with a blanket. We manage to do pretty well in dry weather, but when it rains we get like drowned rats – no nice position for one to be in, holding on to the tent-pole, and expecting that at every moment that tent and everything belonging to the men in it will be blown away! But like everything else we beginning to get used to things now which at first we were disgusted with . . . Cholera is very dominant with us, and generally speaking attacks the new arrivals more virulently than the old . . . We lose a great many fine strong fellows through diarrhoea, dysentery, and febris, but when the attacked recover after a course of calomel [a strong purgative] they become as it were acclimatised to it.[45]

Strange was also struck at how the landscape had turned to churned up mud with 'little green' to be seen:

> We are in a valley surrounded by mountains or high and steep hills, with little green or wood to be seen. In fact it is desolate, and strikes one forcibly with the horrors of war. Where once fruitful

vineyards were, nothing now remains . . . all the ground is cut up with trenches, and the hills surmounted by batteries.[46]

The leading medical journal, *The Lancet,* noted that the LTC suffered from the highest rate of sickness in the British army; the rate of mortality amongst personnel of the LTC amounting to one-third of the entire army. *The Lancet* opined that the high rate of illness was 'owing more to its composition, than either to duty of want of care', but it did admit that during the period May to August deaths amongst the LTC had been 'excessive' largely due to cholera and typhoid fever. The worst cases were amongst the newly arrived recruits from Britain who soon fell prey to 'Crimean fever'.[47] This debilitating level of sickness had knock-on effects throughout the British army, as Russell of *The Times* noted:

> The losses in the Land Transport Corps by death would be extraordinary did we not find a parallel to them in the Sardinian army of Tchorgoun, which has lost in three weeks nearly 1000 men by cholera, dysentery, and diarrhoea. The Turks and French encamped in the valley suffer somewhat from the same diseases, but it is observable that the men who die are recruits and not old men who are mostly acclimatized. At Yenikale the detachment of Land Transport Corps lost in a fortnight 50 men, of whom 25 were English and 25 native drivers. In its present state it cannot supply all the wants of our army. We could not advance any body of troops without running risks of starvation, and even the 10th Hussars are said to have been unable to keep their horses so far from Balaklava, owing to the want of forage.[48]

Not all LTC were taken to hospital due to sickness: despite being escorted by cavalry, 2nd Class Drivers John McHenry and Robert Barrington were injured when they were ambushed by Russian sharp-shooters 'near the Chateau of Prince Woronzoroff, beyond Biadar [sic]'. One of their mules was killed and two were wounded.[49] One of the essential duties of the LTC was to take water to the men in the trenches, and it was dangerous work carrying heavy water bags. On one occasion, 'Some of our chaps got killed, and about 14 wounded.'[50]

Crime and Punishment

The officers and men of the LTC were perhaps not of the highest quality; as Colonel Massé notes, 'Enlistment was not selective and many men unsuitable for other arms were accepted' so that 'many rough characters and physically unfit youths were included'. In order to attract recruits to the LTC very high pay was offered and indeed Captain Vokes, who was responsible for recruitment in the United Kingdom, notes how he tried to persuade 275 men who had been rejected as unfit by the Medical Staff Corps to enlist. What was needed was experienced officers and men but both were lacking.[51] In August Quartermaster O'Reilly, LTC, was tried by court martial, 'For not having accounted for the sum of £57 13s. 9d., part of a sum of £210 Government Money entrusted to the Quartermasters of Brigade.' O'Reilly was found guilty as charged and cashiered. O'Reilly had previously been considered 'utterly unfit for service' due to being nearly blind, which had previously led him to retire from the 99th Regiment on grounds of ill-health.[52] First Class Driver James Dempster was tried by court martial on 22 October for 'having made use of disgusting and insubordinate language' to his superior, one Corporal William Timms, and 'having struck a violent blow' at Timms with 'a clenched fist'. He was sentenced to fifty lashes, 'and imprisoned with hard labour for 12 months'. Second Class Driver Alexander Webb was court-martialled the same month for having stolen food and money amounting to 207 sovereigns and 3 £5 notes from the tent of Mr George Harding, Chief Accountant's Clerk, LTC. He was sentenced to two years' imprisonment with hard labour.[53]

But it was not just out in the Crimea that the LTC found itself in trouble: William Harris 'absconded from the barracks' in Bristol which housed the LTC Depot with £30 in silver in October 1855. By autumn 1855, nearly 3,000 men of the LTC were billeted in Bristol, many of whom were 'the rawest recruits from the different regiments of Irish militia'. In order to manage these 2,334 men there was only 1 field officer, 2 captains and 8 quartermasters. Moreover, the barracks could only accommodate 300 men, meaning that the remainder were scattered about the city, billeted on the civil population. On 25 October a 'serious mutiny and riot' occurred at the LTC barracks. A detachment of men from the Galway Militia who had volunteered for service in the LTC had recently arrived in Bristol. Expecting their full £5 enlistment bounty, they were informed that their uniform would be deducted from it, and they would not receive the full amount. 'The Adjutant remonstrated with them' and threatened to have them arrested whereupon 'the insubordinate recruits . . . commenced an attack upon him, and . . . knocked him down'. When an attempt was made to restore discipline, the disgruntled recruits armed themselves with stones from the parade ground and 'threw them in thick volleys at the officers'. Urgent requests for help were sent to the nearby artillery barracks and help soon arrived in the shape of gunners and a howitzer which was 'brought out and placed on the parade' in order to intimidate the mutineers. Not having the desired effect, the order was given to load 'an operation which had the desired effect of restoring something like order'. Between twenty and thirty of the 'principal ringleaders' were arrested and were to be court-martialled.[54]

When a draft 600 LTC recruits were ordered to be despatched to the Crimea, 'quite a mutiny occurred'. On arriving at Bristol station for onward travel to Plymouth for embarkation, 'a large number of them positively refused to set foot in a railway carriage unless they were paid the remainder of their [enlistment] bounty'. A 'large number of the men' then 'dispersed to various public houses' where they got uproariously drunk. Despite the 'entreaties of their officers' only a 'small number ... consented to go quietly'. The remainder were all arrested.[55] Violence by men of the LTC broke out again on 7 November 1855. 'Staves, stones, and knives were used' and the police were 'sadly ill-used by the ruffians' in their attempt to restore order. Peace was short-lived however, as the streets of Bristol erupted into violence again on 10 November, when four members of the LTC were wounded and taken to the infirmary. The rioting continued into Sunday, 11 November in the neighbourhoods of Lewins Mead and St James's Back. Such was the 'continued uproar' that 'the entire police force at the central station ... had to be more than once turned out'. The citizenry of Bristol were 'loud in their complaints' toward the LTC and the apparent inability of its few depot officers 'to enforce discipline'. Recruiting for the LTC was, for a time, suspended until the depot could be brought into some form of discipline.[56] Worse was to come out in the Crimea, however, when in September 1855 the *United Service Gazette* (25 September 1855) reported 150 men had deserted:

> The Land Transport Contingent was diminished two days ago by the sudden desertion of about 150 men. This is attributed by the Officers to a sort of conspiracy, and to the instigation of Russian agents ... Active measures are being taken to fill up the void thus occasioned, and which, though considerable, is not of grave importance.

Whilst the LTC was certainly a step in the right direction, its heterogeneous personnel, many of them the 'rawest recruits from

Ireland', were not of a particularly high standard. It had been quickly and somewhat indiscriminately recruited up to strength. The officers were too few, and many of them having transferred from the cavalry gave themselves 'airs of a combatant corps'. None of this helped the LTC gain popularity or much official support at a time when many conservative commentators thought it a 'prominent and costly evil' which was probably better replaced by hiring Messrs Pickfords to move the army's supplies.[57] How the LTC coped under the strain of active service in the Crimean climate will be explored in Chapter 10.

Chapter 8

The Ambulance Corps

Not only were the LTC entrusted with moving supplies and ammunition but also with carrying and tending to the sick and wounded. Frenchman Dominique Larrey had pioneered battlefield medicine and ambulances during the Napoleonic Wars. Britain lacked any equivalent organisation, despite the common sense suggestion made by a Dr Milligan to raise an Ambulance Corps in 1819 which sadly came to naught.[1] The British army medical services had historically been divided into the Army Medical Department and the Ordnance Hospital Department, the latter part of the ancient Board of Ordnance which was responsible for all the fortifications, artillery and Engineer soldiers of the British army. The two separate medical organisations were merged in 1853. Dr Andrew Smith was appointed as its head and it was he who proposed the formation of a specialist 'Ambulance Corps' in February 1854. Dr Smith aimed to emulate the French system of *Ambulance Volante* (literally 'Flying Ambulances') introduced by Baron Larrey more than half a century earlier. Unfortunately, design of the vehicles was passed to the Royal Arsenal at Woolwich, which produced cumbersome, heavy designs using gun-carriage wheels rather than the lightweight vehicles Smith had originally intended. As one commentator noted, the French had been using field ambulances for fifty years which 'we are only [now] beginning to employ'.[2]

Every regiment in the army had its own surgeon and small hospital, usually manned by the 'Hospital Sergeant' and a handful of orderlies, many of whom were considered useless. However, the French appeared years ahead of the British: the French medical services (*Service de Santé Militaire*) had been formed in the 1790s as a single, unified military organisation. The French had used battlefield ambulances and stretcher-bearers (*brancadiers*) from as early as 1812, and by the time of the Crimean

THE AMBULANCE CORPS

Dr Andrew Smith designed these large, four-wheel ambulances for service in the Crimea but they were too large and heavy and needed at least four horses to pull them. Many sick and wounded men refused to use them since they looked like hearses.

War the system was well-established, with mules carrying folding iron litters to carry two patients (one on each side) for battlefield evacuation. Whilst the British army had just fifty-three wheeled ambulances of which only fourteen were taken to the Crimea, every French division had thirty ambulance mules and forty stretcher bearers. In addition, there were teams of trained nurses (*infirmiers*) as well as the nursing Sisters of St Vincent de St Paul – the 'Sisters of Charity', whom Florence Nightingale dismissed as merely 'consolatrices'. The French army even offered the services of fifty of these nursing sisters as well as medical personnel to the British army during the outbreak of cholera whilst the two armies were camped around Varna, but the offer was declined. Finally, both armies could call on their bandsmen to act as stretcher-bearers.[3]

Despite Dr Smith's urgent call for the creation of a 400-strong 'Hospital Conveyance Corps' formed from able-bodied men to transport the sick and wounded he was overruled by the government, largely on the grounds of cost, and instead the superannuated Chelsea and Greenwich Pensioners were to be employed for this work, none of whom in Smith's opinion were fit for duty. A War Office circular dated 30 March 1854

Members of the Brigade of Guards carrying their wounded, a role traditionally given over to the bandsmen and regimental boys.

invited Out-pensioners under the age of 50 to enrol.[4] Despite Smith's misgivings, *The Times* thought the Out-pensioners 'healthy, robust fellows, well able to perform the duties assigned to them'.[5] Two officers were placed in charge, Captain John James Grant, Staff Officer of Pensioners at Waterford in Ireland, and Captain John Pelling Piggot, Staff Officer of Pensioners for the Salisbury District. Usefully, Grant was fluent in French, Italian and Persian. The third officer was Adjutant William Henry, late of the Royal Artillery.[6]

In total 324 All Ranks were recruited by April and they sailed on board the *Tynemouth* on 13 June, having been reviewed in Hyde Park on 30 May. The corps was organised into four companies and a troop of drivers. Arriving in Varna thirty-nine days later, the corps was dispersed with half the number being used as hospital orderlies and 'servants to medical officers'. The remaining 150 or so remained to man the ambulances. Between July and September the corps suffered from 32 deaths due to cholera; by the end of October Captain Grant had 288 men under his command of whom 150 were 'unfit for duty'. Of their vehicles, 53 had been embarked onboard *Tynemouth* and only 14 had been sent with the army to the Crimea. The remainder, including forge carts, were still at Varna. The drivers were not 'of even moderate ability' and the troop of drivers never reached its establishment strength.[7]

The reputation of the 'Hospital Conveyance Corps' was not high amongst the men at the front. They were 'superannuated Chelsea Pensioners' who 'killed themselves by drinking' and thus proved an abject failure.[8] Grant was unable to maintain discipline and drunkenness was widespread. The Inspector General of Hospitals, Dr John Hall, argued for the establishment of an Ambulance Corps organised and equipped on French lines.[9] Dr John Wood, surgeon to the 42nd Highlanders, recommended its 'immediate' adoption in January 1855.[10]

As 1854 came to a close with freezing mud and snow, Grant was planning a major re-organisation of the 'Hospital Conveyance Corps' as the Ambulance Corps. The wheeled ambulances designed by Smith had not been a success. Two designs had been employed, a large four-wheeled vehicle devised by Smith and a light, small two-wheeler created by Dr Guthrie, President of the Royal College of Surgeons and who had served as a surgeon during the Peninsular War. These light two-wheelers were reported to weigh as little as 10cwt. Contrary to the wishes of Smith, they had been fitted with heavy gun-carriage wheels which did little to aid their mobility. Lieutenant Colonel E.B. Hamley of the Royal Artillery described them as being like a London omnibus, with racks for stretchers on each side, and 'eased by high springs'. Staff Officer Somerset Calthorpe thought them 'decidedly' inferior to the French designs, lacking comfort for their occupants whilst others thought them rather like a hearse or 'the conveyance used by Messrs. Broadwood for the transportation of pianofortes'. It was their resemblance to a hearse which led to many soldiers refusing to travel in them. Even *The Lancet* could not find any praise for them.[11] On 25 October 1854 Smith wrote to the Military Secretary at Horse Guards informing him that the 'Hospital Conveyance Corps' had 'totally failed'. In its place he proposed forming a new unit of 400 specially selected volunteers but this was turned down. Smith also urgently requested augmenting the number of officers in order to improve discipline, but this too was rejected. In a report of 27 December 1854 to General Airey, Smith noted he had 12 ambulance waggons, 1 stores cart and 1 forge cart. There were 3 waggons still onboard the *London* and of the rest of the wheeled rolling stock, 5 ambulance waggons, 19 ambulance carts, 9 Flanders waggons and 2 stores carts were still at Varna, with the exception of the forge cart which had been given over to the Inniskilling Dragoons. For the vehicles he did have in the Crimea he had no serviceable horses or mules and the number

Above and below: Lighter, four-wheel ambulances were also designed for Crimean service. These were inspired by the French light two-wheel *Ambulance Volante* of Baron Larrey from fifty years earlier, and were far more successful than the lumbering four-wheelers.

of effective drivers was just 24. He recommended the purchase of new horses and mules and the raising of a new troop of drivers of 110 effectives, aged 25 years or older and taller than 5ft 3in. He also recommended that drivers from the Royal Artillery, men who were used to handling horses and vehicles, be seconded to 'contribute materially to its efficiency'.[12]

By spring 1855 the 'Hospital Conveyance Corps' was 'quite *hors de combat*': 'men and horses were nearly all gone or unfit for duty, or sick'. To the aid of their allies came the French *Train* with their teams of mules carrying litters for transportation of the wounded. The whole corps required rebuilding from the ground up as the Ambulance Corps. Placed in command was the now Major Grant assisted by Captain Pigott, Captain Bainbridge LTC and Adjutant Henry. By 19 April 1855 Grant had managed to scrape together '12 waggons and cattle for them complete for the conveyance of sick and wounded'. From this pool, the Ambulance Corps was able to send 8 waggons daily, each capable of carrying 10 men, so that 80 sick or wounded soldiers could be carried down from the camps to Balaklava, 'leaving one third the number in Camp daily for present' to rest and maintain rolling stock but *in extremis* could also be put into service. A further memorandum was sent by Grant to HQ complaining about the overloading of the ambulance waggons as 'in addition to the arms, accoutrements, knapsacks' there were 'blankets, sheepskin coats, long boots and extra winter clothing which render incommoding the sick and wounded'. Grant recommended that two *bât* ponies from the LTC be seconded to the Ambulance Corps to carry this additional clothing.[13]

Dr John Hall had sent an urgent request to Dr Smith in London in November 1854 for new ambulance waggons. These were new light-

Instead of wheeled ambulances, and based on their North African experience, the French army preferred to use mules – the cross-country 4x4 of their day.

weight rolling stock designed for the Ambulance Corps, and they began to arrive from May 1855, but were scarcely enough to replace the number of broken down older vehicles, and the army's full requirement would not be met until winter 1855.[14] McMurdo completed a lengthy memorandum on the new vehicles. He reported on 24 May that there were available 24 'Irish Jaunting Cars', each drawn by 2 horses and capable of carrying 6 men sitting down and 1 man lying. There were 6 in the Crimea and '18 on their way out'. McMurdo thought that these 'Irish Cars':

> Are not intended as <u>Principal</u> – but more as an <u>Aid</u> in the Ambulance Service; and in this light I consider them exceedingly useful & economical, carriages. The present siege operations, for example, the daily Calculations [for wounded] have been few; and an Irish Car has therefore been found to be sufficient in the rear of each attack – where forward a large ambulance with six horses and three drivers were posted.[15]

There were also twelve 'Maltese carts' carried on springs which had originally been intended to carry commissariat supplies but could in an emergency be used to transport the sick and wounded. Each cart was 'well calculated to carry with comfort – two bad cases (recumbent) or 4 to 6 in a sitting posture according to the gravity of their hurts'. In January 1,000 French-style litters were ordered. The French system of ambulance mules carrying litters was systematically and 'universally admired' by the British in the Crimea due to their rapidity of deployment and the comfort they offered the wounded.[16] The French ambulance mules could carry two patients in an 'iron chair, or litter . . . hooked to the packsaddle . . . hinged . . . to support the head, which could be fixed at any angle desired . . . and a foot-board . . .'.[17] In addition to the patients each mule carried medical supplies to treat the wounded, as well as the personal kit of the *infirmier* who attended each mule and its patients.[18] Unlike wheeled ambulances, these mules could cross a wide variety of terrain and also presented a smaller target than a wheeled ambulance.[19] British observers believed them to be able to clear a battlefield rapidly ('in an afternoon') of wounded, and such was the 'humanity' of the French that they evacuated French, British and later Russian wounded, for treatment.[20] The French also displayed 'great kindness and gentleness' to the wounded, in contrast to the British orderlies and bandsmen.[21] British officers thought of the French that 'if they had been women they could not have behaved more tenderly'.[22]

Above and right: The French army used mule litters like these to carry the sick and wounded. They could be arranged so the passenger laid down or sat up and had a folding hood to keep off the rain or sun. The British army copied the design for its own use.

By 24 May only 200 pairs of French-style litters had been completed, of which McMurdo had 33 pairs in the Crimea. McMurdo 'immediately fitted them upon mules – and drilled the Drivers in managing these conveyances'.[23] There were 36 pairs of litters and 15 pairs of chairs landed at Balaklava for the ambulance service and taken up to the front on 15 June; a further 26 pairs of litters returned from the Kertch expedition 2 days later and were forwarded to the front so that McMurdo had 77 pairs of litters ready in time for the Assault on 18 June. These litters required 1 officer, 3 NCOs, 49 drivers and 51 Mules.[24]

The number of mules and litters gradually crept up during the summer, eventually totalling 149 pairs by the time of the capture of Sebastopol in September 1855:

Pack mules	92 (77 'in charge of LTC'; 15 attached from LTC)
Litters and pack saddles complete	75
Litters and pack saddles needing repair	15
Spare litters and chairs	59[25]

Of the newly designed rolling stock were forty-three 'Bianconi Cars'. These were somewhat idiosyncratic vehicles designed by an Anglo-Italian entrepreneur Charles Bianconi (1786–1875) for the postal service in Ireland. They were small, lightweight two-wheelers carrying about a dozen passengers on longitudinal bench seats, the passengers sitting back-to-back, facing outward, with space between the seats for luggage. Dr John Hall also approved of the adoption of these Bianconi Cars for the transportation of the sick, and proposed to attach one to every battalion 'upon the march for the purpose of taking up the weakly men who fall out of the ranks'. Because they offered no protection from the elements, McMurdo recommended the fitting of a hood or awning to protect the passengers. Despite *The Times* optimistically describing how a 'number of jaunting cars *à la Irlandaise*' had arrived at Balaklava at the end of April 1855, McMurdo notes at the end of May that *none* had in fact arrived in the Crimea.[26] They were each capable of carrying eight wounded men; very 'light easy and manageable' and 'very much approved of' compared with the old lumbering Ambulances of Dr Smith. Accompanying these Bianconi Cars were 'a body of artificers and drivers, with quaint looped hats and sleeves with the devices of their craft embroidered thereon . . . for the Land Transport Corps.'[27]

On 16 July Major Grant was granted three months' leave in Britain and five days later the Ambulance Corps was ordered to be merged

THE AMBULANCE CORPS

The British army emulated the French ambulance mules and litters: here personnel of the Land Transport Corps accompany the sick and wounded to the hospital at the Monastery of St George, high above Balaklava.

with the LTC so that transport of stores and the sick were under the aegis of a single organisation *à la francaise*.[28] The few remaining Chelsea Pensioners were to be discharged and new men were to be recruited for what was now the 'Ambulance Division' of the LTC, placed under the command of Captain Pigott. Twelve additional officers would be required – six Quartermasters and six Assistant Quartermasters, the former being recruited from officers already serving in the Crimea in order to bring the establishment up to strength.[29] This hard work by McMurdo and Grant meant that by the time of the final Assault on Sebastopol on 8 September, the British army was far better prepared, and able, to deal with casualties. The hard lesson had been learned that caring for and carrying sick and wounded soldiers on the battlefield could not be done on the cheap, and had to be done by well-trained professionals using specialist vehicles and equipment designed for the task. It was another step in the right direction for the British army.

Chapter 9

Running the Railway

Organisation and Manpower

James Beatty, Kellock and Campbell were in charge of the railway but acting under the orders of McMurdo regarding personnel, including officers, supplied by the LTC. Captain, later Major, Powell (39th Regiment) was seconded to the LTC as Chief Superintendent of the railway. He had under his command 3 officers and about 200 other ranks. Powell was one of the first officers to be appointed to the railway. In July he was promoted to 'Captain of Division'. McMurdo warmly welcomed this as: 'For several months past, [Powell] has served under my orders at the Terminus of the Railway; and I have great satisfaction in bearing the highest testimony to his practical work as an officer; and I may add that the late Field Marshal [Lord Raglan] was fully aware of the character of this excellent officer.'[1]

Amongst these officers was Lieutenant Lamb (50th Regiment), appointed on 31 July. McMurdo thought him 'in every way qualified' to take on the task as 'Superintendent of one of the Railway Dépôts'. He was 'attentive and unremitting in his duties'. The appointment of Lamb as superintendent of the 'upper terminus' meant that Powell could be 'removed to the Centre Station, in charge of the Line'. In this he was assisted by the young Ensign Clancy (14th Regiment). Lamb was succeeded in early November 1855 by Lieutenant Grace of the 57th Regiment who was then with his regiment at Kazatch. McMurdo thought it imperative to replace Lamb as 'the locomotive is about to run, and that the railway will be carried on a much larger scale'.[2] Lieutenant Grace was in charge of 'that portion of the line from the Col de Balaclava to the Forks' which was opened for traffic on 13 November 1855. In October Captain Collinwood (21st Regiment) was attached to the railway, and in November Lieutenant Norman, 'a most quiet and painstaking officer', was added to the roster.[3] Those officers 'specially attached' to run the railway on 1 January 1856 included Lieutenant Grace, Ensign Clancy and Ensign Rance (14th Regiment).[4]

Sergeant Aston (20th Regiment) was appointed as Assistant Paymaster. There was no clerk to deal with the administration of the railway and proper management of its stores until November 1855 when it was ordered that: 'The following establishment is sanctioned for the office of the chief superintendent of the railway – One clerk, receiving the difference between his regimental pay, and 4s. 4d. One clerk, with an allowance of 6d. per day, in addition to his pay.'

Sergeant Henry Benson of the 39th Regiment was appointed as clerk on 26 November 1855, to be paid by the railway establishment.[5] Additional NCOs were needed to superintend the seventy-five Turkish porters at the 'engine station' under the command of Lieutenant Powell, with Sergeant James Garnett 39th Regiment, an 'intelligent,

The Railway Yard in the centre of Balaklava town photographed by Roger Fenton. The crude nature of the permanent way is apparent, the sleepers being laid directly on the old road surface. (*Library of Congress*)

young, trustworthy' NCO being recommended to the position of 'superintendent'.[6]

Service on the railway must have been attractive as in May William Colquhoun Grant (1822–61) who was then serving as Captain Commandant of the Mounted Staff Corps, wrote to McMurdo applying for a position as assistance engineer, and was even willing to resign his appointment with the Mounted Staff Corps if his services were required by McMurdo for the railway, or any other service for which he was qualified, but in this he was not successful. Captain Grant, Royal Artillery, was appointed to 'take charge and Superintend the horses and mules employed on the Railway' in July 1855.[7] In order to take care of the railway horses, McMurdo required the services of a veterinary and a farrier, having been recommended the services of William Hurford of the 12th Lancers 'as a temporary measure' to the railway, receiving an 'additional salary of 5% a day while performing to the duties'.[8]

The railway under construction at the wharf side in Balaklava. The route has been roughly levelled and tamped, ready to receive sleepers and rails with a minimum of ballasting. (*Library of Congress*)

Farrier Major Adye of the 5th Dragoon Guards was attached to the railway in August 1855.[9]

During the same month, McMurdo requested ten smiths and ten carpenters under the supervision of a sergeant be temporarily seconded to the LTC 'for the service of the railway at Balaklava'. The men would receive 4s. per day and free rations.[10] A saddler sergeant and four saddlers or harness-makers were also required to keep the tack and harness of the railway horses in good order; McMurdo wrote to HQ at the beginning of August seeking permission to temporarily attach those men with the required skills to the railway workshops of the LTC. He also required a further three NCOs 'acquired with stable duties' to take charge of the railway stables. One Sergeant Rafferty of the 13th Foot had applied for the position of saddler sergeant.[11]

Railway Operations

Horses, later locomotives, were used both to shunt and pull loaded waggons from Balaklava Harbour on the level stretch of line a far as the depot at Kadikoi and thence to the foot of the inclined plane at Frenchman's Hill, a distance of about 2 miles. The line was double throughout, allowing for Up and Down working. The first engine-worked inclined plane was also double track, operated by two steam engines, although the artist of *The Illustrated London News* shows both the Up and Down line sharing a common centre rail. The inclined plane rose at 1 in 15 and was about ⅓ mile long. The winding engines were capable of raising eight loaded waggons at a time.[12] From the top of this incline, horses took the waggons forward up a second inclined plane of '1 in 25, for about 1½ mile to the Col de Balaclava'.[13] Such was the severity of the second incline that six horses were needed to pull only two loaded waggons. This second incline was single track which would later prove something of a bottleneck. Upon reaching the summit, the line was pretty much level, but it had to cross two deep gulleys. Due to lack of time and equipment these had not been bridged and so a rather unique – and dangerous – operating procedure was adopted: 'These were crossed by the rather primitive method of detaching each wagon in succession and making it run down one side and run up the other side by its own gravity; when there, horses were again used, and so the munitions arrived at Forks Depot, the terminus of the line.'[14]

It appears that 'Down' trains were worked via gravity, under the control of a brakesman, at least down the shallower of the inclined planes. This had already resulted in one fatal accident in March when the brakesman had lost control. Sadly, it was followed up by a second accident a few days later. A colour sergeant of the 71st described what happened:

> Camp, Balaklava, 9th April 1855. My dear Brother – I duly received yours of the 12th March, and was glad to hear you were all in good health at the time you wrote . . . Since I last wrote you – on the 2d March – nothing worth mentioning occurred to us up to the 5th inst., when 300 of the 71st were ordered to the front to assist in the siege operations. Accordingly we paraded and marched a short distance to where the Land Transport Corps keep their mules, soon we all got mounted on cattle they had prepared for us. This being the first time the Land Transport Corps had been called in to requisition for the conveyance of troops, you may guess there was some good laughing at us when we first got mounted. Thanks to the practice I had riding out with the 8th Hussars in Carlow, I felt quite at home on my mule; but many a poor fellow who had to mount for the first time looked droll enough. However, as we managed to get up to the heights over Sebastopol without any casualty, and were immediately marched to the advanced trenches, and commenced work – some filling sand-bags, others carrying gabions, &c. The place we were sent to being next to the enemy's sharpshooters, made us feel rather uncomfortable, as they kept up a constant fire of musketry on us the whole day, and now and then a shell would burst much closer to us than we had any fancy for. We left off work at 4 PM the only casualty being one of my company shot through the arm, as he was in the act of raising the pick he was working with, when the ball struck it and glided off and entered his arm. It was soon extracted, and he is now doing well; his name is Hugh Gourlay. After our work was over we were marched from the trenches to Lord Raglan's (a distance of five miles), where coffee was prepared for us, his Lordship coming out and superintending the distribution of it himself.[15]

Disaster struck as the last train load of the 71st was descending the incline:

After we were all served we were marched about half a mile to the railway, and were put into carriages to be conveyed to Balaklava. Up to this every one of us was quite delighted with what we called our first day's real soldiering (it being the first time we were under fire). Many of us remarked that it would be a memorable day for us, as we had been the first in the service who had been conveyed by the Land Transport Corps or Crimean Railway; but what follows will show you that we had not long cause to congratulate ourselves with the latter arrangement. From when we started into Balaklava is by rail about six miles. It being an incline the whole way, no engines are required coming down. We were accordingly divided into three parties; the two first, I think, hail four trucks, each having 15 men in them. They started, with an interval of about five minutes between the first and second, and both parties arrived in safety at a place about two miles from Balaklava, where the railway people have their principal station. We were then halted until the third and last party would come up. I believe in it there were six trucks, including one covered car for the officers. Most fortunately I belonged to the second party; for no sooner had we got halted to wait for the last to come than the cry was raised for us to jump out. It appears that the break that was used for stopping the carriages of the last party had given way, and on they came down the incline at a rate that threatened the destruction of all that were in them. I will leave you to imagine what were our feelings on seeing the train coming rushing along with all our officers and so many of our comrades about to be hurled into eternity. All the trucks in which the two first parties came in were standing right in their way, and had the last been allowed to run into them God only knows what would have been the result; but with great presence of mind, one of the railway officials put a plank of wood across the rail, and turned the carriages off. Of course the speed they were going at soon smashed some and upset the others. The one the officers were in (a covered one) was smashed to pieces, but only one of them was slightly injured. Our poor men were not so fortunate; one a nice young lad, Lance-Corporal H. Wilson, belonging to Westmuir, was killed on the spot, and 12 others more or less hurt. One (Private P. Loughelry, belonging to Bridgeton) has had his leg amputated; the others, I believe, are all likely to recover. Corporal Wilson was very intimate with Leishman; his son, who is in the band of the 14th Regiment, called on me the day after, and told me he was just come to see the poor fellow, whose body was then just

Officers and an NCO of the 71st Regiment (Highland Light Infantry), photographed by Roger Fenton in spring 1855. (*Library of Congress*)

brought down from where the accident occurred. This sad affair has cast a gloom over the whole regiment. It was the first casualty those of us who have came from Corfu have had. . . . I remain your affectionate brother, J. M.

A sergeant of the 71st informed his brother in Glasgow:

> We started all right; but after getting down a short distance I observed the speed getting too great for my notion of safety, and prepared for a smash. I was not wrong in my calculation, as, after running a short distance with great velocity the trucks ran off the rails and threw most of us upon the bank at the next station, where I believe the officials shifted the rails purposely to throw us off and prevent us running into the other division which had gone down in front of us, and was at a stand at that place . . . I never lost my presence of mind, and jumped off in time to escape scot free.[16]

Riding in the second carriage were the officers, including the Regimental Surgeon Dr Charles Ricketts. None of the officers were injured but received a 'severe shaking'. Ricketts immediately attended to the wounded men and had them taken to the regimental hospital of the *27e de Ligne*, where they were 'treated with the greatest kindness'. In the accident one man was killed, Lance Corporal H. Wilson, and a further twelve injured, with wounds varying from a compound fracture of the lower leg resulting in amputation to a 'contused back and cut forehead'.[17] Amongst the wounded civilians was James Beatty, who was thrown from one of the overturned waggons and suffered internal bruising which took several days of convalescence to overcome. Sadly, these were injuries that would later kill him.

Sous Lieutenant Alfred Minart of the *27e de Ligne* was an eyewitness to the accident:

> The railway is very curious. It is worked by horses for most of its length, the other means is by a steam engine which works a cable drum that pulls the wagons. Three days ago there was a terrible accident: 5 wagons carrying English soldiers coming back from the Trenches were struck on the descent by another train which had lost its brakes. We shout to the men who had come down, but despite this, there were a dozen of them who had survived in the trenches who were unfortunately

crushed or crippled. The rest of the men returned to camp by foot. The phlegm of the English is so great that five minutes after the accident, everything was cleared away and the traffic recommenced. I expressed my astonishment at this carelessness and was told: 'there were only four men killed. It could have been fourteen.'[18]

French staff officer Émile Vanson notes that 'they did not know how to use the brakes. In short, thanks to the indefinitely accelerating speed, several wagons carrying soldiers came off the tracks and were overthrown when arriving [at the bottom of the incline]'. Some of the wounded were transported to the French first-aid post where they were treated by French army doctors.[19] Surgeon Robinson of the Scots Guards wrote in his diary how 'owing to remissness in not putting on the break early enough, whilst going down the inclined plane' the waggons derailed and were overturned. 'Three men, it is said, have been killed, and seven wounded.'[20]

Raglan tried to shift the blame onto Beatty, writing in his despatch of 7 April:

> I caused 300 of the 71st to be brought down from Sir Colin's position yesterday on baggage animals, and send them back by railway. This produced a fatal and very serious accident, which has given me great pain. Mr Beatty assured me that there was no danger whatever, and that he had selected experienced and steady hands to take charge of the brakes, and he would accompany them himself, not from fear of any accident, but to ascertain how so many men could be well conveyed. He did go with them, but from some cause or other the last set of carriages, upon one of which he was, upset, and I grieve to say a corporal was killed, a private had his leg smashed, poor fellow, and ten or eleven others were more or less hurt . . . But the accident is unfortunate and much to be lamented, and will I fear stop the free use of the railway to the extent contemplated, unless Mr Beatty can place the brakes under far better control.

W.H. Russell, however, believed that the blame for the accident lay with Raglan who had delayed the departure of the 71st until night had fallen, and that it had started to rain making the rails greasy.

The Duke of Newcastle records during his visit to the Crimea in July 1855 that 'the railroad comes down to where the hospital ships lie, so that the sick can be carried straight on board'. Furthermore, a party of the Scots Guards had gone up to the heights by mule but had come back down by railway, showing that the railway was still used for the conveyance of troops despite the 71st' accident. The varied duties of the railway are listed in the following table:[21]

Distribution of Railway Service, 17 April 1855			
Corps or Department	No. of Waggons	Service Required	Place and Hour for Landing
Commissariat	32 'and ten half waggons of fuel'	2 waggons Fuel	For Kadikoi
		4 waggons Hay	For Kadikoi
		2 waggons Corn	For Kadikoi
		10 waggons Fuel	For the Front
		8 waggons Hay	For the Front
		6 waggons Corn	For the Front
Engineers	6 'and 6 half waggons of gabions on shot waggons'	2 Oak Scantling	Ordnance wharf, 9am
		4 Platforms	Engineers Yard
Artillery	22	6 waggons Powder	Diamond Wharf
		16 waggons Shot and Shell	Ordnance Wharf
71st Regiment	15	Conveyance of 300 Men to Balaklava	Head of Rail in Camp, 8am
Sick	10	Conveyance to Balaklava	Head of Rail in Camp, 12 o'clock noon

Another indication of the work asked of the railwaymen and the loads transported is given in a written order from McMurdo of 23 June 1855:[22]

Loads Conveyed, 23 June 1855			
Corps or Department	No. Waggons Needed	Stores Required	Place and Time for Landing
Qaurtermaster General	4	Huts	Diamond Wharf
Commissariat	40	Supplied to the depot at 'The Col'	
	10	For hay	
	4	For corn	
	4	For porter	
	1	Rum	
Artillery	20	Shot	Diamond Wharf
	20	Shell	Ordnance Wharf

Beatty had reported back in May about the tension and frustration with the commissariat. This continued in June with a furious McMurdo reporting to General Airey that:

> The Commissariat Officer at Kadikoi was in the habit of stopping wagons of corn intended for the front. This circumstance now accounts to me for the extraordinary discrepancy between the departure and arrival reports. The Railway allotment was made for Kadikoi and the Commissariat Officer was not justified in taking corn from wagons which were distributed by me for another service.[23]

William Filder wrote to Airey that 'McMurdo appears to have been misinformed that the wagons were stopped by the Commissariat at Kadikoi' and provided a written report from John Power, the storekeeper. Power reported that five waggons containing corn and barley had been 'put in a siding here [Kadikoi] about a week since (not by my orders)'. It was only when they were unloaded that it was discovered they were intended for the front because the despatch notice was found in the bottom of one of the waggons. Occasionally waggons had been stopped when they had been over or poorly loaded, causing a sack of corn (or similar) to fall from them, in which instance 'the managing man at the Railway Station said it was no use sending it on'.[24]

All was not well with the railway. In mid-June McMurdo reported violent quarrels between the different groups of navvies, and that the 'Railway Drivers had struck work' leaving McMurdo 'stumped'. The navvies had struck work because their six-month period of enlistment had come to an end and they refused to work. 'The whole system of getting up provisions by the railway', noted the *Leeds Intelligencer*, was 'deranged and valuable time is lost in also bringing up shot and shell to the trenches.'[25] McMurdo invited Romaine to act as arbitrator, who found that Beatty had been sick for ten days: 'Mr Camidge who is sick in a hut . . . lacks energy. Mr Parker the next cannot manage them at all & Mac [sic McMurdo] says he can get no work done.' Romaine 'answered their complaints' and 'promised to get set right by Lord Raglan and me, as the officers refused . . . from fear of responsibility'.[26] It was reported to Lord Raglan that 'the drivers and breaksmen [sic] and some others of the workmen employed . . . have openly refused to do their duty and mutinied against their officers'. It was therefore ordered that 'to take steps to inforce obedience to the lawful commands of the officers of the Railway . . . That tomorrow morning [24 June 1855] at six o'clock the Provost Marshal and his assistants will attend with sufficient force and the first and every instance of mutiny and disobedience will be instantly and severely punished.'[27]

As the railway wound its way toward Kadikoi it was susceptible to flooding. On the evening of 23 June there was a 'tremendous storm of lightning'. Rain 'fell in torrents', and the sky was lit up by 'electric disturbances'. Flash flooding damaged 'several stores' and huts at Kadikoi as well as the railway itself due to the ballast being washed away and some sections being flooded. The *Daily News* reported railway traffic was at a standstill and it would be 'several days . . . before the injury can be repaired'.[28]

The worn-out state of the railway and rolling stock resulted in several nasty accidents. On Saturday, 11 August two railway waggons carrying hutting material came off the line 'between Mrs Seacoles' and the Col'. The accident was reported by Captain Gerald Goodlake who witnessed a second accident three days later causing considerable delay to the transportation and thus erection of wooden stable huts.[29] Lieutenant Powell was ordered to carry out an investigation, reporting that 'neither myself, Lieut. Lamb, or Ensign

Glancy knows anything whatever about Waggons . . . having ran off the line'. Nor did he think it likely a waggon could have come off the line without his knowledge. Further questioning was carried out by Lieutenant Powell of Sergeant William Torke, of the Coldstream Guards, who was supervising the unloading of the waggons at 'The Col'. His testimony to Powell in fact differed from his sworn statement in which he categorically mentioned that two waggons 'were off the line between Mrs Seacoles and The Col' and could provide a sergeant from the Royals as witness; two loaded waggons had also 'ran off the Line at Balaclava'. Upon being asked about waggons running off the line he denied such an accident had happened but then admitted that:

> Two waggons had arrived at The Col laden with timber attached to a shot waggon, and that as soon as the shot waggon was disengaged from the other which it supported, that the weight of the timber was so great behind that it lifted off up the fore-wheels and that it had to be unloaded on the spot.

The incident was considered to be of a trivial nature, and because it had not interrupted the regular working of the line it had not been reported. Captain Goodlake, however, '<u>saw</u> the trucks go off the line' and that some of his men had helped to get them back on the track and was unhappy with Powell's explanation.[30]

This investigation, however, did reveal flaws in the operating practices of the railway and that the second, horse-worked incline up to the heights was a considerable bottleneck. Powell noted that waggons were usually loaded early in the morning and would typically reach 'The Col' at about midday. However, this delay was due to the line on the second incline being single so that 'the waggons cannot pass by each other, all must take their turn' to be worked up the incline. This led to railway waggons sometimes having to wait for up to 6 hours. There was a lack of porters to load and unload the waggons and furthermore the loading of them appears to have been very haphazard with 'want of care': 'only a few days ago he had to unload two, and reload them before he could allow them to proceed.' Waggons had been badly or incorrectly labelled. This all added to the delays in getting material to the front. Furthermore, sometimes loads would shift on the move, necessitating trains of waggons being stopped so that they could be reloaded en route. Even worse, 'I also found pieces of hutting material, which had fallen off the Waggons, coming out of the incline.' In order

Detail of the incline up to Frenchman's Hill. Note the double-track incline shares a common centre rail which meant only one train could use it at a time.

Detail of the winding engines, both of which were supplied by Clayton & Shuttleworth and rated at 14hp. Note the large diameter winding drum and artesian well for supplying the boilers with water.

to ensure waggons were correctly loaded, Powell had stationed NCOs at 'various parts of the Line with orders for them to see Everything that falls off the Waggons put up and sent on by the first one that passes'.[31] In reply Captain Goodlake noted that the timber of the huts he had ordered had been loaded before noon on 8 August but did not in fact arrive at 'The Col' until two days later, and told a similar story about a load of hutting materials ordered before noon on Saturday, 11 August which arrived on Sunday evening. Furthermore, there had been a strike amongst the Turkish porters and 'Turkish labourers told off to load them [the waggons]'. In reply to this criticism, it was noted that a corporal and two privates were 'always present to superintend the loading'.[32] In order to amend this, a few weeks later it was proposed that the LTC drivers assist with the loading and unloading of waggons, a suggestion that McMurdo disagreed with. He felt it would be 'attended with much risk and frequently with damage from the animals running away'. But the question of the irregular loading and delays in getting railway waggons up to the front had resulted in him receiving 'constant complaints'. He also received complaints from officers commanding that their men had to be detailed to assist in loading and unloading the waggons 'without the aid of a single fatigue man or labourer'. McMurdo thought it was asking too much of the already over-tasked drivers to help with the loading and unloading of waggons and McMurdo informed General Airey he would take immediate steps to better regulate the loading and unloading of waggons.[33] General Orders of 4 September confirmed McMurdo's view, and probably to the chagrin of those officers commanding, 'the loading of the carts, or animals, belongs to those for whose use they are supplied'. In other words, the unit to whom the cargo was transported were to assist with the loading and unloading duties.[34] This issue of transhipment became a source of friction and delay with stores arriving by railway to the depot at 'The Col' but then having to be physically manhandled into waiting waggons and carts for onward transport. A road would have avoided this issue.

There was another accident on the evening of 21 August when '2 trucks with heavy guns turned right over near the shot and shell Depot, killing one breaksman and injuring another'. Major Evans blamed this on the railway waggons being 'rotten and out of repair', and the 'line itself shaky'. It was 'any wonder' that more accidents did not occur. New railway waggons were 'daily expected' as was the first detachment from the Army Works Corps and it was hoped that the latter would be able to 'put the line in repair'.[35]

By the fall of Sebastopol, McMurdo reported that the 'Railway Detachment' of the LTC consisted of 4 officers, 25 NCOs and 178 privates:

State of Railway Detachment, 16 September 1855

Distribution	Officers	Superintendents	Sub-Superintendents	1st Class Drivers	2nd Class Drivers	Civil Artificers	Horses	Mules	Spanish Mules
Superintending line	3	3	6	7		3			
Engineers						3			
Assistant engineers					2				
Assistant quartermasters			1		1				
Brakesmen					6				
Pointsmen					3				
Drivers on the line					65				
Signalmen					2				
Chaff cutters					4				
Sawyers					1	2			
Carpenters					4	3			
Stable men				2	18				
Quartermaster General					1				
Oil men					1				
Blacksmiths						3			
Orderlies				2	7				
Cooks					12				
Engine drivers					2				
In charge of lamps					1				
Other duties				2	26				
Servants					1				
Animals effective							58	84	14
Sick	1				11	1	8	3	4
In hospital				2	16				
Total	4	3	7	15	178	21	66	87	18

The Army Works Corps

The navvies sent out in January to build the railway had only signed up for a period of six months, so they began to return home during July and August; the last navvy had left the Crimea by 27 August with only Beatty, Campbell and two or three of his principal railway superintendents remaining in the Crimea to take charge of things. The first party of navvies returned home in early June on board the *Prince of Wales*, landing at Gravesend. With the exception of two, all were invalids but in 'excellent health and spirits' and apparently 'none the worse' for their six-month stay in the Crimea. They 'expressed themselves perfectly satisfied with the treatment they had received from Mr Beatty'.[36] Not all of the navvies came home, some forty-six of them dying in the Crimea, including Mr Gyngell, the missionary and 'tract reader'.

To replace the navvies, Sir Joseph Paxton put forward the suggestion for another civilian corps, the Army Works Corps, to be officered by civil engineers with the manpower drawn from artificers, labourers and navvies. It was a cross between the French *Troupes d'Administration* and the Royal Sappers and Miners and can be seen as the ancestor of the Labour Corps (1917–21) and Royal Pioneer Corps (1939–93). The first serious suggestion for the Army Works Corps (AWC) as a 'Corps of Navigators' was made in a letter from Paxton to Lord Panmure, the new Secretary of State for War, on 24 April 1855. Paxton proposed to recruit 1,000 navvies 'to be employed in the Crimea in the duty of forming entrenchments and other earth works'. Two days later Paxton was given permission to proceed with his novel scheme. Paxton was to undertake much of the organisation personally and together with Panmure was responsible for the selection of the officers and staff and the terms of enlistment which were to be 'upon precisely the same scale' as the navvies who had built the railway. Rations were to be supplied by the commissariat whilst Paxton was to make the contracts for all the clothing, equipment and tools used by the AWC, as well as organise its transport to the Crimea. In the Crimea the AWC was to be placed under the command of General Sir Harry Jones, the Chief Royal Engineer. The total cost of forming and equipping the AWC was estimated to be £50,000.[37] Whilst in London Paxton and Panmure were enthusiastic, out in the Crimea the idea of forming another corps of non-combatant civilians to support the army was met with scepticism and doubt by Lord Raglan and Sir Harry Jones.[38]

Punch Magazine's take on the Army Works Corps – navvies presenting arms with the tools of their trade.

The duties of the AWC were laid out by Paxton in a memorandum to Panmure:
1. To execute field works of any kind, the training and habits of the men qualifying them to do so with a rapidity and efficiency which cannot be attained by the solider.
2. To perform other works connected with the Camp, not included in the strict routines of military duties . . . the construction

or repair of roads, the formation of reservoirs, the sinking of wells, the construction and repair of huts, kitchens, hospitals, latrines . . . and the digging of pits for the burial of the dead.[39]

Placed in charge was the Irish civil engineer William Thomas Doyne (1823–77). It seems that command was originally intended for James Beatty, but despite writing to Peto in London on 28 May 1855 with his observations on the AWC, his letter doesn't appear to have reached Lord Panmure's desk until 16 June, by which point Doyne had been in command for two days. Originally styled 'Chief Engineer', this title was soon changed to 'Chief Superintendent' to avoid any conflict or confusion with the Royal Engineers. Doyne's staff included David Doeg and Russell Shaw as his 'Sub-Assistant Superintendents'. William Pope was appointed as 'Superintendent of the Works'; Samuel Barrett as 'Superintendent of Stores, Commissariat and Quarters'. In addition, were 7 'Assistant Superintendents', 11 foremen, 70 carpenters and smiths, 65 artificers, 32 gangers and 800 navvies.

Not all of these recruits were of the highest quality. For about three weeks in July 1855 men of the AWC were collected in the grounds of the Crystal Palace at Penge, the gardens turned into a massive army camp. Here they had money to buy drink and time on their hands. Sadly, nine of them and one woman named Ann Maria Pooley were brought before the Lambeth Magistrate for making a 'murderous assault' on police constables Canon and Wiles on 20 July. The pair were so seriously injured in the fray that it was feared one of them might die. The navvies had been drinking; one of them was armed with a table leg, and had attacked the two constables. Six navvies were remanded in custody.[40]

There never appears to have been enough of the AWC. The first detachment of 406 men and 6 officers of the AWC left London via the South Eastern Railway 'for Dover for the Crimea' travelling onwards by rail via the *Chemin de Fer de Paris à Lyons et à la Meditérranée* and Marseilles for the Crimea. They arrived in the Crimea onboard the *Simoom* on 11 August 1855. A further 300 arrived in the middle of September on the *Barrackpore*. Lord Panmure authorised the formation of a second division on 1 September 1855; Paxton had 222 men ready to sail only 11 days later and a further 500 men were authorised to be recruited on 19 September which were sent out on board 2 steamships, the *Pacific* and *Azoff*. By 1 October some 2,700 men had been despatched for the AWC in the Crimea. A further expansion took place in November when the 'Commissariat Branch Army Works Corps' was raised.⁴¹ Eventually the AWC would consist of 65 officers and 2,363 other ranks organised in 3 divisions, and 12 officers and 464 men in the Commissariat Branch. There were 104 members of the AWC who lost their lives on active service and 84 invalided home.⁴²

Doyne 'quickly found that... his Corps certainly was not viewed with favour' by the military authorities, just as Beatty had six months before. There was constant friction between Doyne and Beatty, especially when Beatty was able to take charge of the floating factory ship the *Chasseur*. The 'Floating Steam Factory for the Army', under the command of Captain Charles Brightman, with the workshops being managed by Mr R.S. Fraser, had been attached to the AWC in July 1855 and placed under Doyne's command. *Chasseur* had been launched on 17 April 1855 on the Tyne at the yard of T. & W. Smith. She was 175ft long overall, with a beam of 26ft. Her engines were supplied by R. Morrison & Co. of Ouseburn Foundry, Newcastle. Originally intended as a collier, she was purchased by the Admiralty on 28 May 1855 and immediately fitted up as a floating workshop. The *North & South Shields Gazette* of 16 August 1855 reported that she was fitted with 'almost every variety of machinery, lathes, slotting and planing machines, and ship and carpenters tools have also been provided'. There were 'two double smiths hearths worked by a fan rather than bellows and two

Departure of the Army Works Corps from London for the Crimea, as depicted by the *Illustrated London News*.

steam powered saws with benches 40 feet long'. The *Newcastle Journal* (19 September 1856) boasted that these two sawmills could cut '3,000 superficial feet of wood daily'. On shore was an additional sawmill as well as 'two iron foundries, one a brass furnace and one a cupola for cast iron' meaning castings up to 25cwt could be produced and 4 tons of metal could be melted every 12 hours. The *Leeds Times* described her in glowing terms:

> The factory comprises an engineers' fitting shop, a smithy, a foundry, a saw mill and a carpenter's shop, and has on board the mechanics, and all the most improved machinery for carrying on each of these branches effectually. There are on board, also, other useful workmen, including a brickmaker, well-borer, and miner. The internal arrangements . . . include a bathroom, ventilation by fan-blast, messing and sleeping galleries, a manager's office, and foremen's apartments, and factory storerooms.[43]

Chasseur sailed from North Shields on about 27 August and arrived in the Crimea on about 6 October.[44]

Sadly, during December there was an outbreak of cholera on board the *Chasseur* and two men, Elliot 'a hammerman from Newcastle' and Nelson a private in the 82nd Regiment, died. The workshop staff numbered thirty-nine civilians and ten soldiers 'sent on board daily as a fatigue party' and employed either on board or onshore in the sawmill or the foundry. A correspondent to the *Yorkshire Gazette* noted that between October and December 1855, 'no less than seventy five requisitions have been made' including repairs to locomotives, waggon wheels and axles: 'In every branch, the floating factory has proved so eminently successful.' Also worthy of note were the floating flour mill and bakery, named *Abundance* and *Bruiser*, which had also arrived in October.[45]

Relaying the Railway

The railway had been built quickly and cheaply. By summer 1855 it was becoming a victim of its own success and was creaking under the enormous loads carried; instead of the predicted 112 tons per day it had been carrying close to 700 tons per day. The rails were too light for the loads carried and many of the waggons that had been second-hand when supplied back in January were worn out. The main line needed relaying with heavier rails and new sleepers, an operation that took place at night so as not to hinder the passage of stores and materiel to the front during the day. The work was supervised by Beatty but undertaken by Doyne and the men of the AWC, which led to a considerable amount of friction between the two.

As soon as Doyne and the first detachment of the AWC had landed in the Crimea, they had been informed that 'the reconstruction and maintenance of the Railway were of paramount importance', and that as many men as possible were to be put over to that task immediately.[46] On 15 August, Beatty sent requisitions for 2 gangs of 25 navvies and 1 ganger which was to be increased to 100 'as soon as possible'. Eventually Beatty had 9 gangs of navvies at work, with 2 foremen, to 'assist in setting out the works'. A tenth gang began work on the railway when 280 reinforcements for the AWC landed in September. General Sir Harry Jones reported in the same month that out of the 760 men available to Doyne, 600 of them were seconded to the railway: 200 'for the extra repairs on the line', i.e. the relaying programme, 260 'for the traffic' and 140 'for repairs', i.e. the day-to-day maintenance. This left Doyne, much to his great annoyance, with only 160 for camp and other duties. Carpenters from the AWC were put to work erecting wooden stables for the horses of the LTC, and Doyne was even requested to provide 'breaksmen, pointsmen, and others, who possessed the experience necessary' to work on the railway. This sapping of the strength of the AWC by the railway would have a damaging effect when it came to road building.[47]

General Simpson wrote to Lord Panmure in London expressing his doubts about the AWC. He wrote in a despatch, 'The trouble caused here by Mr Doyne's corps and his disputes with Mr Beatty, annoy me very much.' The Army Works Corps was 'by far the worst lot of men ever yet sent here. It is ruin to our soldiers to be placed in contact with such a set of people, receiving higher pay than themselves.'[48]

Simpson was equally critical of the railway and transport arrangements:

> I beg to call your attention to the railroad. It is not answering to its purpose, because engineers and navvies have in great numbers refused to work, and it is plain that they all wish to leave the country. If the Army winters here, it will be just the same as last year – there will be no road. Two days' rain renders it quite impassable for wheels. We have no hands to make roads, which ought now to be in progress.[49]

The arrival of the Army Works Corps following the departure of many of the navvies meant that work on relaying the railway could commence in earnest. Lieutenant Harvey of the 77th Regiment sketched some of his men at work on railway duties.

Doyne shared a similar opinion and wrote to Paxton toward the end of September:

> The works of the greatest importance for the Army for the winter are the roads from Balaklava to the Camp, it is upon them that they must depend, not on the railway, for however perfect it can be made it can never carry more than a very small portion of the traffic. However I see no hope of its being put in a safe state of repair.[50]

Reporting to London on 4 August, Simpson noted how he had ordered Sir Harry Jones to carry out an inspection of the railway; Simpson was 'certain that much of it will in winter sink in mud'. On 19 July Beatty had telegraphed home requesting the delivery of 130 railway waggons, 40 drivers, 10 shoeing smiths 'and a supply of iron for [horse] shoes'. These were provided by Peto, Brassey and Betts and despatched to the Crimea within four days.[51] He also requested that two small-wheeled locomotives be sent out, to relieve the burden on the poor horses. Beatty reported home on 27 August that, 'The horses which were sent out from

England, diminished in numbers and overworked, are not equal to the development and the possibilities of the line.'[52] One correspondent of the *North British Agriculturalist* observed that, 'Whilst the French have made excellent roads, in our camp ones sees mere tracks.' As for the 'much-vaunted' railway, 'it will be useless in a short time after the bad season sets in. It is a very convenient summer construction, but the ground on which it rests will be converted into mud by the winter's wet.' Prophetic words indeed.[53] On the last day of August 1855 Romaine reported progress on the relaying of the railway:

> The new Railway Wagons are arrived & a few more men. The road is being made, and if McMurdo had another thousand drivers, we should be almost safe for the winter even if the railway failed – I have no fears for the Railway myself, [although] the Times persists in saying that the rain stopped the traffic for ten days – One line of rails was repaired & worked in less than 24 hours and the other in 48 – There will be men set apart as in all lines, called 'Repairers' whose business it is to go up and down the portion of the line entrusted to them and put every thing in order as soon as a defect begins to show itself.[54]

In London Edward Betts reported that 'the line has been doubled, and is now being effectually drained and ballasted'. He added: 'The present railway is on the best site that can be obtained, and when effectually drained and ballasted, which is being done, will be quite free from floods.' It was further reported at the beginning of September that Lord Panmure in London had ordered a further 150 railway waggons to be sent out to the Crimea, as well as 100 more horses – all of them coming from the firm of Peto, Brassey and Betts, of course.[55]

However, there were problems and setbacks again. The 'new' waggons were another batch of cast-offs from Peto, Brassey and Betts. They were not in the best of condition and, to make matters worse, had been sent out dismantled. General Codrington, who succeeded Simpson as commander-in-chief in the Crimea, fumed to Lord Panmure in London:

> The Railway Carriages! [waggons] – the idea of sending them out so that forges, coals, carpenters are positively necessary to repair, and sometimes to materially alter, them before they can be of use! They have now to occupy sound trucks to get them away from encumbering the wharf, and require days and days and labour at another spot before they can be useful to us.[56]

In reply, Panmure informed Codrington, 'I have sent to the maker to call him into court for their malconstrusion.' He could not comprehend 'how the apparently shameful cases occur'.[57] The technical journal *The Engineer* remarked caustically that the waggons were worn out 'ballast waggons . . . from Coleraine and elsewhere, of no use to any but the owner', Peto, Brassey and Betts. Worn-out rails and sleepers has also been sent out as yet more 'cast-offs'.[58]

The *Cumberland Paquet* reported on 4 September 1855 that the steamer *Surprise* was being despatched to the Crimea with sleepers and heavy rails for the Balaklava Railway and *The Examiner* (22 September 1855) reported, 'The Pasha and the Chanticleer are now lying in Lowestoft Harbour for the purpose of taking in more huts and 12,000 sleepers for the Balaklava Railway.' The *Norwich Mercury* reported on 5 September that the 'ballasting &c. is proceeding well'. Two branches were also being built serving the French and Sardinian camps:

> They are not only putting the Balaklava Railway into a state of some durability, but about to construct two other lines to run at right angles with this – one from the Col de Balaklava to Kamiesch, to be worked by horse power, and the other from Kadikoi to the Woronzoff Road, near the Sardinian position over Tchorgoum. The latter . . . will be worked by locomotive power. The labour of both lines will be supplied by the French and Sardinians.[59]

In order to further the work on relaying the railway, in September McMurdo requested that a pile-driver then standing idle in the recently captured docks in Sebastopol be put over to his use. It had been formerly used to drive piles in the harbour and was, he thought, 'to be complete, and of a size capable of being moved'. It was small enough to be easily dismantled by a party of Royal Sappers and Miners and transported on two waggons down to Balaklava by road. This was finally agreed to on 4 October.[60] He also sought permission to excavate around 30 tons of stone 'from the neighbourhood of the Redan' for the erection of a 'suitable building' to house a steam-powered sawmill next to the engine house at the top of the incline from Kadikoi.[61] A steam-powered sawmill was also erected at the LTC Depot at Sinope, the machinery having been sent out from Britain. Due to shortages of manpower, McMurdo requested Doyne of the AWC provide the personnel, which were despatched, together with the machinery, on board the *Belbeck* on 20 November.[62] Captain Powell reported to McMurdo on 12 October that the relaying of the railway between 'The Col' and the artillery depot was completed and the line ballasted, and that work was soon to commence on ballasting the section to 'The Forks'. He was concerned, however, about railway waggons and material being used to build roads which would limit his ability to complete the railway as far as HQ and thus carry items for making huts up to the front. McMurdo had been 'apprehensive' about the use of railway waggons and materials to build the road and wrote that Doyne of the AWC should supply 'some of his lumber wagons' to carry road-building and hutting materials so that the railway could get on apace.[63] Doyne was frustrated he had hardly any of his own men under his command. He wrote to Sir Joseph Paxton on 29 September that the AWC would be only a 'disorganised remnant, unproductively employed upon works over which I have no control'. Whilst he admitted that the railway was of the utmost importance, he felt that Beatty 'should be supplied with the necessary means of making a railway', or that if the AWC were to find the labour to do so, it should be under his orders, and not Beatty. Doyne also wrote to Lord Panmure in London to a similar effect, urging that the agreement with Peto and Betts regarding the railway be terminated as soon as possible. On 3 November 1855, Lord Panmure approved a system recommended by Paxton that in order to prevent future friction between the railway and the AWC that a fixed portion of the AWC be placed under Beatty and Campbell's orders to be wholly employed on the railway. Furthermore, Beatty and Campbell were attested as members of the AWC in December to facilitate this, followed by twenty-four of the remaining men from Peto, Brassey and Betts in January 1856.[64]

The road from the stationary engine on the incline where McMurdo had his HQ down to Kadikoi was in very poor repair. It was 'so slippery, and so worn down, as to be positively dangerous' and a party of the AWC was put to work to effect a 'temporary repair' until the 'new railway line', i.e. double track, was in full operation as without the road there was 'constant stoppage' to rail movement and even some accidents. This work wasn't done quickly enough for McMurdo, who fumed that despite the urgency of the repairs such work had not taken place and it was 'becoming worse then ever'. He was also unhappy with Doyne's attitude.[65] Doyne and Beatty constantly clashed heads. McMurdo complained to General Airey how Beatty seemingly opposed every move Doyne made. When the AWC was employed in 'removing a portion of the ground below the Stationary Engine' over which the new road was to run, Beatty informed him that he required the spoil thus created 'for the construction of the railway bank', which meant Doyne had to 'bring materials from another place to fill up the excavation he is

A pile-driver captured during the assault on the Malakoff (8 September 1855) was used to sink the foundations for bridges of the railway as it headed toward Kadikoi.

making'. He had already had to divert the road away from the railway, thus making it steeper than he had originally planned. He complained to Paxton how he had managed to avoid a quarrel with Beatty but 'he now complains I do not furnish him with sufficient officers and foremen' who were to 'look to him [Beatty] as their master for their time being' meaning Doyne had no say in the matter, yet Doyne was 'to design and execute the works, leaving him [Beatty] to gain any credit . . . while we are to bear the blame of all failures and deficiencies'.[66]

The stream that wound its way along the valley from Balaklava to Kamiesh was re-routed and culverted, to prevent the railway from flooding during heavy rain. 'This work will materially add strength to the railway', reported the *Bradford Observer*, 'and will carry off the surface water which turned the whole . . . into a lake last winter'. At the same time, the Sardinians were 'at work on the railway from the Woronzoff Road to the main line at Kadikoi'.[67] The 'special correspondent' of the *Morning Chronicle* wrote:

> Nov. 13 Our Italian allies are also busy preparing to lay down their branch line of railway from our own at the head of Balaklava

harbour out to their encampment in the plain, and a considerable quantity of their 'plant' has already arrived and been landed. Their railway waggons seem altogether of a superior quality to our own, being fitted with springs and other aids to locomotive smoothness which we have not thought requisite. Last week, our first engine, the 'Alliance' was landed, and is now upon the rails ready for use as soon as the alterations and repairs at present in progress along the line are completed.[68]

The *Manchester Courier* reported that:

The railway is now assuming an appearance of great solidity. There are divisional roads in progress, which will also communicate with the divisional depots. When the railway is worked by locomotives, instead of horses, the permanent way will endure much better, and a great deal more work will be got out of the line. All these preparations are being made to enable the army to exist comfortably in its winter cantonments, to bring up huts, food, clothing, and fuel, and to remove guns, mortars, and materiel from the front.[69]

The tiny twin-kingdom of Piedmont-Sardinia sent a contingent of 18,000 men to fight in the Crimea. They were excellent soldiers, and their camp would be served by the Balaklava Railway.

Whilst it was 'highly creditable' to Beatty and Campbell, some commentators thought the surveying and poling out of the branch lines was perhaps too good, too much time spent 'elaborating, polishing, and finishing off' the drawings than the physical act of building the railway. Lawrence Godkin of the *Daily News* reported on 13 November that the Sardinians had already started work on building their branch line: 'A considerable quantity of their "plant" has already been landed. Their railway waggons seem altogether of a more superior quality to our own being fitted with springs and other aids to locomotive smoothness.'[70] Progress on the Sardinian branch, however, was very slow as only five men had been detailed to lay the rails.[71]

The construction of one of these branch lines 'led to the discovery of an ancient temple in a tolerable state of preservation'. To prevent any further damage, a palisade was 'placed around it for protection'. Elsewhere workers unearthed a recently buried body in a shallow grave 'in a state of decomposition, and was dressed in rather elegant clothes' and in their boots were found several English sovereigns. The discovery was considered quite a mystery since 'there was no mark of any wound' and the grave was so new and shallow.[72]

Locomotives Arrive

The logical solution to the ever-increasing weight of trains was the locomotive. The first two locomotives were second-hand and arrived by November 1855. Placed in charge of them was the Yorkshire Civil Engineer, Godfrey Oates Mann (1829–1903) who sailed on board the SS *Powerful* in September 1855. He arrived at Gibraltar after a 'very stormy passage' on 8 October 1855, finding himself: 'During the worst of it for two or three days I was along with one of the Medical Staff the only two passengers who mustered at meals and those we had to eat whilst the dishes and plates were flying about from one side of the table to the other'.[73] Finally arriving in the Crimea on 26 October 1855, he found the harbour a 'confusion of tongues at the building of the tower of Babel'. The village was filthy and 'nearly demolished to make way for the Quays' Stores and the Railway'.[74] The railway itself was in very poor shape: it had been hastily laid and 'very rough so far as I have seen it' and the 'ballasting very rough' but the two locomotives (*Alliance, Victory*) in the hold of the *Powerful* would be able to assist in the work of getting the track into good condition. He notes that two stationary engines were already at work on the incline above Kadikoi and that a third was to be set up and put to work as soon as a 'second line of rails, which is being formed' was laid to allow the incline to work bi-directionally meaning waggons could be worked up and down it simultaneously.[75] There were problems unloading the two locomotives and other heavy machinery as the *Powerful* was not equipped with appropriate lifting gear. This meant that Mann had to wait several days for a 'perfect calm, to proceed alongside the Leander Man-of-War', as suitable lifting tackle had 'been rigged on board that ship to take out our Locomotives'.[76] These two locomotives, like their superintendent, were also from Leeds. The *Leeds Mercury* reported on 8 September 1855:

> As any novel fact connected with the conduct of the War has a peculiar interest at the present time, and as a good deal is being said about the miserable state of the Balaklava Railway, it may be gratifying to many to learn that the Government are by no means disposed to allow this peculiarly British creation to be 'washed out' or a stick-in-the-mud. The Government had decided to send out another locomotive engine of a make suitable to the heavy gradients on the above line, and last Thursday week, Lord Panmure gave instructions for such an engine to be procured. Messrs. Peto & Brassey immediately despatched an agent, who, by Saturday morning, was fortunate enough to meet with and purchase an engine in this town. It is one constructed a short while ago by Messrs E. B. Wilson & Co., of Railway Foundry, and has been working a few months. It is a tank engine, namely one which carries its own water in a tank placed on top of the boiler. All the wheels are coupled, so that although its weight with fuel and water will not exceed 12 tons it will be able to draw very considerable loads, say thirty tons, at an average speed up the inclines. Its lightness will make it admirably adapted for the soft foundation of the railway. The engine which leaves here for Southampton today has had a thorough renovation, and repainting at the Railway Foundry. Her 'Iron Sides' are adorned with the English, French Turkish and Sardinian flags conspicuously painted thereon, and she is called the 'Alliance'. She will be embarked for the Crimea by the middle of next week, so that her whistle may in two or three weeks be blended with the other notes of defiance hurled against the common foe, and her shrill voice shall not be the least emphatic declaration of the Allies to carry on this war with the utmost vigour.

The *Leeds Intelligencer* also carried the following:

> A Locomotive for the Crimea. We understand that a small locomotive engine, called *The Alliance*, was yesterday forwarded from the Railway Foundry, Leeds, to Balaklava. The engine was what is called a tank engine with 11 inch cylinders, 17 inches stroke, six wheels of three feet diameter, all coupled. The engine was originally made for Messrs. Leather, coal owners, for use on the tramway to and from their pits, and was purchased on Saturday [1 September] by a government agent. During the interval the words *The Alliance*, and the national flags of England, France, Turkey, and Sardinia have been painted on it.[77]

On the same day that *Alliance* was despatched from Leeds, 'A telegraphic message was received at the Railway Foundry, Leeds' ordering a second tank engine for the Crimea. Sir John Lister Kaye volunteered the nearly new locomotive that worked on his colliery line at Denby Grange – now part of the National Coal Mining Museum. *Victory* was purchased at a cost of £1,680, and was 'Brought down to the Railway Foundry on Saturday night, and after being overhauled will be forwarded to its destination.' This locomotive had originally been named *Fairy Queen*, but patriotically had been re-named *Victory*. She was similarly adorned with national emblems: 'On Thursday Morning, a beautiful little engine, decorated with the flags of England, France, Turkey and Sardinia passed through Pontefract Station en-route for the Crimea.'[78]

Alliance was first steamed in the Crimea on 8 November, two months after the fall of Sebastopol and thus too late to play any major role in the siege. Lawrence Godkin of the *Daily News* reported to his readers at home how the railway caused amazement to the locals:

> Since last week two additional locomotives (old ones) have been landed at Balaclava and placed upon the railway. The little 'Alliance' has already begun to run on the line, and, as she puffs and screeches along at the rate of eight or ten miles an hour, with her cumbrous tail of some half-dozen heavily laden trucks, intense is the gaping wonderment, and multitudinous are the Allahs! of many a crowd of Tartars, Croats, Bulgarians, pure-blooded Turks, Arabs, Hindoos, and Heaven knows what other nationalities besides, whom heavy wages and light work have attracted to this Crimean Babel. The wire rope so long used by the stationary engine to pull the waggons on the incline near Kadikoi, has been removed,

and the entire traction of the line will, it is hoped, be done by three locomotives now upon the rails. Until this can be accomplished, the gain to our transport campwards will be immense, and the scores of heavy animals hitherto employed on the line solely, will be available for the branch labours through the various divisions, and other parts of the camp not immediately connected with the railway.

Godkin was, however, mistaken in his observation that the wire rope and stationary engine for the incline above Kadikoi would be abandoned. Another newspaper correspondent described that *Alliance* had started work on the railway by the second week of November:

> Nov. 10 The second 'bit of information' I have to communicate is the bodily appearance of 'The Alliance' locomotive on the Balaklava Railway. I saw it thereon about an hour since. It is a pretty piece of puffing, snorting, clicking, vapouring machinery as ever traversed a line of railway. Last night, and with success, it was tried for the first time. A second locomotive is already at Balaklava, but for the present we must not quite expect the rival to the Blackwall & Greenwich Railway. The Crimean Tatars cannot at all understand the locomotive.[79]

These two little tank engines may not have been up to the task asked of them. General Codrington complained that, 'The locomotive railway engine, by Colonel McMurdo's account to me will scarcely do the work expected of it. He thinks we shall have to trust to horse-power on the rail principally.'[80] This was an opinion shared by Lieutenant Colonel Lefroy who informed Panmure in London that *Alliance* and *Victory* were insufficiently powerful. According to Lawrence Godkin, there was a third locomotive, *Swan*, at work in late November 1855; this latter engine (also second-hand) coming from the St Helens Railway at a cost of £1,303. This locomotive was built in 1848 and sold to the Balaklava Railway in August 1855. The St Helens Railway replaced it with a similar locomotive of the same name, which worked until 1864.

Mann notes on 28 December 1855 that, despite the freezing temperatures, he had 'three locomotives now running' and that he would have 'four in a day or two'.[81] A fourth locomotive was put in steam on 5 January 1856 by which point he had over thirty men under his command. This fourth locomotive was probably one of the ex-LNWR Burys (below).[82] Godkin of the *Daily News* described that the 'four locomotives will be employed solely on that portion of the line which extends from Balaklava to the spot at which the rope takes up the waggons'. In other words, they worked on the relatively level section of track from Balaklava to Kadikoi with loads being worked up the incline by stationary engine as heretofore. The remainder of the line was to be: 'Done by horses, and not, as I had previously been informed, by a couple of the moveable engines, for all of which employment will be found between Balaklava and Kadikoi. A second of the new engines – the Victory – has been landed, and will commence sharing the labours of the Alliance tomorrow.'[83] *Sous Lieutenant* Alfred Minart wrote home in January 1856 noting that, 'Locomotives now work on the Balaklava Railway, it's very curious, I would be interested to know the opinion of the Russians on the subject!'[84]

Two locomotives were also purchased from the Southern Division of the LNWR, a pair of 2–2–0s built by Benjamin Hick & Son of Bolton in 1838 and 1840 for the London & Birmingham Railway. The pair, originally LNWR No. 13 and No. 50, had 5ft 6in driving wheels and inside cylinders measuring 14 x 18in. They were rebuilt in 1846–7 with larger 5ft 9in driving wheels. No. 50 had been working on the North London Railway and had returned in May to the LNWR 'minus all wheels' suggesting it may have been shipped to the Crimea in a similar state. As McConnel, the LNWR Southern Division Locomotive Superintendent, observed, although they were not on the 'condemned for sale list', they would soon be suggesting both were in very poor condition and close to being worn out. The pair were sold for use on the Balaklava Railway on 14 September 1855, and cost £800 each, including 'fittings to connect them with a rope for working an incline' and 'all duplicate parts supplied'. The tenders appear to have cost £100 each as the two locomotives are entered into War Office accounts as having cost £1,800.[85] Quite how useful these decrepit little four-wheelers would have been in the Crimea compared with the modern 0–6–0s from Leeds is unknown. Whilst they had larger cylinders, having only a single, large-diameter pair of driving wheels would have given them less tractive effort than the two saddle tanks. They were probably purchased at a bargain price in an attempt to provide additional motive power quickly and cheaply.

The first of the pair, No. 13, was despatched from on board the *Levant* from Ipswich on 11 October 1855. She had been partially dismantled and in addition to 'ten cases containing machinery for the engine' was despatched with 'one spar wheel; two couplings; one pinion; one clutch handle and stud . . . and one shaft'. These were probably those 'fittings to

Two former LNWR Bury type locomotives were purchased for use on the Balaklava Railway. Quite how useful they would have been with only single, large-diameter driving wheels is not clear. At least one of them was used as a stationary winding engine.

connect them to a rope' suggesting that No. 13 was used as a stationary winding engine, probably the third stationary engine mentioned by Mann.[86] The *Falkirk Herald* reported in January 1856 how another locomotive had been despatched to the Crimea from Greenhithe on board the *Great Northern*.[87] Supposedly two 0–8–0s were planned for the Crimean Railway and built by the Haigh Foundry Co. intended to be able to work up inclines as steep as an unlikely 1 in 10. They apparently had outside cylinders (15 x 20in), driving the third pair of coupled wheels, the middle pairs of driving wheels being flangeless. The boiler reputedly had a marine-type firebox and a working pressure of 120psi. The duty of these engines is recorded as 'to run the guns out to the ends of a row of short sidings turning off a line of single way . . . up a gradient of 1 in 10'. The sheet-iron cab was supposedly perched on top of the boiler rather like one of Ross Winans's 0–8–0 'Camel Back' locomotives in the United States, and one of them was supposedly damaged by Russian case shot 'smashing a cylinder and another carrying away the cab, and so injuring the driver's arm that it had to be amputated'. Despite these tall stories emanating from the often unreliable pen of Clement Stretton, there is no evidence that they were ever built.[88]

Summary of Locomotives Working on the Balaklava Railway								
Name	Type	Driving Wheels	Cylinders	Builder	Date	Date Purchased	Price	Purchased From
Alliance	0-6-0ST	3ft 0in	11in x 17in inside	E.B. Wilson & Co., Leeds	1854	September 1855	£1,500	Messrs Leather & Co. Leeds
Victory	0-6-0ST	3ft 0in	11in x 17in inside	E.B. Wilson & Co., Leeds	1855	September 1855	£1,500	Sir John Lister Kaye
Swan	Unknown	Unknown	Unknown	Unknown	c. 1848	August 1855	£1,303	St Helens Canal & Railway Co.
LNWR 13	2-2-0	5ft 9in	14in x 18in inside	B. Hick & Son	1838	September 1855	£800 minus tender	LNWR, Southern Division
LNWR 50	2-2-0	5ft 9in	14in x 18in inside	B. Hick & Son	1841	September 1855	£800 minus tender	LNWR, Southern Division

Railway Regulations

There was constant friction between the army authorities and the civilian railway and between the railway and the AWC. Romaine thought, 'Beatty is a fidget – He has a super-civilian dread of being under the "orders" of an officer of the Army, but has no objection to be under his "direction".' That said, however, Beatty and McMurdo enjoyed an excellent working relationship and the two 'get on capitally'. In September, the railway and its workshops had been taken over by the Royal Engineers under General Sir Harry Jones, who had succeeded Sir John Burgoyne as Chief Engineer. As soon as the civilian navvies began to leave the Crimea, General Jones 'in accordance with his orders began to make preparations to take over the workshops stores &c.' but was unable to do so as they 'still remain in McMurdo's hands'. Beatty had been happy to serve under McMurdo, and wanted the railway to be formally 'attached to the strength of the Land Transport Corps . . . as part of the permanent means of transport of the army'. Jones, however, believed the railway and its workshops, etc. should be under *his* orders as senior Royal Engineer. Happily, for all involved, despite all three (Beatty, McMurdo and Jones) being 'peppery' with strong opinions, they were all 'sensible . . . and there has been no hitch'. Beatty was outraged when, in September 1855, it was proposed to withdraw the men of the LTC who had hitherto been seconded to the railway in favour of a detachment from the AWC so that the LTC could take to the field for a proposed field campaign. Beatty was of the opinion that 'nothing but the most urgent necessity should induce the Commander in Chief to take the working of the Railway out of the hands of Col. McMurdo'. He and his men were 'accustomed to the work' and 'fresh men would require a considerable time to learn' their new duties.[89]

McMurdo had been faced with a mammoth task, of both organising the LTC in a combat theatre and keeping the waggons rolling. He reported his successes and failures on 16 November 1855:

> Nothing but the application of science could enable the British army to exist in its present situation. The little harbour Balaklava, which I can liken to nothing but the eye of a needle through which the camel *must pass* is now embraced on either side by the railway – its branchlines loading from the various wharves and storehouses to depots outside the town, where room (though not sufficient) is afforded to the transport to load up. Waggons and their teams are thus allotted for the special service of drawing up fuel, hay, corn to these depots, independent of the trains which proceed to the front . . .
>
> I reckon that every waggon, with its horse, harness, and driver, must travel on an average fourteen miles a day . . . and this wear and tear must extend over a period of six months . . . neither wagons nor harness in a serviceable state. It is absolutely necessary, therefore, that reserves of wheels, axles, shafts, poles, and harness of every kind should be [made] ready.

He was deeply impressed by the floating factory, the *Chasseur*, which with its steam-driven machinery, was able to 'turn axles . . . saw timber' and press wheels onto axles. Similarly, he was also thankful for 'the arrival of young English Drivers' because the locally hired natives had 'begun to desert in great numbers'.[90]

McMurdo resigned due to ill health on 27 November 1855. He was replaced as Director General of the LTC by Colonel Edward Robert Wetherall. In a final lengthy report to Lord Panmure in London, McMurdo notes that the railway had been carrying 225 tons daily. The railway included:

4 Officers
53 NCOs
257 Other Ranks
26 Artificers
215 Horses
17 Mules

4 Locomotives
3 Fixed Engines
190 Waggons

New orders for operating the railway were issued on the day McMurdo resigned, suggesting that the railway had been somewhat rough and ready. These instructions are quoted at length below:[91]

Head-quarters, Sebastopol, November 27.
No. 1. The increased development of railway traffic caused by the arrival of the locomotive engines, renders it necessary that corresponding regulations should come into operation, to ensure the more perfect, safe, and satisfactory working of the line.
First. The chief engineer will be responsible for the stability, and the chief superintendent for the management of the railway, under the orders of the Director-General of Transports.
Second. All requisitions for railway transport are to be sent to Captain Powell, Land Transport Corps, chief superintendent, by three p.m., on the day previous, who will make, thereupon, the necessary distribution of the traffic of the line. These requisitions are to specify the precise nature of the stores required to be sent to the front. The Commissariat Department will, in their daily requisitions, state particularly the number of puncheons of rum, or barrels of porter, and other stores required to be sent up, with a view to the necessary measures being taken, as well for the security of the stores, as the allotment of the proper transport for their conveyance. The stores which are more urgently required at the front than others should also be specified, in order that arrangements may be made accordingly, in the event of any insufficiency of transport.
Third. No requisitions are to be made for the conveyance of stores not yet landed from onboard ship; but all stores required to be sent to the front are to be ready for the inspection of the traffic manager, at three p.m., on the previous day, who will thus be enabled to judge of the description of waggon that will be necessary for the conveyance of the various stores, and make his allotments accordingly.
Fourth. The traffic manager wilt be solely responsible for the distribution of the waggons, and that they are properly loaded. He will also be responsible, through his assistants, that no waggon is allotted for service which is unfit to convey its regulated load.

A pair of warmly dress sentinels stand guard over a flurry of activity at Diamond Wharf, Balaklava, where stores and components for wooden barrack huts are being unloaded.

> And, lastly, that every waggon is properly labelled as to its destination, &c.

A fully codified set of rules and regulations was issued, suggesting that hitherto the line had been run at less-than-optimal efficiency. Beatty drew up a complete set of regulations for working the 'Balaklava Railway', outlying the duties and responsibilities of all its personnel, and getting rid of much bad practice. A full timetable was instituted, with two trains an hour from 8am until 5pm, departing alternately from Diamond Wharf or Ordnance Wharf, Balaklava. Every train was to consist of 'no more than ten waggons' and under the control of the head guard and his two assistants. Every guard was issued with a pocket watch, a red (danger) and white (all clear) flag. Each guard was to keep a journal and logbook of train movements throughout the day, noting starting time, composition, cargo carried and any incidents that occurred. The head guard was to ensure that every waggon was correctly and safely loaded, that the brakes were in working order, waggon sheets were properly secured and every waggon correctly coupled. 'Upon arrival at any station', the guard was to 'deliver over the charge of the train to the Superintendent of that place'; the guard was also to report 'any faulting loading &c. that may have shown itself during the passage of the train'. The head guard was responsible for the safety of the train; in case of any accident he was to 'send back one of his assistants, with a red flag, at least 250 yards' in order to stop the following train. 'On no account' was he to 'leave the spot until the chief guard has signalled to him that he may come on.' If any accident occurred owing to the negligence of the chief guard – and that included his assistants – he was to be court-martialled and 'punished accordingly'.

Waggons had obviously been unloaded whilst standing on the main line, thus bringing the system to a standstill. Beatty ordered: 'No waggons to be loaded or unloaded on the main line, under *any circumstances*, during train hours. All trains to be made up opposite the Grenadier Guards' store, Balaklava, and at the Diamond Wharf.'

When the train arrived at the foot of the incline at Frenchman's Hill the head guard was responsible for the safe coupling and uncoupling of the locomotive:

> The Engine to be detached, and crossing over, brought in front of the empty wagons to return to Balaklava; and it will be the duty of the Guard and his assistants to break these wagons down. But the Engine Driver will direct when the breaks are to be put down and when to be released; and the wagons, under any circumstance must not be allowed to come down the line except in charge of the Guard.
>
> Any person infringing this regulation will be immediately taken into custody and handed over to the provost marshal.

As on civilian railways back home, the Balaklava Railway worked on a 'One Engine, One Driver' basis: no driver was allowed to operate another's engine unless with express permission of the Chief Engineer. Every driver was to: 'Examine his engine carefully before commencing work in the morning, and report any damage that may have occurred to the superintending engineer . . . The engine-driver to have his engine with steam up at the places where the trains are made up at least ten minutes before the time specified for the departure of each train.'

Two of the three locomotives were in steam daily to work the section from Balaklava to the incline at Frenchman's Hill. This was on rotation basis so that one locomotive could undergo a period of maintenance:

> The engine from Balaklava will proceed with its train to the junction of the Diamond Wharf Branch, and there be detained, leaving the

Ordnance Wharf at Balaklava was also served by rail, and shot, shell and powder was taken to the front by the railway. Locomotives were not allowed to work close to the powder magazines.

train on the Balaklava side of the junction. It will then be moved a sufficient distance in advance to allow the train from the Diamond Wharf to clear the junction. The Diamond Wharf train will then be joined by the Balaklava train; both engines will proceed with the train to the foot of the incline, and return on the down line in front of the empty waggons. On arriving at the Sardinian depot each engine will proceed with its proportion of waggons to the Diamond Wharf at Balaklava.

A speed limit of 10mph was in force, with 4mph over any level crossing and through the streets of Balaklava. The whistle was 'to be used freely whilst going along the line'. In case of any accident, the engine driver was liable to trial by court martial.

To ensure the safety of the trains, Railway Police were appointed to daily inspect the track and keep any straying animals or soldiers away from the track and trains:

> The gatekeepers are to shut the gates across the road from the time the train is in sight until it passes the level crossing, taking care that the railway is perfectly clear, and that no stones or gravel be

allowed to collect between the rails and the check-rails. The duties of the police will be to see that no person except those engaged on the line be allowed on it, under any pretence whatever. They will see that no obstructions exist on the railway, and will note particularly the passage of the trains, and call the attention of the guards to any-thing that may appear improper in the loading or calculated to endanger the safety of the train. They will endeavour, to the best of their ability, to afford such assistance to the guards and engine-drivers as will enable them to carry out their duties according to their several instructions, and it will be their duty to report to their inspector any infringement of these regulations that may come under their notice.

Copies of the regulations were to be issued to all railway personnel who then had to read them (or have them read to them) and sign them, stating that they had understood them and would obey them. Copies were also 'Posted up in the Engine Shed, Railway-Yard and Huts of the Men'.

Chapter 10

The Second Winter

The Crimean Railway and the Land Transport Corps had been built and established to prevent a second winter of crisis in the Crimea. Yet, despite McMurdo's best efforts, the LTC had never been fully organised or equipped. As early as September 1855 there were proposals to carry out root and branch reform of the LTC 'to further [its] military character'. The first reform was in the harmonising of LTC ranks with those of the regular army, which came into effect in October:[1]

Regimental Superintendent, to be styled, Troop Sergeant Major

Assistant Quartermaster Superintendent	Paymaster or Quartermaster Sergeant
Sub Superintendent	Sergeant Major
1st Class Driver	Sergeant
2nd Class Driver	Corporal
3rd Class Driver	1st Class Driver
	2nd Class Driver

McMurdo resigned as Director General of the LTC in November 1855 due to ill health. He was replaced by Colonel E.R. Wetherall as Acting Director General. In his report on his new command he noted that it 'has been almost reduced to annihilation' through sickness and over work. It was not large enough to 'meet the extraordinary demands placed upon it'. Men and rolling stock were worn out. Reveille usually sounded at 3am for men 'to water and feed their animals' and they returned to camp after dark after watering and feeding their horses again, and 'generally reach their tents about 9pm or 10pm' utterly exhausted having had little time to eat or wash properly. No time could be found for the appropriate care of horses, harness or vehicles. There were only 3 surgeons and 15 assistant surgeons to look after 8,000 men, which was a lower proportion of medical provision than an infantry brigade. Wetherall also noticed that the overwhelming majority of administration and office work had been carried out by McMurdo, the HQ staff being very weak to non-existent. The LTC was a heterogeneous organisation, recruited from 'the rawest recruits' and the 'worst sort of men'. What was needed was a complete re-organisation and new officers who 'better knew their trade'. Whilst McMurdo had given an optimistic view of the LTC, Wetherall and the 'Special Correspondents' painted an entirely different picture. There were too few officers and NCOs, insufficient artificers such as wheelwrights, harness-makers and saddlers, and only a single veterinary surgeon for 2,100 horses. Wetherall made four immediate recommendations:

1. For an extended period of rest for the men and horses of the LTC so far as the 'wants of the army' permitted and 'with the assistance of the Railway' in replenishing the army.
2. Complete the establishment of officers and NCOs.
3. Dismiss the 'native' drivers and to form them into an auxiliary transport corps.
4. Re-organise the LTC as a corps of two regiments, each commanded by a lieutenant-colonel, numbering up to 6,000 men each.[2]

The LTC was ordered to be thoroughly re-organised, and the personnel sifted in an attempt to remove the worst offenders. McMurdo had been concerned that so many 'ragged rascals' had been recruited and that, as was seen when many mutinied in Bristol, they were far from 'amenable to discipline'. The LTC had been rapidly formed and brought up to strength with little care or attention in selection of recruits other than finding the sufficient number. In the Crimea, General Codrington urged the dismissal of the 'native' drivers as soon as possible because 'they are not to be trusted'. Even in the corridor of powers in London doubts were being expressed about the LTC: Lord Granville wrote that the LTC was 'a complete failure' whilst even Queen Victoria thought that 'instead of being an assistance [it was] only a clog to the army'. The Duke of Newcastle concluded that: 'I think the corps will require to be organised on a still more military plan than it now is' and towards the end of 1855 plans for a complete reorganisation of the LTC were considered. Colonel Wetherall presented his plan for re-organisation on 14 December 1855 to the Minister for War. In his scheme he estimated that the army would require at least 17,000 horses, the total equine strength of the army including cavalry horses and regimental *bât* ponies being 30,000. Wetherall suggested reductions could be made in the number of *bât* ponies, saving some 2,000 animals. Existing LTC nomenclature of 'Division' and 'Brigade' were 'liable to cause confusion' and were abolished in favour of 'Battalion', 'Squadron' and 'Troop', each battalion consisting of 860 all ranks, with one battalion attached to each division of the army. Finally, Wetherall suggested that the name of the LTC be changed to the 'Military Train being satisfied that the greater the military feeling and tone that can be given to the corps, the greater will be the chance of success'. General Codrington was of the opinion that such re-organisation was much-needed: there was a 'want of organization' within the LTC as it then stood and lack of superintendence.[3] Codrington further suggested that the LTC have 'the establishment of a little army' so that it be entirely self-contained, with 1,000 officers and other ranks attached to each division of the army on a permanent basis. Lord Panmure also argued for a similar organisation. To emphasise the more military nature of land transport, the title 'Military Train' was to be adopted. General Codrington wrote to Lord Panmure in December 1855 arguing for a complete reorganisation, and was given 'full powers to deal with your transport as you please'.[4] On 11 January 1856 the new organisation came into effect with the officers and men of the LTC being formed into regiments, each 800 strong, commanded by a field officer. The NCOs and privates were to receive a higher rate of pay and their prior service would still be counted toward their pension. One regiment of the LTC was to be attached to each division and it was the additional responsibility of the general or division to maintain and enforce discipline in the LTC regiment attached to their division. There was to be greater scrutiny of the men than previously, and especially officers who volunteered into the LTC, officers not being formally appointed until 'it is know that they suit the service, and the service suits them', suggesting many officers who had volunteered from the Line into the LTC had not been up to the task.[5] The complete re-organisation of the LTC was estimated to require 19,000 horses and mules bringing up the equine population of the British army in the Crimea to 40,000, all of which had to be supplied by sea. There would be one driver per animal, and whilst excellent in theory these horses and mules simply could not be found either at home or in Turkey and Bulgaria. The French army had been shipping horses from Algeria and Spain for their army but the Allied armies, and indeed the Russians, were all trying to find draught and remount horses from the same limited pool in the eastern Mediterranean. Then there was the problem of supplying forage as even the largest steam vessel could only carry 500 tons, the equivalent of feeding 40,000 horses for one day.[6] According to Codrington, this reorganisation had been completed by the beginning of February and Colonel Wetherall had now assumed command as Director General, rather than Acting in McMurdo's stead. Wetherall, however, noted later in the same month, that this re-organisation was still on-going under his guidance. On 1 March 1856 a new organisation was put forward, mirroring in many respects the organisation of the French *Train*. Recognising that each division required its own attached transport, Colonel Wetherall proposed that the LTC be formed into a single corps commanded by a Director General, consisting of seven regiments, each of two battalions. One regiment was to be attached to each division; thus six regiments were attached to the infantry divisions and one to the single cavalry division. The first battalions were to be responsible for military stores, and the second for commissariat stores. Each battalion was to be formed from three squadrons, each of two troops.[7] It seems Wetherall never really achieved his aim to have 8,000–10,000 men organised into the same number of battalions as there were divisions in the army. The Treaty of Paris (30 March 1856) meant that any further investment and re-organisation of the LTC came to an end. The LTC was to be wound up and a new Royal Warrant issued on 4 August 1856 established the Military Train creating a 'permanent formation of a land transport corps for the service of our army at home and in the field'.[8]

Preparing for Winter

In order to prepare the LTC for the coming winter, McMurdo ordered the building of wooden barrack huts and warm clothing to be issued to the men. In July he ordered sufficient timber to construct wooden huts for 12,000 'European' drivers and 5,000 'natives' as well as to build wooden stable accommodation for 10,000 horses, but this scheme never appears to have been fully realised.[9] There was already increasing sickness within the ranks of the LTC, especially amongst the men from Malta. The men's uniforms were ragged and new clothing was requested for the 400 Maltese drivers – including new 'under clothing'. The 1,000 Italian and Spanish muleteers were also in want of uniforms and McMurdo requested his men be issued with warm winter clothing in time for winter.[10] Things were not much better in terms of medical provision: at the end of August the corps' surgeon, Dr G. Taylor, complained how a 'want of tent pegs' had prevented the pitching of three hospital marquees. Dr Taylor also urged McMurdo to establish a hutted 'winter hospital' and to take advantage of the then fine weather to build roads, dig latrines, build cook-houses and stores before winter set in in earnest. Unfortunately, many of the existing latrines had been badly dug (of insufficient depth) and had been poorly maintained and therefore were unsanitary. The majority of the men were living in tents, and even here Taylor found fault and he recommended a 'model tent' be erected to show how tents should be put up. He also reported that the men were filthy and hungry. They had not been washing themselves properly and their hair was long and unkempt and he immediately recommended the hair be cut 'sufficiently short'. Steps were to be taken to 'ensure a clean shirt, flannel, and two pairs of socks weekly'. It is little wonder that they were suffering with lice and skin infections.[11] Furthermore, not only had the men insufficient time to wash but also to eat. Dr Taylor ordered that: 'The greatest attention and care be paid not only that the men have a good and sufficient breakfast provided, but also that sufficient time be given them to partake of it before leaving the camp every morning.'[12]

Toward the end of October, the men of the LTC were supplied with 'good fur lined jackets' made from sheepskin with the fleece still on, the fleece side being worn inside. In November McMurdo requested that warm winter clothing be supplied to the native drivers.[13] Corps surgeon Dr G. Taylor ordered on 1 November 1855: 'Every man be completed with a coatee, two flannel [vests], two pairs of drawers, three pair of socks, and waterproof clothing.'[14] Despite these recommendations, there had been little progress on the erection of wooden hospital huts and the provision of warm winter clothing, especially to the natives. None of the huts had arrived despite sites for their erection being cleared and levelled. New latrines had also not been dug. To make matters worse, on 1 December 1855 Dr Taylor reported that the hospital marquee had been blown down in a gale. Wooden huts finally started to appear three days later.[15]

It wasn't just the men who were suffering from want of proper accommodation but the horses and mules, too. In order to prepare the horses for winter, wooden stable huts had to be built to provide cover for the 8,000 animals in his care. To this end McMurdo requested pre-fabricated wooden stable huts and the tools to build them at the beginning of October 1855. He needed, for example, 50 crowbars, 500 picks, 500 shovels, 125 saws and 50 hammers. His request went unheeded and on 11 October McMurdo wrote again requesting tools and parts to build wooden stables. Without the necessary tools work was considerably slowed on the stables, and he wanted all his animals

A general view of Balaklava Harbour, with components for barrack huts being unloaded in earnest ready for the coming winter.

under cover by winter. It also transpired that the request by Captain Powell for the parts for two wooden stables huts to be built for the railway horses had not been correctly worded and had been rejected.[16] McMurdo also requested twelve wooden hospital huts to be supplied 'for the accommodation of the sick and public stores' which hitherto had been under canvas. This request does not appear to have been granted as, in almost a repeat of the previous winter, eight of the tents were blown down in a gale on 1 December 1855. Colonel Wetherall wrote to HQ requesting hospital huts be immediately supplied. He also noted that some of the men were still in tents despite winter setting in in earnest.[17]

Yet, something went wrong as a month later work on the stables was 'at a stand still' for want of nails and tools. Furthermore, McMurdo had to requisition 1 million feet of planking to make these wooden stables. In a strongly worded letter of 17 November Wetherall criticised the Quartermaster General's Department for being tardy in fulfilling an earlier requisition for parts for huts for horses and men. Parts for twenty stable huts had already been delivered but he was short of nails, tools and other components with which to complete them. It was a 'matter of some urgency' that these stables were built, 'I cannot conceal from myself that unless speedy measures are taken, a very large mortality must be expected amongst the Draught and Pack animals.' Whilst the Italian and

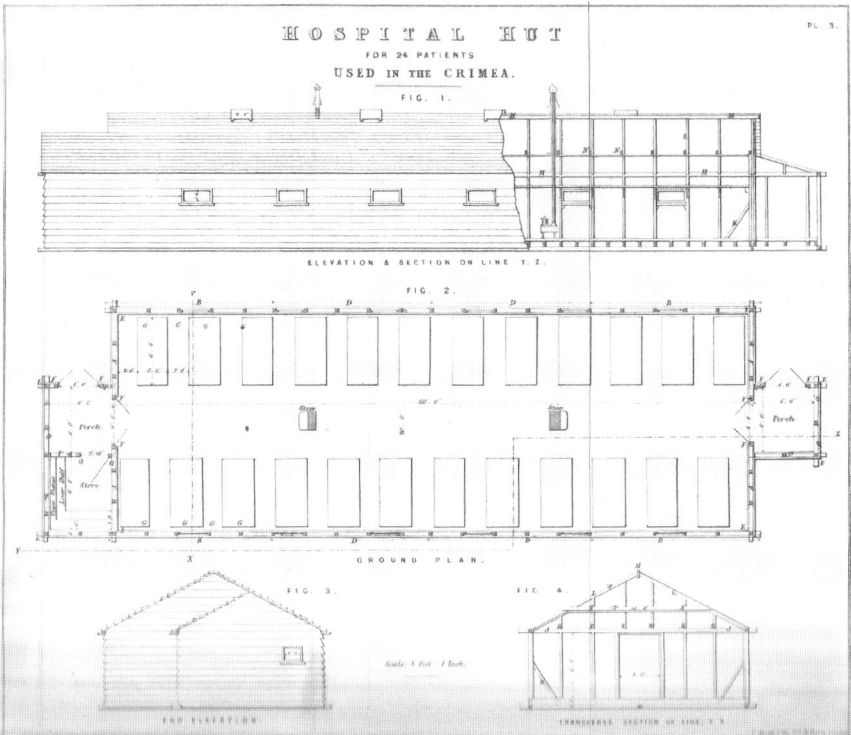

Prefabricated barrack and hospital huts like these were sent out in their hundreds to the Crimea, the biggest provider being Messrs Potter & Price of Gloucester.

Spanish mules were better suited to the rigours of the Crimean climate – especially the hot summer – they needed to be brought under cover in order to survive the winter. If such stables could not be built, McMurdo proposed to send away the vast majority of his animals to warmer climes at Sinope. As he wryly noted, 'winter has already commenced' leading to great anxiety as to the survival of his transport animals especially as 'the strain upon the Corps has not yet relaxed'.[18]

W.H. Russell reported in *The Times* on 11 December 1855:

> Mules and carts are fast disappearing; I have been told that of the former not less than 1,200 have perished or have been destroyed since the rains began ... Col. Wetherall has called a Board to inquire into the condition of the carts, wagons, harness, pack saddles, and horses and mules, with a view to condemning such as may be unfit for use, and to supply others.

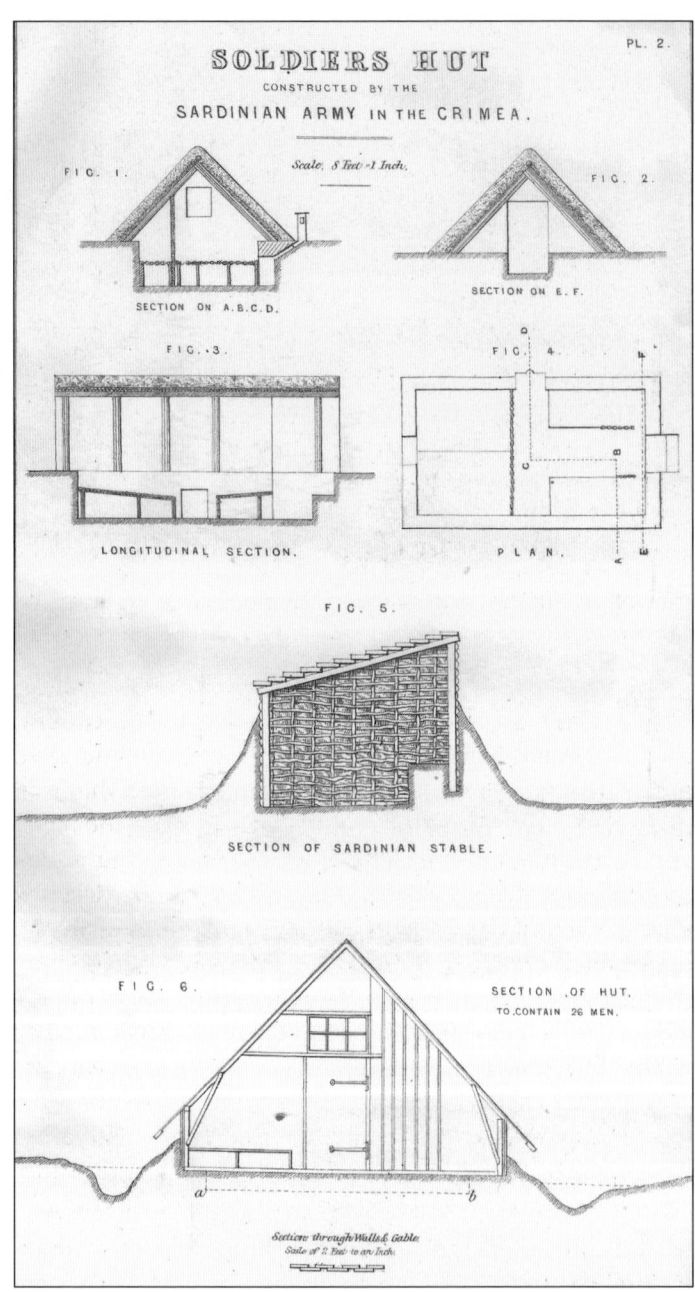

The French and Piedmont-Sardinian armies also used wooden barrack huts and stables, like this Piedmontese example. Despite French huts also being made in Britain by the same suppliers as those for the British army, many commentators considered them superior.

The interior of an officer's hut, winter 1855. Somewhat cramped but with a roaring fire and an iron camp bed, this was far superior to the ragged bell tents of winter 1854.

Thus it was a sickly, over-worked LTC that faced the on-coming winter, one that would stretch its resources to the maximum and result in the corps having the highest rate of sickness and mortality of the entire British army. Much to the consternation of the military men, the civilians and those officers seconded to the railway were enjoying high-quality food and a good night's sleep. Godfrey Mann wrote home describing how he, Captain Powell of the LTC and Veterinary Surgeon Weston shared a wooden barrack hut. Each officer had their own bedroom and there was a sitting room 'papered with the Engravings from the Illustrated London News'. His bed was a 'very comfortable' iron camp bed with a mattress, five blankets, a rug and a waterproof sheet. Meals were three times a day, 'in fact we get as much of everything as we like' – other than milk so tea was taken black. The railway officers and staff and those of the AWC spent Christmas Day together enjoying 'Turkey, side of beef, mince pies etc' in stark contrast to the lot of the serving soldier.[19]

Road Building

The French had watched the progress of the 'Balaklava Railway' with a mixture of admiration and scepticism. One French officer wrote, 'Toujours les Rossbeefs! They have brought everything with them, even their railway. It is like they are making a colony.' Whilst much labour and energy had been spent in building the railway – which had promised to cure the transport crisis – the French Corps of Engineers stuck to tried and tested ideas. They had built a metalled road from their port at Kamiesch to their HQ and camps on the Chersonese Plateau, and moreover created a metalled road down to Balaklava. And it was to roads, rather than the railway, that the British army looked for its transport needs during autumn and winter 1855.

Even before Sebastopol fell to the Allies thoughts were turning toward a second winter in the Crimea. In July McMurdo applied for 200 Turkish army labourers for road-making duties 'between the Transport Camps and the main roads'. He also requested to have loads of timber which had recently arrived put over to his use 'for the construction of necessary public works'. Whilst General Airey declined to allow McMurdo to use the Turkish labourers, he did agree to him having the next load of timber that landed.[20] On 8 August McMurdo sent a lengthy memorandum proposing to build three new roads: two 'one on each side of Vinoy's Hill' and the third down to Balaklava. He wrote such a measure would be 'highly desirable' to prevent a repeat of the previous year's disaster. McMurdo was also of the opinion that the roads and landing stages at Balaklava needed urgent attention, especially regarding traffic flow:

> I only wish that something of the kind could be done in Balaklava . . . in reference to that spot where the planking &c. for the huts landed and loaded and which indeed is nothing but the street. I think it not inappropriate that an upper road for going might be made while the town road might be with greater convenience be used for loading and bringing out the wagons.

He also questioned the methods of unloading the boats in Balaklava Harbour:

> I have been watching with some anxiety the state of the Depots of Supplies at Balaklava. For many days past there has been a dearth of fuel on the shore as well as a corn; and tho' throughout has sometimes remained the entire day there loading by dribbles from boats as they arrive. All this is a matter for grave consideration. In fact, Balaklava is the eye of a needle through which we have to thread immense supplies (for the country produces nothing) – and I consider that it is mathematically impossible to get much ahead in our Depots in our present circulation.

Such was the delay and confusion at Balaklava, that of the fifty-four railway waggons allotted daily to move commissariat stores to the front only thirty-one were used 'owing to supplies not having been brought on shore' which meant that the unused waggons couldn't be employed on other duties. He also proposed the use of Kazatch Bay as a landing place during the good weather and that he would put waggons to work to carry supplies from there. McMurdo urged that road-building commence quickly.[21]

Captain Gerald Goodlake was instructed to 'superintend the formation of a large road from Balaklava to Sevastopol, having 4,000 men set to work'.[22] Road building ignited many of the frictions between the AWC and the railway. Despite the AWC supposedly being there to provide the navvies, engineers and equipment to build the roads, and thus alleviate that burden on untrained fighting men, due to the number of AWC personnel who had been seconded to the railway, the reality was that soldiers once again found themselves hard at work building roads. On 10 September at a meeting with Generals Simpson, Jones and Airey, Doyne admitted that out of his entire force he had only twenty men from the AWC who could be employed on road building. This meant that soldiers had be to seconded for road-building purposes, the very contingency which the AWC had been formed to avoid.[23] Doyne believed that the efforts to rebuild and keep the railway going were syphoning off men and material which would be better placed in road building. He also believed a road was far more suitable since it did not require specialist rolling stock, materials or skills to build and maintain. And in this he was correct. Doyne fumed to Joseph Paxton:

> The Roads can be made to carry the whole traffic, the Railway cannot, the inference is clear that if one must give way from lack of labour it ought to be the railway. Without the roads the winter will be even more fearful than the last, and I am very anxious . . . I have about 200 of our men at work on them, and nearly 5,000 soldiers, which are to be increased in numbers as soon as tools can be got of which the army are very short . . . With the assistance well directed and vigorously worked for another month I feel no doubt of completing the roads, but there can be no certainty of the assistance from the Army being continual, and my remaining men . . . will soon be required to reinforce Mr Beatty. But even when the roads are made I estimate that it will require at least 500 of this Corps to maintain them through the winter.[24]

Captain Gerald Goodlake VC of the Coldstream Guards was placed in charge of road-building operations in autumn 1855. (*Library of Congress*)

On 4 September – four days before the final assault – McMurdo was ordered to place at Goodlake's disposal twenty-one lumber waggons for carrying road-making materials. Goodlake was 'prepared to take over 40 wagons' if they could be spared and hoped he could find drivers from amongst the Croatian labourers, supervised by officers and NCOs from the LTC. He was uneasy as to the success of the road and thought to build a decent, metalled road would require between 4,000 and 5,000 'native labourers' to complete before winter set in. On 11 September McMurdo was requested to place a further fourteen waggons and ten workmen at Goodlake's disposal 'for the purpose of conveying material for road making'. McMurdo was unable to spare any workmen or artificers as they were all busily employed in repairing or building railway waggons. Instead, he recommended artificers from the AWC be detailed in their place. He was reluctant to hand over waggons or use the railway for road-building purposes as he was already 'in much want of transport' to carry stone for properly ballasting the railway. McMurdo reluctantly agreed to make up a further seventeen lumber waggons; he had already supplied waggons to the AWC bringing up materials for the railway and huts for the men of the AWC. He was not impressed by the way the men of the AWC cared for his vehicles. He fumed that 'if they could repair more which they break it would add to the existing means greatly'. On 28 September a disgruntled McMurdo was required to hand over another thirteen lumber waggons, their teams and harness to Goodlake to carry stones and other materials for the construction of this new road. Further LTC vehicles were put over to the AWC for road building.[25] The railway was also put to work carrying road stone, which McMurdo was not happy about. He was also unhappy that the new road to the heights from Kadikoi mirrored that of the railway. He predicted 'much confusion and damage' to the railway and from the mules 'and other harness animals unaccustomed to the hissing and screaming a railway engine in motion' being panicked. He strongly recommended the road be re-routed or some regulation put in force to prevent accidents to road users.[26] General Airey wrote to McMurdo requesting the railway be used to assist in the transport of 'hutting materials and planking ... at once' to the front. Divisional transport would be used to carrying the various parts of the huts to the various camps. McMurdo replied on 24 September that he was still busy ballasting the line from 'The Col' to 'The Forks' and that service on the line would be suspended for ten days so that, all being well, 'everything will go as far as the forks' from the beginning of October. He could however spare two lumber waggons for carrying planks and timber, but most of them had been passed over to Captain Goodlake.[27] The scale of shortages of rolling stock and other materials in the Crimea is shown by an order placed in January 1856 by the Royal Carriage Department at Woolwich Arsenal inviting outside contractors to deliver:

Carts	2,600
Waggons	1,600
Lumber Waggons	100

Maltese Carts	300
Pads for Pack Saddles	10,000
Pack Saddles	3,000[28]

By October there were some 6,500 soldiers, 6,750 Turks and a mere 200 men from the AWC at work on road building. There was a 'miserable deficiency of tools and materials' and the rate of sickness was high but the main road from Balaklava to Kadikoi (6½ miles) was opened in forty-eight days. Russell of *The Times* was, predictably, full of praise for a 'great military road which will last for centuries.' It was an 'enduring mark of our presence' akin to a Roman road. A stone tablet was erected 'let into the solid rock by the roadside at Kadikoi reading: "This Road was made by the British Army, assisted by the Army Works Corps, under the direction of Mr Doyne, C.E., 1855".'[29] How well the road would stand up to the rigours of the Crimean winter, however, would be something else entirely. Lawrence Godkin of the *Daily News* described how:

> Roadmaking has begun on an extensive scale both with the French and ourselves. Large fatigue parties are everywhere to be seen throughout the camp, and along the main routes from Balaclava busy with pick and shovel, constructing new tracks and repairing old ones against the necessity of rainy and snowy months now near at hand. Evidently no greater value is attached to the make-shift Railway than a trumpery character deserves; and this is well, for, were our winter transport confined to it, I much fear the Commissariat Stores would be often like the shop of Romen's Apothecary; reduced to a 'beggarly account of empty boxes'.[30]

He had more praise for the AWC who seemed 'likely to render valuable service'. Their hard work was 'formidable' and 'contrast[ed] with the scheming idleness of the navvies whom they have succeeded'.[31]

An inkling of the coming transport problems came toward the end of September 1855. On 24 September it was ordered that '6 men from the line' be attached to the transport of their respective division and in order to increase the number of transport animals available, it was hoped to borrow them from the Ambulance Corps. McMurdo, however, was not in favour of this as the Ambulance Corps had no mules to spare. Instead, more mules and drivers were to be trained up for transport duties.[32] Similarly, it was proposed to withdraw the LTC detachment working on the railway and replace them with men from the AWC. This

A member of the Mounted Staff Corps (a precursor to the Royal Military Police) supervises a fatigue party bringing stores through the mud up to the heights.

The first 'caterpillar tracks' were invented by James Boydell in the 1840s and were experimented with in the Crimea, with limited success.

would have freed up 200 carts for the army but neither McMurdo nor Harry Jones could sanction such a measure.[33] Although road building seemingly dominated winter preparations, on 5 November 1855 an agreement was reached with the Turkish government for the British army to purchase 500 trees at Sinope to be used for sleepers for the Balaklava Railway.[34] Although Colin Robins has denied Boydell wheels were used in the Crimea, they were certainly used on an experimental basis.[35] Due to the poor state of the roads and in an attempt to improve the manoeuvrability of large field guns and sling carts for moving siege-gun barrels, an experiment was made by fitting them with James Boydell's patent wheels. These were a primitive form of caterpillar track using hinged plates around the circumference of the wheel. 'No better place than in Crimean mud' could have been desired by those carrying out the experiment. They were fitted to a 95cwt gun sling, drawn by five horses which were able to drag their massive load with ease, 'convincing proof of its capabilities'. But whilst considered useful, and safe, on the level and going uphill, going downhill was a different matter with the wheels literally sliding on the slippery mud, requiring at least twenty men to hold it back.[36]

Return to Transport Chaos

By the middle of November the Crimean winter was beginning to bite: torrential rain and heavy frosts had turned many of the roads, despite the lavish praise of *The Times*, into impassable quagmires. Where four horses had been used to pull the waggons, six or even eight had to be used to drag them through the mud. Even the railway was affected, Russell reporting that the 'Railway is nearly useless' owing to the weather and broken-down nature of the rolling stock. In order to try and ease the burden on his new command, Wetherall ordered that: 'Until further orders, no portion of the Railway or Land Transport Corps shall be employed in the transportation of huts, except for the purpose of covering their own horses.'[37] The poor men at the front would have to carry up the heavy parts of their pre-fabricated winter huts themselves, repeating the situation that the railway had been intended to avoid nine months earlier. Given the very low temperatures encountered Godfrey Mann found that the water pumps on the stationary engines and locomotive froze, causing them to burst.[38] Despite having enjoyed his 'jolly parties' at Christmas 1855, with the change in the weather and transport chaos, rations even for the railway officers deteriorated: 'The beef is of poor lean quality, stewing being the only means of making it at all fit for mastication'. The mutton was 'very poor' and the bread 'slightly brown, or rather dirty grey' was very sour. This was more than compensated for, however, by tea, ersatz coffee, cocoa ('more than we require'), potatoes and onions. Alcohol could be purchased from the French at 'exorbitant prices' but the champagne was 'cheaper than in England' and 'good quality'.[39]

Even though Official Despatches stated that the railway was 'In Excellent order' and that 'locomotives to Kadikoi run up and down incessantly with trucks' the transport situation was descending into chaos. The *Caledonian Mercury* reported:

> ROADS, HUTTING, ETC. Although the heavy rains and storms which prevailed last week have ceased since Sunday, the country is in a very heavy state; and, as the . . . roads have failed, and have become in a very bad condition . . . Under present circumstances, Colonel Wetherall, the Director-General of the Land Transport Corps, has felt himself obliged to lighten the burdens on his corps as speedily and as much as possible, and in compliance with his recommendations orders have been given to suspend the carriage of hutting materials to the front, so that many thousand men will have to pass the winter under canvass, unless the huts be sent up before the bad weather sets in with severity. In fact, mules and carts were fast disappearing; I have been told that of the former not less than 1200 have perished or have been destroyed since the rains began, and I should be afraid to repeat the number given to me as that of carts, &c., broken down . . . Not only is the carriage of hutting suspended, but officers are obliged to carry up the forage for their bat animals and horses from the divisional and other depots; and those who have gone home on urgent private affairs, and have left horses for the public service on condition of the issue of rations of forage to them, are informed by a general order that such issue will be suspended after the 1st of January.[40]

The railway waggons were falling apart and mostly destroyed. Russell, of *The Times*, bristled that the vehicles sent out to the Crimea for the LTC had been badly and cheaply made: they were 'discreditable, worthless, and rotten'. The bad weather was also having a 'distressing' effect on the horses and mules. Despite all the preparations made for the second winter, the LTC horses had no stables or shelter from the elements. There were two drivers assigned to every three horses or mules, but they were 'barely sufficient to perform long marches, from the divisional camps to

Balaklava and back again' and then have time and energy to spare to look after the horses. They were ill-groomed and badly fed and many sank 'beneath their load' and died.[41]

General Codrington fumed to Lord Panmure in London on 10 December how he had:

> Ordered that every available smith and carpenter of the Army Works Corps . . . should begin to-morrow morning to put together and get on the rail the heap of railway trucks which had been on the wharfs and different places. Wonderful to say, these railway trucks cannot be brought together, put on the wheels, and made commonly serviceable, without coal, forges, bellows, and smiths, besides carpenters; and this at a time when hours are valuable to us, and when the rail is wanted to relieve the enormous consumption of horses by work and weather, and want of shelter.

He was furious that the railway waggons had been sent out dismantled and had held a meeting with Doyne and Campbell where it was arranged that 'the utmost number of hands will be working at the railway trucks tomorrow morning'.[42]

The transport situation had deteriorated to such a point that on 30 December 1855 the commander-in-chief ordered that '500 men and

Heavy rain and hard frosts soon turned the newly built roads into impassable quagmires, seeing a return to the transport chaos that the Balaklava Railway had been built to avoid. A French *cantinière* and cart struggle through the mud.

20 serjeants from each division of the army should be attached to the Land Transport Corps of their Divisions' in order to keep the stores and supplies moving. These volunteers were to work alongside the LTC and assist with loading and unloading of stores and formation of depots. Lists of volunteers for this duty were to be furnished by commanding officers. 'The supply of the Army is so important, that the character of these men must be good' and if possible they were to have experience of caring for horses. Officers who 'felt inclined' for the duty could also volunteer.[43] One correspondent to the *Fifeshire Journal* described 'the dirty carts and men' of the LTC. They had 'little opportunity to look out for themselves', their animals went uncared for 'picketed in the open air, wallowing in mud'. The LTC was to be pitied.[44] An indignant letter in the *Manchester Courier* called the LTC a failure, 'still a subject of conversation in the camp':

> It is said last month that the loss in mules and horses missing and dead amounted to twelve hundred or upwards, and that in one week, after the bad weather had set in five hundred animals were lost . . . On riding through the camps . . . many of the divisional transport animals are without a shed, roof, or any other protection . . . As many as 60 animals in the land transport corps, it is said, die daily.[45]

The *Daily News* confirmed the high equine mortality of the LTC and that a board had been convened by General Codrington to investigate the state of the LTC. The *Daily News* reported that this board had found that only 2 out of 100 horses 'purchased and landed in the Crimea' for the LTC were fit for duty. The remaining 98 were either dead or so ill as to be useless: 'The principal cause of the sickness and mortality appears to have been want of due care', and lack of proper shelter for the horses. The *Daily News* doubted that, come spring, the British army would be able to take to the field.[46] *The Examiner* was deeply critical of the LTC, especially its organisation and personnel. Whilst it could not praise the British officers and NCOs highly enough, the rank and file 'have been unfortunately filled from the off-scourings of all nations, Maltese, Italians, Spaniards, Levanters, Greeks, Tatars and nondescripts from Turkish provinces'. The work required of the LTC was far harder than the duties of the infantry or cavalry, and rather than filling the ranks with anyone, the LTC therefore required far more due diligence in the selection for its personnel. They were expected to take care of their horses and vehicles, but 'they have scandalously neglected them'. The men were not sufficiently well trained nor had sufficient time to carry out all their duties, resulting in the horses and mules becoming so neglected. Nor had any higher-ups been able to organise proper stabling for the horses, in stark contrast to the horses of the French *Train des Équipages*. In the opinion of *The Examiner*, the *Train des Équipages* was far superior to the LTC both in terms of organisation and especially in selection of its manpower. The *Train* was 'not inferior' to any other unit in the French army and above all had a regular, military organisation, rank structure and personnel, who had a high *esprit de corps*. They were *soldiers*, whilst the LTC was 'a body of men whom we could not have turned into soldiers, who had not pride nor self-respect . . . and who have no care for the animals they attend'. The LTC needed to be dismantled and started again based even more closely on the model of the French *Train des Équipages*.[47]

The men of the LTC were exhausted from over work and malnourished from eating too much salt pork. Their surgeon, Dr Taylor, noted that they often had no time for breakfast. As late as February 1856 many of them were still living under canvas, and where wooden huts had been provided to replace the leaky bell tents, they were too few in number. To prevent drafts, the men had stuffed up the ventilators and hung their 'packs, boots, &c. over the windows'. The blankets were damp, filthy and covered with vermin. Nor were the huts particularly waterproof, with leaky roofs covered with sheepskins in an attempt to keep out the rain. The bedding was soiled and full of vermin, and wet washing was hung up to dry inside many of the huts. Even worse, the wooden hospital huts were 'in a very unsatisfactory state' and because of a lack of nails the waterproof roofing felt had not been fitted and instead tarpaulins and sheepskins were used to try and keep the huts watertight. The cook houses had not been completed and cooking took place in the open air. Despite Dr Taylor ordering in October that each man have a clean shirt, flannel and two pairs of socks a week, there was still no regular system of washing the men's clothes. Nor had personal hygiene been attended to with men failing to wash and needing their hair and beards cutting when admitted to hospital.[48] Dr John Hall, Inspector General of Hospitals, noted on 21 December that half of all the deaths in the army occurred in the LTC alone.[49]

To the rescue of many LTC personnel came Mary Seacole, whose 'British Hotel' was established close to their camp. Here she doled out not only rice pudding and hot, sweet tea, but remedies and cures for dysentery, diarrhoea and fever which she had learned over many years treating British soldiers in the Caribbean. Many of the men Mary treated wrote to thank her for the care she had given them. Even Dr Hall was impressed by her work:

I have much pleasure in bearing testimony to Mrs Seacole's kindness and attention to the sick of the Railway Labourers' Army Works Corps and Land Transport Corps . . . She not only from her knowledge she has acquired in the West Indies was enabled to administer appropriate remedies for their ailments, she charitably furnished them with proper nourishment, which they had no means of obtaining.

Florence Nightingale wrote on 10 May 1856 that some 242 men had already perished during the 21 weeks the LTC had been on active service. Even she thought this 'excessive'. The conditions in the LTC hospital 'reminded her of the first winter of the war'.[50] Florence

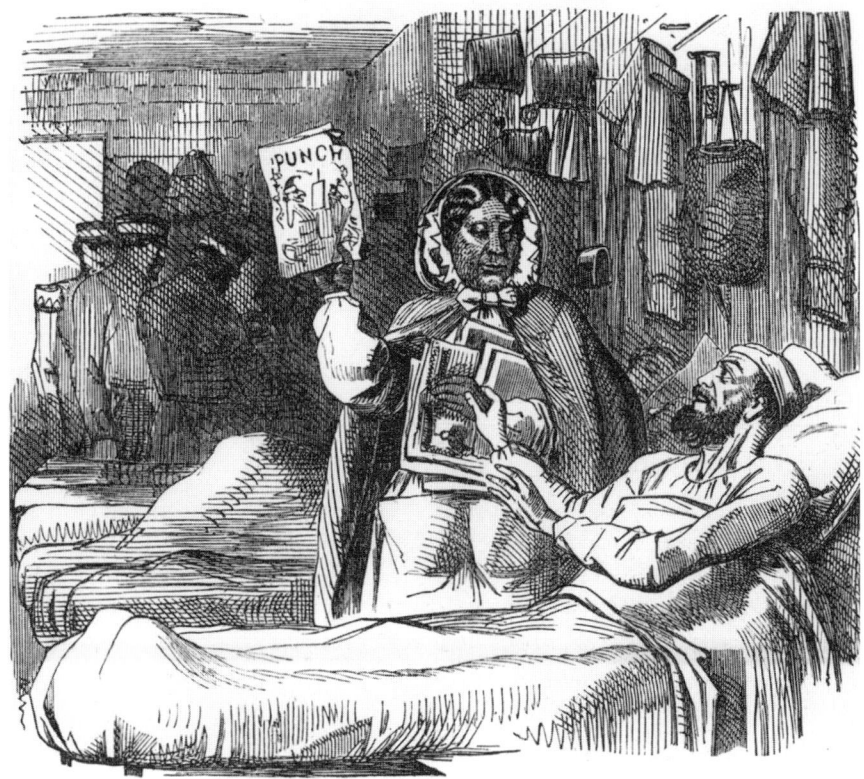

Mary Seacole was a self-trained nurse with considerable experience gained in treating sick soldiers and sailors in the West Indies. Whilst not welcomed by Florence Nightingale, she was adored by the ordinary soldiers.

noted: 'Had they been recruited from country carters, accustomed to exposure in all weathers, they could have stood it. But they [are] chiefly discarded gentlemen's servants, trades-people and townspeople. At least one half never ought to have come out, were unfit for work under any circumstances.'[51] She outlined the daily routine for the LTC, 'They get up at 5A.M., watered the Mules, went down to Balaklava without breakfasting, had no means of drying themselves, no means of cooking their food.'[52] Dr G. Taylor, the surgeon attached to the LTC, wrote that, 'The Land Transport Corps is . . . the hardest worked branch of service, and from the nature of their duties exposed to all kinds of weather'. The report of the Sanitary Commissioners sent to the Crimea noted how the high sickness and mortality of the LTC had, even by March 1856, not been addressed 'satisfactorily'. What struck the Commissioners most was the sharp contrast between the personnel of the LTC and rest of the army, a direct result of the recruitment policy:

> Many of the [LTC] were puny, ill nourished, and badly developed. Altogether they were . . . inferior . . . a large proportion of whom would not have been accepted as recruits; many bore the marks of intemperance and bad habits . . . most of those we examined had not been such as to fit them for the severe duties and exposure incident to the service.[53]

Confirming both Taylor's and Nightingale's observations, the men frequently went without breakfast; they had little time to wash themselves or their clothes and 'though there did not appear much drunkenness, there was drinking, . . . relieving exhaustion by stimulants instead of food'. The work was 'excessive', the men were too few in number and their duties too great, and they didn't even get a rest day.[54]

Despite this high rate of sickness and overwork, the railway managed to keep moving. In December General Codrington noted that 'the efficiency of the locomotive engines was impaired' due to the frost and exceedingly cold weather and that the track had been damaged due to the cold weather. But by January this damage had been made good.[55] The *Manchester Courier* reported in February that during the previous month the three locomotives – *Alliance, Victory* and 'one old one, named the Swan' – had been hard at work between Balaklava and Kadikoi. The daily traffic for the month was as follows, the total load carried per day being 330 tons, the load carried by each waggon being on average 2½ tons.[56]

The railway through Balaklava, as sketched by the artist William Simpson in spring/summer 1855. The post office (with its veranda) is visible on the left, the variety of rolling stock in use and the large packing crate labelled 'PBB', for Peto, Brassey and Betts, a reminder of the firm that built the line.

Daily Returns of Railway Waggon Mileage			
	Miles	Number	Tons Carried
Waggons running	6	20	50
Waggons running	4	32	80
Waggons running	2	16	40
Waggons running	1½	24	30
Waggons running	Less than 1½	40	100

The branch line towards Canrobert's Hill serving the Piedmontese camp and the Highland Brigade was opened and in operation by February, worked by locomotives. And, with peace in the air, there was talk of the railway being sold lock, stock and barrel to a mining company 'in the neighbourhood of Heraclea ... to be used in connection with coal mines'.[57]

Peace

Peace was formally declared at the Treaty of Paris signed on 30 March 1856. Even before this troops and materiel were being shipped home. Evacuation of the Crimea began on 4 April and was to be completed by 12 July 1856. Absolutely nothing was to be left behind, including the railway. The special correspondent of the *Morning Herald* wrote on 8 April how all the roads toward Balaklava and Kamiesch (where the French had their port) were 'encumbered by carts and waggons conveying military stores'. The railway was 'employed on the same errand' reversing, almost, the role for which it had been built. Everything seemed to be 'melting away' and 'immense fatigue parties' were employed in 'recovering' and 'removing the iron shot' which was to be put on ship and sent home as ballast. About 4,000 shot were recovered per day. Sadly, on one occasion a fatigue party sent to recover spent shot from the Redan had one man killed and several wounded when an unexploded shell 'suddenly went off' whilst being loaded on to a railway waggon.[58]

The AWC began to leave the Crimea in May, and 'several hundred' had already embarked. Sadly, their embarkation proved to be a scene of 'general drunkenness and misconduct' with General Codrington feeling powerless to do anything as the AWC was not subject to military discipline. Many of the civilian railway staff had also returned home, including one James Appleford, engineer, who after returning to Southwark assaulted his wife, Eliza, a 'very decent-looking female'. Eliza alleged in court that as soon as war was declared James 'went to the Crimea, and acted as an engine-driver on the Balaklava Railway'. During this time, she received not a penny from him and Eliza had to find her own employment to keep herself out of the poor house. On his return home, James was violent toward her and on one occasion 'without the least provocation, dragged her out of bed by the hair of her head, and kicked her on the head and body' until she nearly passed out. Thankfully her screams attracted the attention of neighbours and the police and James was arrested and sentenced to six months' hard labour.[59]

On 7 April 1856, Lord Panmure noted that 'A company which means to establish a railway from Joppa to Jerusalem' had put in a bid for the Balaklava Railway and plant; on the following day he ordered that the railway was to be dismantled as soon as it had finished being of use. General Codrington wrote to Panmure on 19 April that he was busy disposing of the railway and the horses of the LTC. The Turks had declined to purchase any horses, and instead he wrote to General Niepotoititchsky offering the following horses and mules and materiel:

1,200 first-class mules or horses at £25 to £30.
2,000 second-class mules or horses, about £10.

3,000 inferior mules or horses, at £2 or £3 each.

Huts, about 3,000 in all — a total price of about £60,000.

The Russians had also expressed interest in purchasing the railway, as had the Turks, but as yet 'he had no answer from them about the Railway'. The sale of the horses to the Russians, however, fell through as 'The Queen and Government have a horror . . . that the . . . Russians would parade them through Russia as trophies of war'. Codrington also remarked that the railway had been offered to the Turks but that no firm offer had been received. Lord Palmerston informed Panmure in May that General Codrington had agreed the sale of the Balaklava Railway and its plant to the Turkish government 'for a good price'. He reported on 13 May that dismantling of the railway had already begun, just over a year after it had been completed:

> The railway – that part of it at least beyond the 'forks' – will be taken up now that all shot is pretty nearly gone down to Balaclava. That part of it to the 'left siege train' is already begun: I have kept part of the Army Works Corps for this purpose: the rails, etc., will remain in readiness for embarkation at Balaclava.[60]

On 17 May 1856 it was reported that in order to expedite the sale of the railway and its plant, the British were willing to reduce the 'price by '57 thousand gold, which is the construction cost, will be given to 38 thousands liras'. Furthermore, the Ottoman authorities were hopeful that 'If the negotiations continue, it was reported that there would be a further discount.' Somewhat oddly, Ottoman documents refer to the railway as being 21½ miles in length.[61] The sale was concluded by 30 May 1856 when, 'It was requested from the relevant officers that the railroad materials loaded on the ships from Balaklava were purchased by the Ottoman State and brought in quickly by ships and placed in a suitable place in the shipyard.'[62]

By 26 May 800 men of the AWC were busy dismantling the railway, the sale of which to the Turks had been confirmed by the ambassador at Constantinople, Lord Stretford de Redcliffe.[63] The *Morning Chronicle*, however, reported that the Balaklava Railway including track, locomotives and rolling stock had been sold to a coal-mining concern in Heraclea, with the railway to be dismantled after it had finished being used by the army.[64] During this dismantling process, Russian military engineers visited and inspected the railway overseen by Campbell. By 9 July 1856 the railway had been completely dismantled. Some 19,000 tons of railway equipment was loaded on 'a dozen vessels, the Buffalo, Olinda, Forster, Aztec, and others'. The last mile of track 'which had been used almost to the last' being loaded on board the *Sea King* bound for Constantinople and the track and equipment used to build a railway between the port of Izmir and Manisa, the work underway by March 1857.[65] There is a persistent myth, however, that the Balaklava Railway was sold for use in Argentina and that it was laid to a gauge of 5ft 3in or 5ft 6in rather than the standard gauge as specified by Beatty, but there is absolutely no foundation for this.[66] *Victory* apparently made her way back to Denby Grange Colliery where she was re-named *Balaklava* and continued to work for several more years. Just as they had helped the troops embark for war, so too the railways helped them get home, with the LSWR providing special trains to London from Portsmouth carrying recently returned soldiers to a rapturous welcome.[67]

James Beatty who had engineered and managed the railway returned to Britain in December 1855. He was an ill man, but his physician could identify no cause for his symptoms. In February 1856, however, he took a turn for the worse with difficulty breathing and swelling of the throat and left arm. He died aged 35 on 11 March 1856 from an aneurysm, the result of the accident on 5 April 1855. He is buried in Kensal Green Cemetery.

Conclusion

A New Weapon?

Military observers had seen the potential of rail transport from the dawn of the main-line railway in the 1830s, but the Balaklava Railway was the first time the railway had gone to war, although it was not the first railway to be used in battle: the Tranent to Cockenzie Waggonway built in 1722 was fought over during the Battle of Prestonpans in 1745. The Balaklava Railway was the first railway built in a combat theatre and the first to be run by the army. In its brief history it is a microcosm of how railways had evolved over the last century and a half. The railway was constructed due to the inadequacies of existing transport infrastructure. At first, this horse-worked single-track railway soon proved its worth but within months increasing traffic led first to it becoming a steam-worked railway and finally one which was double track and operated according to a timetable and a strict set of regulations, identical to those of main-line railways.

But was it really necessary? The British army's transport system simply did not exist before the LTC was formed in spring 1855, and even then, some conservative commentators believed it to be an unnecessary expense. The complete lack of any military transport contrasted sharply with the French with their apparently successful *Train des Équipages*, and well-made metalled roads courtesy of *Génie Militaire*. The apparent success of the French system inspired the study of the French *méthode* (as well as that of other continental armies). Several detailed reports were commissioned on the French land transport, but in his desire to be 'seen to be doing something' during the political crisis of January 1855, the Duke of Newcastle authorised the formation of the LTC without any reference to what Britain's allies, the French – or anyone else – were doing and did so over the heads of the commissariat and the Quartermaster General's Department. It is little wonder that

McMurdo struggled to get the LTC to work, being faced with the twin, synchronous, tasks of both forming the unit from scratch and trying to provide the army's land transport. It was only with the appointment of Wetherall and reorganisation of the LTC and later replacement by the Military Train (1856) as a copy of the French *Train* that the British army found a working organisation for its transport.

The Balaklava Railway falls into the same category. Faced with a complete lack of militarised transport, and a lack of men and materials to keep the road system working, the Duke of Newcastle jumped on any suggestion to get supplies to the front. The use of civilians and 'men of business' to do the army's work for them was a victory for those self-same reform-minded 'men of business' who believed through organisations such as the Administrative Reform Association that the country and indeed the army would be best served by being run on the lines of business by the middle class. Against this background, the railway was undoubtedly a success. There was nothing else with which to move supplies to the front, and it filled a very immediate need.

It had not necessarily been welcomed by the army authorities, especially Commissary General Filder, but had won a grudging admiration, even from old Sir John Burgoyne, who believed it had shortened the siege and alleviated the suffering of many of the hard-worked men at the front. It also saved the life of the few remaining cavalry horses available to Lord Lucan, more of which had died carrying stores and ammunition up the hill from Balaklava to the trenches than in action. By carrying heavy guns and ammunition to the front, the railway alleviated congestion on the road system, ultimately carrying more than 90 per cent of all the ammunition used in the siege up to the fall of Sevastopol. This freed up the road system and the horses and waggons of the LTC to move rations and supplies.

Although not a conspicuous success, the Army Works Corps was able to build a new metalled road, running alongside the railway, further helping to alleviate the transport situation. Simply because the British army did not have enough men, civilian navvies and labourers freed the men at the front from the back-breaking duties of road building and mending. The French, in contrast, who had mobilised a million men by the fall of Sevastopol, could count on the services of their military engineers to build and maintain their roads for them through two Crimean winters. Roads, which unlike a railway which required specialist vehicles, personnel and construction, could be used by any vehicle or pack horses and could be built and maintained by relatively unskilled labour.

Notes

Introduction

1. Y. Bektas, 'The Crimean War as a technological enterprise', *The Royal Society Journal of Science*, via: https://doi.org/10.1098/rsnr.2016.0007, accessed 8 February 2021.
2. A.L. Dawson, *The Siege of Sevastopol 1854–1855* (Barnsley: Frontline Books, 2017), p. xiii.
3. Ibid.
4. Ibid., pp. xiv–xv.

Chapter 1

1. A.L. Dawson, 'British Army Perception of French Army Support Services during the Crimean War (1854–1856)', unpublished M.Res Thesis, University of Leeds, 2012, Chapter 5; see also A.L. Dawson, 'The French Army and British Army Crimean War Reforms', in *19: Interdisciplinary Studies in the Long Nineteenth Century*, 2015 (20).
2. C. Hibbert, *The Destruction of Lord Raglan* (London: Pelican, 1963), *passim*.
3. P. Burroughs, 'An Unreformed Army?', in D. Chandler and I. Beckett (eds), *The Oxford Illustrated History of the British Army* (Oxford: Oxford University Press, 1994), pp. 160–88. See also I.F.W. Beckett, *The Victorians at War* (London: Hambledon & London, 2003), Chapters 17 and 18, and E.M. Spiers, *The Army and Society 1815–1914* (London: Longman, 1980).
4. 'Military Punishment as regards to Non-Commissioned Officers and Privates', *United Service Magazine for 1843*, Part III (1843), pp. 562–3; E.M. Spiers, *Radical General: Sir George de Lacy Evans 1787–1870* (Manchester: Manchester University Press, 1983), Chapter 8.

5. H.F.A. Strachan, *Wellington's Legacy. Reform of the British Army 1830–1854* (Manchester: Manchester University Press, 1984), pp. 29–34; Spiers, *Army and Society*, pp. 90–3.
6. Ibid. It is particularly ironic that in the years 1850–4 the French army was actually reduced in size. This was due to political pressure from the French *Parlement* (which, mistrustful of the new president, cut the military budget) and Napoléon III's wish to appear the 'Napoléon of Peace': reduction in the size of the army fulfilled his famous statement that 'The Empire is Peace' (*L'Empire c'est paix*).
7. J. Sweetman, *War and Administration* (Edinburgh: Scottish Academic Press, 1984), Chapter IV. See also Dawson, 'British Army Perception of French Army Support Services', Chapter 3.
8. G. Douglas and G.D. Ramsay (eds), *The Panmure Papers. Being selections from the correspondence of Fox Maule, second Baron Panmure . . .*, 2 vols (London: Hodder & Stoughton, 1908), Vol. I, p. 48.
9. Hibbert, *Destruction of Lord Raglan*, p. 37.
10. Dawson, 'British Army Perception of French Army Support Services', pp. 29 and 31ff.; Hibbert, *Destruction of Lord Raglan*, p. 37ff.
11. Dawson, 'British Army Perception of French Army Support Services', pp. 32–3; A. Griffiths, *Fifty years of Public Service* (London: Cassell & Co., 1905), pp. 58–9.
12. A. Percy, *A Bearskin's Crimea. Colonel Henry Percy VC and his Brother Officers* (Barnsley: Pen & Sword, 2007), p. 108; West Yorkshire Archive Service (WYAS), Bradford, Acc. SpSt, J. Studholme-Brownrigg, Mss., Brownrigg to Colonel Sencer Stanhope, 9 May 1854; 'The Staff of the English Army as Compared with that of the French', *Daily News* (7 May 1855); A.C. Sterling, *The Story of the Highland Brigade in the Crimea* (London: John Macqueen, 1897), p. 289.
13. National Army Museum (NAM), London, Acc. 1994-03-153, A.M. Earle, Mss., Earle to Father, 11 February 1855.
14. Dawson, 'British Army Perception of French Army Support Services', pp. 24–5 and 35.
15. Via http://cwrs.russianwar.co.uk/cwrs-R-mstevens-drake-letters-054-18550201.html, accessed 9 August 2019.
16. Sweetman, *War and Administration*, pp. 41–8.
17. Ibid., pp. 46–51; Dawson, 'British Army Perception of French Army Support Services', pp. 40–3.
18. Sweetman, *War and Administration*, p. 49; W.N. Funnell, *Pathological Responses to to accounting controls: The British Commissariat in the Crimea 1854–1856* (University of Wallongong Department of Accountancy and Legal Studies, 1988), *passim*.

19. *Royal Warrant and Regulations Regarding Army Services . . . 1st of July 1848* (London: HMSO, 1848), p. 119.
20. C. James, *A New and Enlarged Military Dictionary* (London: T. Egerton, 1810).
21. Ibid.
22. 'Colonel Firebrace', 'Errors and Faults in our Military System', *The United Service Magazine for 1843*, Part 1 (1843), pp. 214–15.
23. *Royal Warrant and Regulations Regarding Army Services*, pp. 119–21.
24. Ibid., pp. 126 and 137.
25. Ibid., pp. 135–41.
26. Sweetman, *War and Administration*, pp. 49–50; Lieutenant Colonel C.H. Massé, *The Predecessors of the Royal Army Service Corps 1757–1888* (Aldershot: Gale & Polden Ltd, 1948), Chapter 2.
27. Lord Panmure, *Sidney Herbert, Lord of Lea. A memoire* (London: John Murray & Co., 1906), pp. 286–8; National Army Museum (NAM), Acc. 1962-10-94, General Sir R. Airey, Mss., Airey to General Wetherall, 29 December 1854; NAM, Acc. 1962-10-95, General J.B.B. Escourt, Mss., Estcourt to General G.A. Wetherall, 28 November 1854, 3 December 1854, 26 December 1854; NAM, Acc. 1962-10-94, General R. Airey, Mss., General Sir G. Brown to General G.A. Wetherall, ND; The National Archives (TNA), London, Acc. WO 43/973, remonstration by the Duke of Newcastle regarding land transport.
28. 'The Army before Sebastopol. Parliamentary Committee of Inquiry. Third Day', *Morning Chronicle* (8 March 1855); Assistant Commissary General F. Wingfield, 'Military Transport', *Journal of the United Services Institute for Defence Studies*, Vol. 13 (1870), pp. 269–71.
29. *Third Report from the Select Committee on the Army Before Sebastopol* (London: HMSO, 1855), pp. 17–23.
30. Panmure, *Sidney Herbert*, p. 311.
31. NAM, Acc. 1962-10-95 General J.B.B. Estcourt, Mss., Estcourt to General G.A. Wetherall, 28 November 1854, Estcourt to Wetherall, 8 January 1855 and 20 January 1855.
32. V. Bonham-Carter (ed.), *Surgeon in the Crimea. The experiences of George Lawson recorded in letters to his family* (London: Constable, 1968), pp. 23–6.
33. F. Robinson, *Diary of the Crimean War* (London: Richard Bentley & Co., 1856), p. 203; NAM, Acc. 1962-10-95, General J.B.B. Estcourt, Mss., Estcourt to General G.A. Wetherall, 6 January 1855.
34. S. Calthorpe, *Letters from Head-Quarters or the Realities of the War in the Crimea*, 2 vols (London: John Murray, 1856), Vol. II, p. 84.

35. E.B. Hamley, 'The Story of the Campaign – Part IV', *Blackwood's Edinburgh Magazine*, Vol. 77 (January–June 1855), p. 353; R. Pack, *Sebastopol Trenches and Five Months in Them* (London: Kerby & Endean, 1878), pp. 55–6; 'Parliamentary Committee: Condition of the Army before Sebastopol. Second Day – Tuesday', *Morning Post* (7 March 1854); NAM, Acc. 1962-10-95, General J.B.B. Estcourt, Mss., Estcourt to General G.A. Wetherall, 9 January 1855.
36. 'The War, from our Special Correspondent', *The Lancet for 1855*, Vol. 1 (1855), p. 112; 'The War, from our Special Correspondent', *The Lancet for 1855*, Vol. 1 (1855), p. 22. See also J. Shepherd, *The Crimean Doctors*, 2 vols (Liverpool: Liverpool University Press, 1991), Vol. 1, p. 79.
37. 'The Neglect of the Wounded at the Alma', *The Standard* (17 October 1854).
38. *Report upon the State of the Hospitals of the British Army in the Crimea and Scutari* (London: HMSO, 1855), p. 89.
39. 'Surgery of the War', *The London Lancet*, Vol. 1 (1855), p. 455.
40. P. Pincoffs, *Experiences of a Civilian in Eastern Military Hospitals* (London: Williams & Norgate, 1857), p. 179. The Medical Staff Corps was disbanded in 1859 and re-organised as the Army Hospital Corps.
41. 'English Dragoons and their horses', *Eclectic Review*, Vol. 64 (January–June 1865), pp. 565–6; L.E. Nolan, *Cavalry. Its history and tactics* (London: Bosworth & Harrison, 1860), pp. 100–1; 'Hints from the Crimea on the Organisation of the British Army', *Colburn's United Services Magazine for 1855*, Part 1 (1855), pp. 258–60; A.L. Dawson, *Real Warhorses* (Barnsley: Pen & Sword, 2016), p. 4ff.
42. Dawson, *Real Warhorses*, pp. 4–14.
43. A.J. Guy and A. Massie, *Captain L. E. Nolan 15th Hussars. Expedition to the Crimea* (London: National Army Museum, 2010), p. 71.
44. Dawson, *Real Warhorses*, p. 4.
45. NAM, Acc. 1962-10-95, General J.B.B. Estcourt, Mss., Estcourt to General G.A. Wetherall, 28 November 1854 and Estcourt to Wetherall, ND; NAM, Acc. 1962-10-94, General R. Airey, Mss., Airey to General G.A. Wetherall, 29 December 1854.
46. A.L. Dawson, *Letters from the Light Brigade* (Barnsley: Pen & Sword, 2014), pp. 193–5.
47. Captain J.W. Thompson, 'Horse Dealing in Syria, 1854', *Blackwood's Edinburgh Magazine*, Vol. 75 (July–December 1859); *Morning Chronicle* (1 June 1854).
48. Guy and Massie, *Captain L. E. Nolan*, p. 44.
49. Ibid., p. 45.

Chapter 2

1. Spiers, *Army and Society*, Chapter 1; W. Serman, *Les origins des officiers francais, 1848–1870* (Paris: publications de la Sorbonne, 1979), pp. 149–63.
2. Dawson, 'British Army Perception of French Army Support Services', pp. 36–7.
3. Percy, *A Bearskin's Crimea*, p. 109.
4. Dawson, 'British Army Perception of French Army Support Services', Chapter 2.
5. H. Ortholan, *L'Armée du Second Empire* (Saint Cloud: Éditions Napoleon III, 2010), p. 181; V.L.J.F. Belhomme, *Histoire de l'Infanterie en France* (Paris: Charles Henry Lavauzelle, 1892), Vol. 5, pp. 111–12; P. Griffith, *Military Thought in the French Army 1815–1851* (Manchester: University of Manchester Press, 1989), pp. 153–4.
6. Panmure, *Sidney Herbert*, p. 287.
7. *Reports from Commissioners on the Purchase and Sale of Commissions in the Army with Evidence and Appendix* (London: HM Stationery Office, 1857), p. 123.
8. *Royal Warrant, dated 28 October 1858, and Report of the Committee Appointed to inquire into the Commissariat Department with Evidence and Appendix* (London: Harrison & Sons, 1858), pp. 3, 10–11, 12–13.
9. Dawson, 'British Army Perception of French Army Support Services', Chapter 3.
10. 'Our Troops at Gallipoli', *Bury and Norwich Post* (3 May 1854); NAM, Acc. 1962-10-65, General J.B.B. Estcourt Mss., Estcourt to General G.A. Wetherall, 13 December 1854.
11. Ortholan, *L'Armée du Second Empire*, pp. 204–5; Major General G.B. McClellan, *European Cavalry* (Philadelphia: J.B. Lippincott & Co., 1861), pp. 173–4.
12. Dawson, 'British Army Perception of French Army Support Services', pp. 80–2.
13. Ibid., p. 84.
14. Ortholan, *L'Armée du Second Empire*, pp. 208–10.
15. Dawson, 'British Army Perception of French Army Support Services', pp. 87–8.
16. Ibid., pp. 68–71.
17. C.F.M. Rousset, *Histoire de la Guerre de Crimee* (Paris: Libriarie Hachette et Cie, 1877), Vol. 1, p. 83; Dawson, 'British Army Perception of French Army Support Services', pp. 52–3.
18. Dawson, 'The French Army and British Army Crimean War Reforms'.

Chapter 3

1. House of Commons, *Reports from Committees, (1854–1855), Vol. III, Part II*, 'Minutes of Evidence taken before the Select Committee on the Army Before Sebastopol', evidence of Sir C. Trevelyan, p. 18.
2. Massé, *Predecessors of the Royal Army Service Corps*, pp. 23–4.
3. 'Minutes of Evidence Taken before the Select Committee on the Army Before Sebastopol', pp. 15–22, 37–8, 381, Memo, Filder to Trevelyan, 2 September 1854.
4. *Third Report*, pp. 35–6, 38, 40, evidence of Sir Charles Trevelyan; W. Filder, *The Commissariat in the Crimea* (London: W. Clowes & Sons, 1856), pp. 33–4.
5. *Third Report*, p. 38.
6. Ibid., p. 40 and 386–7, Memo, Filder to Raglan, 5 October 1854, Raglan to Filder, 6 October 1854.
7. Ibid., pp. 385–6, Memo, Filder to Trevelyan, 8 October 1854.
8. Hibbert, *Destruction of Lord Raglan*, pp. 250–1.
9. *Third Report*, p. 389, Memo, Filder to Trevelyan, 23 October 1854, 8 November 1854.
10. Filder, *Commissariat*, pp. 43–4.
11. Ibid., p. 45.
12. Hibbert, *Destruction of Lord Raglan*, p. 256.
13. *Third Report*, p. 389, Memo, Filder to Trevelyan, 8 November 1854.
14. Ibid., pp. 389–90, Treasury Minute, 28 November 1854, pp. 390–1, Memo, Filder to Trevelyan, 8 November 1854.
15. Hibbert, *Destruction of Lord Raglan*, p. 256.
16. V.I. Samsonov, *English Railroad in Balaclava during the Crimean War* (Sevastopol: Gos. voen.-ist. Muzej, 1931), pp. 3–5, trans. Vladimir Serdiuk, email, 15 September 2019.
17. Ibid., pp. 5–7ff.; *Report of a Board of General Officers Appointed to Inquire on the Report of Sir J McNeill and Col. Tulloch* (London: 1856), p. 515, evidence Colonel Gordon RE; Hibbert, *Destruction of Lord Raglan*, p. 252.
18. *Third Report*, pp. 391, Memo, Filder to Trevelyan, 11 November 1854, pp. 392–3, Treasury Minute, 28 November 1854.
19. Ibid., p. 397, Memo, Filder to Trevelyan, 22 November 1854, pp. 398–9, Treasury Minute, 22 November 1854, p. 399, Memo, Filder to Trevelyan, 27 December 1854.
20. Ibid., pp. 398–400.
21. 'Royal Agricultural Society of England. Exeter Show', *London Evening Standard* (18 July 1850), p. 1; advertisement, *Lincolnshire Chronicle* (14 July 1854), p. 11.

22. Filder, *Commissariat in the Crimea*, pp. 38–9.
23. Hibbert, *Destruction of Lord Raglan*, p. 250.
24. B. Stuart (ed.), *Soldier's Glory Being 'Rough notes of an Old Soldier' Major General Sir George Bell* (Tunbridge Wells: Spellmount, 1991), p. 251.
25. 'Letter from the Crimea', *Wakefield Journal & Examiner* (15 December 1854).
26. *Third Report*, Appendix 3, the Commissariat, p. 395, evidence W. Filder.
27. *Third Report*, pp. 394–6.
28. Ibid., p. 401.
29. Ibid., p. 402.
30. Hibbert, *Destruction of Lord Raglan*, p. 252.
31. Marquess of Anglesey (ed.), *Little Hodge. His letters and diaries of the Crimean War 1854–1856* (London: Leo Cooper, 1971), p. 64.
32. Dawson, *Real Warhorses*, pp. 128–9; Dawson, *Letters from the Light Brigade*, p. 192; Anglesey (ed.), *Little Hodge*, pp. 62–4.
33. 'Our Horses in the Crimea', *North British Agriculturalist* (20 December 1854), p. 10.
34. 'Minutes of Evidence taken before the Select Committee on the Army before Sebastopol', evidence of Sir C. Trevelyan, p. 89.
35. Anglesey (ed.), *Little Hodge*, pp. 69, 78–9.
36. Ibid., p. 61.
37. Dawson, *Real Warhorses*, p. 128.
38. 'The Horses in the Crimea', *North British Agriculturalist* (10 January 1855), p. 11.
39. Anglesey (ed.), *Little Hodge*, p. 62.
40. Dawson, *Real Warhorses*, p. 128.
41. Sweetman, *War and Administration*, pp. 51–7.
42. Herefordshire Record Office (HRO), Acc. E47/G/IV/A, Richard Airey papers, Mss., Lord Hardinge to General R. Airey, 4 May 1855.
43. Douglas and Ramsay (eds), *The Panmure Papers*, Vol. I, pp. 48–9.
44. Dawson, 'British Army Perception of French Army Support Services', *passim*.
45. NAM, Acc. 1962-10-95, General J.B.B. Estcourt, Mss., Estcourt to General G.A. Wetherall, 17 December 1854.
46. WYAS, Acc. SpSt/10/4/1, J. Studholme-Brownrigg, Mss., J. Studholme-Brownrigg to Major General Spencer Stanhope, 2 January 1855.
47. Dawson, 'British Army Perception of French Army Support Services', pp. 74–5; Douglas and Ramsay (eds), *Panmure Papers*, Vol. I, p. 53.

48. NAM, Acc. 2002-05-2, Thomas Bell, Mss, Bell to father, 18 January 1855.
49. A.L. Dawson, *Wakefield Voices from the Crimean War* (Wakefield: 2012), pp. 18–19.

Chapter 4

1. F. and M. Palau, *Le Rail En France: Les 80 premières lignes, 1828–1851* (Paris: Editions F. & M. Palau, 2003), *passim*.
2. Chemins de Fer du Nord; CF d'Est; CF l'Ouest; CF Paris-Orleans; CF Paris a Lyons et à la Mediterannée; CF du Midi.
3. A.C. Rath, *The Crimean War in Imperial Context* (New York: Palgrave MacMillan, 2015), Chapter 1.
4. H. MacDonald, 'The Rideau Waggonway that never was: Rail vs Canal', in G. Boyes (ed.), *Early Railways 4* (Newcomen Society, 2010), p. 210ff.
5. T.J. Donaghy, *Liverpool & Manchester Railway Operations 1831–1845* (Newton Abbot: David & Charles, 1972), pp. 74–5.
6. E.M. Spiers, *Engines for Empire: The Victorian Army and its use of railways* (Manchester: Manchester University Press, 2017), Chapters 1 and 2.
7. The modern passenger will find the same journey takes an hour between Paris and Versailles by train and 40 minutes by road.
8. L.A. Unger (trans.), *Essai sur les Chemins de Fer considere comme lignes d'operations militaire* (Paris: J. Correard, 1844), p. 31.
9. 'Riots in the Country', *Illustrated London News* (20 August 1842), pp. 230–3.
10. Unger, *Essai, passim*.
11. Griffith, *Military Thought in the French Army*, pp. 165 and 181; Capitaine R. de Coynart, 'Emploi Militaire des Chemins de Fer', *Journal des Sciences Militaires*, Vol. 1 (1847), pp. 389–415; 'Une experience de plus importantes', *Journal des Chemins de Fer* (6 Fevrier 1847), p. 92; 'Chronique de Semaine', *Journal des Chemins de Fer* (15 Fevrier 1847), p. 107; 'Chronique de la Semaine', *Journal des Chemins de Fer* (20 Mars 1847), p. 204; 'Le problème du transport de cavalerie', *Journal des Chemins de Fer* (15 Mai 1847), pp. 371–2.
12. 'Correspondance', *Journal des Chemins de Fer* (18 Septembre 1847), p. 713; J.B. Krantz, 'Études sur l'application de l'armée au traveaux d'utilité publique', *Journal des Chemins de Fer* (18 Septembre 1847), pp. 713–14.
13. M. Nilsen, *Railways and Western European Capitals* (New York: Palgrave MacMillan, 2008), pp. 114–15ff. and 122; J.-D.G.G. Lepage,

Military Trains and Railways (Jefferson: McFarland & Co., 2017), pp. 10–11.
14. G.I. Kogatko (ed.) and N.V. Starostenkov, *Railway troops of Russia. Book 1. In the service of the Russian Empire: 1851–1917* (Euroservice-SV, 2001), courtesy Vladimir Serdiuk, email 19 September 2019.
15. 'Passage of English Troops through France', *Morning Advertiser* (4 April 1854), p. 3; 'Transit of English Troops through France', *Illustrated London News* (1 April 1854), p. 2; 'The English Cavalry in France', *Illustrated London News* (8 April 1854), p. 2.
16. 'Despatch of English Cavalry Through France', *The Advocate* (29 March 1854), p. 2, citing *The Times*; 'France, from our own Correspondent', *Daily News* (22 August 1854), p. 5; 'Conveyance of Troops by Railway in France', *Manchester Times* (26 August 1854), p. 6.

Chapter 5

1. Dawson, 'British Army Perception of French Army Support Services', pp. 4, 8, 90–100.
2. A.F. Nisbet, 'Brunel the Hospital Builder', *Backtrack*, Vol. 33, No. 9 (September 2019), pp. 541–3.
3. 'Crosskill's Patent Portable Railway', *Southern Reporter* (16 February 1854), p. 4, citing *Hull Advertiser* (3 February 1854).
4. 'Farm Railways', *Bucks Herald* (13 April 1850), p. 7; 'Railways for Farms', *Nottinghamshire Guardian* (2 May 1850), p. 4.
5. 'Portable Railway', *Dublin Evening Packet* (6 May 1854), p. 3; 'Portable Railway', *Hull Packet* (3 February 1854), p. 4; 'Crosskill's Patent Portable Railway', *Southern Reporter* (16 February 1854), p. 4, citing *Hull Advertiser* (3 February 1854).
6. University of Nottingham Library, Special Collections, Mss. Ne C 10337/1, William Monsall to Duke of Newcastle 6 December 1854; 10337/2 Captain Collinwood RE to Monsall, 6 December 1854; 10337/3, Arthur Gordon to Newcastle, 6 December 1854.
7. M. Robbins, 'The Balaklava Railway', *Journal of Transport History*, Vol. 1, No. 1 (May 1953), p. 30.
8. A.L. Dawson, *The Grand Crimean Central Railway* (Stroud: Amberley Books, 2019), p. 32.
9. Wigan Archives (WA), Edward Hall Collection, Acc. EHC/16, War Department Official letter book, Crimea Quartermaster General's Department, December 1854–June 1855, Henry Roberts to Sir Charles Trevelyan, ND.
10. Ibid.; Robbins, 'Balaklava Railway', p. 30.

11. WA, EHC/16, Henry Roberts to Trevelyan, ND.
12. Robbins, 'Balaklava Railway', p. 30.
13. WA, EHC/16, Edward Betts to the Duke of Newcastle, 30 November 1854.
14. Ibid.
15. Ibid.
16. Robbins, 'Balaklava Railway', p. 34.
17. WA, EHC/16, Edward Betts to the Duke of Newcastle, 30 November 1854. Trevelyan to Henry Roberts, 6 December 1854.
18. WA, EHC/16, Trevelyan to Henry Roberts, 6 December 1854; Duke of Newcastle to Lord Raglan, 6 December 1854.
19. Ibid.; Betts to Newcastle, 30 November 1854.
20. Ibid.
21. Ibid.
22. 'Material for the Railway in the Crimea', *Wolverhampton Chronicle* (3 January 1855), p. 3.
23. 'Portable Steam Engines', *Stamford Mercury* (15 December 1854), p. 3.
24. 'The Balaklava Railway', *Weekly Gazette* (3 March 1855), p. 9.
25. *Preston Guardian* (16 December 1854).
26. *Manchester Courier* (23 December 1854).
27. 'The War', *Bell's Weekly Messenger* (3 February 1855), p. 1.
28. 'The Balaklava Railway Corps', *Halifax Courier* (6 January 1855), p. 7.
29. 'The Balaklava Railway Corps', *Daily News* (3 January 1855), p. 4.
30. Ibid.
31. 'The Balaklava Railway', *Birmingham Journal* (24 February 1855), p. 9.
32. C. Kelly, *Mrs Duberly's War. Journal & Letters from the Crimea* (Oxford: Oxford University Press, 2008), pp. 131 and 139.
33. Robbins, 'Balaklava Railway', p. 30.
34. WA, EHC/16, Donald Campbell to Peto, Brassey and Betts, 29 December 1854.
35. C. Robins (ed.), *Romaine's Crimean War. The letters and journal of William Govett Romaine* (London: Army Records Society, 2005), p. 77.
36. WA, EHC/16. James Beatty to Lord Raglan, 21 January 1855.
37. Kelly, *Mrs Duberly's War*, p. 118.
38. NAM, Acc. 1994-03-153, Captain A.M. Earle, Mss., Earle to Father, 18 February 1855.
39. 'Letter from the Seat of War', *Wakefield Journal & Examiner* (27 July 1855).

NOTES

40. 'Balaclava Harbour and New Water Police', *Illustrated Times* (9 June 1855), p. 3.
41. WA, EHC/16, Memorandum re. Railway Board, 25 January 1855.
42. Via http://cwrs.russianwar.co.uk/cwrs-R-mstevens-drake-letters-052-18550124.html, accessed 9 August 2019.
43. 'The Balaklava and Sebastopol Railway', *Railway Record* (12 May 1855), pp. 3–4.
44. Lieutenant General G.E. Wrottesley (ed.), *Life and Correspondence of Field Marshal Sir John Fox Burgoyne, Bart.* (London: Richard Bentley & Son, 1873), Vol. II, p. 189.
45. Ibid., p. 217.
46. WA, EHC/16, Beatty to Raglan, 22 January 1855.
47. Ibid.
48. Ibid., Romaine to Beatty, 21 January 1855, Beatty to Sir John Burgoyne, 25 January 1855
49. WA, EHC/16, Major General C. Campbell to Romaine, 25 January 1855.
50. Ibid.
51. Ibid.
52. 'Picture of Balaklava', *Nairnshire Telegraph* (1 March 1855), p. 4.
53. WA, EHC/16, Major General C. Campbell to Romaine, 25 January 1855.
54. Sterling, *Highland Brigade in the Crimea*, p. 167.
55. WA, EHC/16, Major G. Hall, Railway Memorandum, 26 January 1855; Sir John Burgoyne to Beatty, 26 January 1855; Beatty to Romaine, 27 January 1855; Captain P. Christie to General Airey, 26 January 1855; Beatty to Airey, 26 January 1855; Christie to Romaine, 28 January 1855; Romaine to Colonel Gordon RE, 28 January 1855.
56. Ibid., Major G. Hall, Railway Memorandum, 26 January 1855.
57. Ibid.; Lieutenant A. Elphinstone RE to Major Gordon RE, 28 January 1855; Betts to Henry Roberts, 16 January 1855; Romaine to Beatty, 3 January 1855.
58. WA, EHC/16, Memorandum, Major Gordon RE, 25 January 1855.
59. WA, EHC/16, Elphinstone to Gordon, 28 January 1855.
60. 'The Balaklava Railway', *North British Daily Mail* (5 January 1855), p. 4.
61. Sterling, *Highland Brigade in the Crimea*, p. 178.
62. Robbins, 'Balaklava Railway', p. 32; WA, EHC/16, Romaine to Beatty, 4 February 1855; Romaine to Beatty, 7 February 1855; Beatty to Romaine, 8 February 1855; Beatty to Romaine, 26 February 1855; Airey to Beatty, 26 February 1855.

63. WA, EHC/16, W.G. Romaine, Report of the Board, 5 March 1855.
64. *Dover Telegraph* (24 March 1855), p. 2, citing *The Times*.
65. Sterling, *Highland Brigade in the Crimea*, p. 163.
66. 'Letters from the Crimea', *Berkshire Chronicle* (17 February 1855), p. 2.
67. WA, EHC/16, Beatty to Romaine, 27 February 1855.
68. Sterling, *Highland Brigade in the Crimea*, p. 191.
69. W. Luscombe (ed.), *Cadogan's Crimea* (New York: Atheneum, 1980), p. 139.
70. C. Fitzherbert (ed.), *Captain Henry Clifford VC, his letters and sketches from the Crimea* (London: Michael Joseph, 1956), pp. 166 and 171.
71. General É. Vanson, *Crimée Italie Mexique. Lettres de campagnes 1854–1867* (Paris: Berger-Levrault et Cie, 1905), p. 104.
72. 'War Summary', *Brighton Gazette* (8 March 1855), p. 5.
73. 'The Regiment of Navvies', *The Globe* (5 March 1855), p. 4.
74. 'The Balaclava Railway', *Illustrated London News* (31 March 1855), p. 16.
75. Ibid.
76. WA, EHC/16, Beatty to Romaine, 3 February 1855, Romaine to Beatty, 6 February 1855; 'The Navvies', *Stirling Observer* (19 April 1855), p. 2.
77. 'Further news from the Navvies', *Carlisle Patriot* (3 February 1855), p. 4.
78. 'Naval and Military Intelligence', *Sun* (2 April 1855), p. 8.
79. Dawson, *Wakefield Voices*, p. 11.
80. 'Letters from the Crimea', *Morning Chronicle* (22 March 1855), p. 6.
81. WA, EHC/16, Beatty to Romaine, 2 March 1855; General Richard Airey to Major C.J. Woodford, 2 March 1855.
82. Sterling, *Highland Brigade in the Crimea*, p. 192; *Dover Telegraph* (24 March 1855), p. 2, citing *The Times*.
83. Sterling, *Highland Brigade in the Crimea*, p. 195.
84. TNA, WO 33/2B/8, Colonel Wetherall on Land Transport.
85. WA, EHC/16, Beatty to Woodford, 10 March 1855, Beatty to Woodford, 11 March 1855, Romaine to Airey, 12 March 1855, Report, 15 March 1855; 'The Balaklava Railway', *Dover Telegraph* (7 April 1855), p. 3.
86. *Dover Telegraph* (24 March 1855), p. 2, citing *The Times*.
87. WA, EHC/16, Beatty to Romaine, 13 March 1855.
88. W.H. Drake to Louisa Drake, 2 March 1855, via http://cwrs.russianwar.co.uk/cwrs-R-mstevens-drake-letters-063-18550302.html, accessed 27 July 2020.

89. Robins (ed.), *Romaine's Crimean War*, p. 93.
90. 'Balaclava Railway', *Illustrated London News* (14 April 1855), p. 2.
91. Capitaine Minart, 'Lettres écrites pendant la campagne de Crimée par les frères Charles, Alfred et Édouard Minart', *Carnet de la Sabretache*, Vol. 9 (1910), p. 88.
92. Ibid., p. 90.

Chapter 6

1. WA, EHC/16, Beatty to Romaine, 16 March 1855, Beatty to Romaine, 19 March 1855; 'Working of the Crimean Railway', *Liverpool Mail* (12 May 1855), p. 3.
2. WA, EHC/16, Memo, W.G. Romaine, 20 March 1855, Romaine to Raglan, 26 March 1855, McMurdo to Romaine, 16 March 1855, Airey to Romaine, 26 March 1855, Romaine to Airey, 26 March 1855.
3. 'The Navvies in the Crimea (from a Correspondent)', *Daily News* (29 March 1855), p. 3.
4. 'The Railway', *Dover Telegraph* (24 March 1855), p. 2.
5. Robins (ed.), *Romaine's Crimean War*, pp. 102 and 143.
6. 'The Campaign in the Crimea', *Bell's Life in London* (22 April 1855), p. 10, citing the *Morning Herald*.
7. Captain W.E.M. Reilly, *An Account of the Artillery Operations in 1854–1855 . . . before Sebastopol*, p. 70.
8. 'The Campaign in the Crimea', *Bell's Life in London* (22 April 1855), p. 10, citing the *Morning Herald*.
9. 'Letters from the Crimea', *Morning Chronicle* (3 April 1855), p. 6.
10. Ibid.
11. 'Letters from the Crimea', *Morning Chronicle* (9 April 1855), p. 6.
12. 'The War with Russia', *Norfolk News* (12 May 1855), p. 6.
13. 'Aristocratic Government', *Leeds Intelligencer* (24 February 1855), p. 4.
14. Ibid.
15. 'The Campaign in the Crimea', *Bell's Life in London* (22 April 1855), p. 10, citing *The Times*.
16. TNA, WO 28/175, Memo, McMurdo, Railway Distribution, 14 April 1855; Memo, McMurdo, Railway Distribution, 16 April 1855; Memo, McMurdo, Railway Distribution, 17 April 1855.
17. TNA, WO 28/175, Memo, McMurdo to Airey, Conveyance of Sick to Balaklava, 10 June 1855.
18. TNA, WO 28/175, Memo, McMurdo, Railway Distribution, 7 April 1855.

19. TNA, WO 28/175, Memo, McMurdo, 'About Conveying Huts to the Monastery', 22 April 1855; Memo, McMurdo, 'Recommending distribution of huts', 26 April 1855.
20. TNA, WO 28/175, Memo, McMurdo 'About confusion in Hutting Material', 24 April 1855.
21. TNA, WO 28/175, Memo, Filder to Airey, 17 April 1855.
22. Ibid.
23. TNA, WO 28/175, Memo, McMurdo to Airey, 18 April 1855; Beatty to Airey, 18 April 1855.
24. 'The Balaklava and Sebastopol Railway', *Illustrated London News* (12 May 1855), p. 2.
25. Ibid.
26. Ibid.
27. *Manchester Times* (7 April 1855).
28. 'The Balaklava and Sebastopol Railway', *Illustrated London News* (12 May 1855), p. 2.
29. Ibid.
30. 'Letter from a Huddersfield Man in the Crimea', *Huddersfield Chronicle* (7 April 1855), p. 8.

Chapter 7

1. Robbins, 'Balaklava Railway', p. 29.
2. J. Sweetman, 'Military Transport in the Crimean War, 1854–1856', *English Historical Review*, Vol. 88, No. 346 (January 1973), pp. 81–2.
3. A. Massie, *National Army Museum Book of the Crimean War* (London: Pan Books, 2005), pp. 138–9.
4. Hibbert, *Destruction of Lord Raglan*, Chapter 14.
5. Sweetman, 'Military Transport in the Crimean War', pp. 81–4.
6. HRO, Acc. E47/G/IV/A/408, Richard Airey papers, Mss., Lord Hardinge to General R. Airey, 5 January 1855.
7. Ibid., p. 84.
8. 'Land Transport Corps. WANTED', *Roscommon & Leitrim Gazette* (18 August 1855), p. 3; 'The Constabulary', *Roscommon Journal, and Western Impartial Reporter* (21 April 1855), p. 2.
9. HRO, Acc. E47/G/IV/A, Richard Airey papers, Mss., Lord Hardinge to General R. Airey, 4 May 1855.
10. TNA, WO 28/175, Memo, McMurdo to General J. Simpson, 12 April 1855.
11. TNA, WO 28/175, Disembarkation Return, Land Transport Corps, 11 July 1855.

NOTES

12. 'The Land Transport Corps', *Morning Post* (9 March 1855), p. 4.
13. Ibid.
14. Sweetman, 'Military Transport in the Crimean War', p. 87.
15. TNA, WO 28/175, Letter, J. Harris to Major Cook, 7 October 1855, re native officer pistols.
16. TNA, WO 28/175, Memo, McMurdo, six cutlasses and 1 carbine, 30 September 1855.
17. 'The Land Transport Corps', *Morning Post* (9 March 1855), p. 4.
18. Sweetman, 'Military Transport in the Crimean War', pp. 85–6.
19. Massé, *Predecessors of the Royal Army Service Corps*, p. 28.
20. Ibid., p. 87.
21. 'Letter from Balaklava', *Roscommon & Leitrim Gazette* (14 April 1855), p. 2.
22. Massé, *Predecessors of the Royal Army Service Corps*, p. 28.
23. Sweetman, 'Military Transport in the Crimean War', p. 88ff.
24. TNA, WO 28/175, Memo, McMurdo to Airey and Raglan, 'Confidential. Memorandum on the Transport Service of the Army', 9 May 1855.
25. TNA, WO 28/175, Memo, McMurdo to Airey, 'Estimate of Transport Required', 11 May 1855.
26. TNA, WO 28/175, Memo, McMurdo to Airey, 'Confidential. Amount of Transport Required by the Army', 11 May 1855.
27. TNA, WO 28/175, Memo, McMurdo, 'Return of Transport', 13 June 1855.
28. Ibid.
29. TNA, WO 28/175, Memo, McMurdo, Misconduct of an Interpreter, 21 April 1855; Memo, Major Evans, Application for 3 3rd class interpreters, 18 August 1855.
30. TNA, WO 28/175, Memo, officers wanted, 1 August 1855.
31. Ibid.
32. TNA, WO 28/175, Memo, McMurdo to Simpson, 1 October 1855; Memo, buglers wanted, 6 October 1855.
33. Ibid., Memo, 6 October 1855, carpenters and smiths wanted; Memo, 22 July 1855, blacksmiths and carpenters wanted.
34. TNA, WO 28/175, Memo, Tents requested, 28 May 1855.
35. TNA, WO 28/175, Memo, McMurdo to Packenham, Deserter from Spanish Army, 22 September 1855.
36. Sweetman, 'Military Transport in the Crimean War', p. 86.
37. 'The Land Transport Corps in the Crimea', *Illustrated Times* (7 July 1855), p. 12.
38. 'Land Transport Service', *Paisley and Renfrewshire Advertiser* (28 July 1855), p. 7.

39. Ibid.
40. 'The Land Transport Corps', *Aberdeen Press & Journal* (23 May 1855), p. 7.
41. TNA, WO 28/175, Memo, McMurdo to Airey, 'Requisition for Tents', 28 March 1855.
42. TNA, WO 28/175, Memo, McMurdo to Airey, 'Extra Clothing', 6 May 1855.
43. TNA, WO 28/175, Memo, McMurdo to Airey, 'Clothing', 19 May 1855.
44. TNA, WO 28/175, Memo, McMurdo, 'Deaths LTC', 1 June 1855.
45. 'The Land Transport Corps', *Norfolk News* (11 August 1855), p. 3.
46. Ibid.
47. 'The Surgery of the War', *The Lancet* (8 December 1855), p. 562; 'The Surgery of the War. The Sanitary State of the British Army in the Crimea', *The Lancet* (29 December 1855), p. 639.
48. 'Scraps from the Camp', *The Globe* (11 July 1855), p. 2, citing *The Times*.
49. TNA, WO 28/175, Memo, wounded men, 10 August 1855.
50. 'Land Transport Service', *Paisley and Renfrewshire Advertiser* (28 July 1855), p. 7.
51. Massé, *Predecessors of the Royal Army Service Corps*, pp. 32–3; Sweetman, 'Military Transport in the Crimean War', p. 86.
52. TNA, WO 28/175, Memo, Quartermaster O'Reilly, 6 August 1855; Memo, QM O'Reilly, 19 July 1855.
53. 'Head-Quarters, Sebastopol October 24', *Sun* (8 November 1855), p. 1; 'At a General Court-Martial', *Morning Post* (15 November 1855), p. 5.
54. 'Serious Mutiny and Riot at the Horfield Barracks Near Bristol', *Sherborne Mercury* (30 October 1855), p. 3; 'Serious Mutiny at the Horfield Barracks, Near Bristol', *York Herald* (3 November 1855), p. 3.
55. 'The Land Transport Corps Service', *Cheltenham Chronicle* (9 October 1855), p. 4.
56. 'Rioting at Bristol', *Western Times* (17 November 1855), p. 6; 'More Rioting by the Land Transport Corps at Bristol', *Sherburne Mercury* (20 November 1855), p. 4.
57. Dawson, 'British Army Perception of French Army Support Services', p. 77.

Chapter 8

1. 'The War, from our Special Correspondent', *The Lancet for 1855*, Vol. 1 (1855), p. 22; 'The War. From a Medical Officer', *The Lancet for*

1855, Vol. 1 (1855), p. 23; C.A. Gordon, *Army Hygiene* (London: John Churchill & Son, 1866), pp. 170–1.
2. Dawson, 'British Army Perception of French Army Support Services', p. 79.
3. Ibid., pp. 83–5.
4. G. Fisher, 'Failure of the Ambulance Corps in the Crimean War', *Journal for the Society of Army Historical Research*, Vol. 91, No. 367 (Autumn 2013), p. 161.
5. *The Times* (4 April 1854), p. 7.
6. Fisher, 'Failure of the Ambulance Corps', p. 165.
7. Ibid., pp. 166–72.
8. 'The War, from our Special Correspondent', *The Lancet for 1855*, Vol. 1 (1855), p. 112; 'The War, from our Special Correspondent', *The Lancet for 1855*, Vol. 1 (1855), p. 22.
9. *Report of the Commissioners appointed to inquire into the Regulation affecting the Sanitary Condition of the Army* (London: George & Edward Eyre and William Spottiswoode, 1858), p. 23.
10. Ibid., p. 42.
11. Dawson, 'British Army Perception of French Army Support Services', pp. 84–5.
12. Fisher, 'Failure of the Ambulance Corps', pp. 175–7.
13. TNA, WO 28/175, Land Transport Corps, Adjutant Henry (Ambulance Corps) to Major Kirkland DAAG, 19 April 1855; Major Grant to Kirkland, 22 April 1855.
14. Shepherd, *Crimean Doctors*, Vol. 1, p. 463.
15. TNA, WO 28/175, Land Transport Corps, McMurdo, Memoranda on Ambulance Carriages, 24 May 1855.
16. NAM, Acc. 1962-10-94, Sir R. Airey Mss., Major Claremont to General G.A. Wetherall, 12 December 1854; 'The War. From a Medical Officer', *The Lancet for 1855*, Vol. 1 (1855), p. 23; 'Surgery of the War', *The Lancet for 1855*, Vol. 1 (1855), p. 24; A. Money and G.H. Money, *Our Tent in the Crimea* (London: Richard Bentley, 1856), p. 88; G.S. Peard, *Narrative of a Campaign in the Crimea* (London: Richard Bentley, 1855), pp. 91–2; 'Camp above Sebastopol', *Morning Post* (5 December 1854).
17. Anon., *Have we the best Ambulance System?* (Boston: Walker, Wise & Co., 1864), p. 12.
18. J. Paynter, 'Report upon the Sanitary Condition of French Troops Serving in Algeria', *Army Medical Department: Statistical, Sanitary, and Medical Reports for 1865* (London: HMSO, 1866), p. 445.

19. Panmure, *Sidney Herbert*, p. 286; Anon., *Have we the best Ambulance System?*, p. 11; 'The Surgery of the War', *The Lancet for 1854*, Vol. 2 (1854), p. 494.
20. Panmure, *Sidney Herbert*, p. 286; 'Heights above Sebastopol', *Morning Post* (24 November 1854).
21. 'The French and English Ambulance Corps', *Medical Times and Gazette*, Vol. IX (July–December 1854), p. 655.
22. C.F. Campbell, *Letters from Camp to his relatives during the Siege of Sebastopol* (London: Richard Bentley & Son, 1894), p. 295.
23. TNA, WO 28/175, Land Transport Corps, McMurdo, Memoranda on Ambulance Carriages, 24 May 1855.
24. TNA, WO 28/175, Land Transport Corps, McMurdo, Memoranda, Iron litters, 17 June 1855.
25. Shepherd, *Crimean Doctors*, Vol. 1, p. 463; WO, 28/175, Land Transport Corps, Captain Pigott, Memoranda on Pack Saddles, 18 September 1855.
26. TNA, WO 28/175, Land Transport Corps, McMurdo, Memoranda on Ambulance Carriages, 24 May 1855.
27. 'Siege Chronicle (from The Times Correspondent)', *Derby Mercury* (23 May 1855), p. 3.
28. TNA, WO 28/175, Land Transport Corps, Grant to Lieutenant General Simpson, 16 July 1855; TNA, WO 28/175, Land Transport Corps, C. Yorke to Simpson, 21 July 1855.
29. Ibid.

Chapter 9

1. TNA, WO 28/175, Memo, Lieutenant Powell, 10 May 1855, Memo, Lieutenant Powell appointed Captain of Division, 11 July 1855.
2. Ibid., Memo, Lieutenant Lamb 55 Regiment [*sic*] 1 August 1855; Memo, Lieutenant Grace 57th Regiment, 9 November 1855.
3. TNA, WO 28/175, Memo, Captain Collinwood, 2 October 1855, Lieutenant Lamb and Norman, 8 November 1855, Memo, Lieutenant Henry Benson, 29 November 1855.
4. TNA, WO 28/175, Land Transport Corps, List of Officers, 7 January 1856.
5. TNA, WO 28/175, Memo, 24 November 1855, Railway Regulations.
6. TNA, WO 28/175, Memo, McMurdo, application for a serjeant from the 39th Regt, 10 May 1855.
7. TNA, WO 28/175, Major W.C. Grant to Estcourt; Major W.C. Grant to Estcourt, 25 May 1855; Memo, McMurdo to Colonel Steele, Military Secretary, 23 July 1855.

NOTES

8. TNA, WO 28/175, Memo, 28 July 1855, veterinary surgeon.
9. TNA, WO 28/175, Memo, 7 August 1855, farrier major.
10. TNA, WO28/175, Memo, 22 July 1855, Captain Grant RA.
11. TNA, WO 28/175, Memo, 1 August 1855, harness-makers wanted.
12. Captain C.E. Luard, 'Field Railways, and their General Application in War', *Journal of the Royal United Services Institute*, Vol. XVIII (1874), p. 2.
13. Luard, 'Field Railways', p. 2.
14. Ibid.
15. *Glasgow Herald* (30 April 1855).
16. *Glasgow Herald* (27 April 1855).
17. 'The Railway Accident at Balaklava', *Sussex Advertiser* (1 May 1855), citing *The Times*.
18. Minart, 'Lettres écrites pendant la campagne de Crimée', pp. 272–3.
19. Vanson, *Crimée Italie Mexique*, pp. 109–10.
20. Robinson, *Diary of the Crimean War*, pp. 292–3.
21. TNA, WO 28/175, Memo, McMurdo, 'Railway State', 17 April 1855.
22. TNA, WO 28/175, Order: McMurdo, 'Distribution of Railway Service for the Day', 23 June 1855.
23. TNA, WO 28/175, Memo, McMurdo to General Airey, 8 June 1855.
24. Ibid., Letters, Power to Assistant Commissary General Lundy, 11 June 1855; Filder to Airey, 13 June 1855.
25. 'The Navvies in the Crimea', *Leeds Intelligencer* (14 July 1855), p. 6.
26. Robins (ed.), *Romaine's Crimean War*, p. 173.
27. WA, EHC/16, Memorandum, 23 June 1855.
28. 'Our Army in the Crimea (From Our Special Correspondent)', *Daily News* (9 July 1855), p. 5.
29. TNA, WO 28/175, Memo, Captain G. Goodlake to General Airey, 16 August 1855.
30. TNA, WO 28/175, Memo, Lieutenant Powell to Major Evans, 21 August 1855; Copy, testimony Sergeant Torke, 17 August 1855.
31. TNA, WO 28/175, Lieutenant Powell to Major Evans, 17 August 1855.
32. Ibid.
33. TNA, WO 28/175, McMurdo to Airey, 2 September 1855.
34. TNA, WO28/175, Memorandum for General Orders, 4 September 1855.
35. TNA, WO 28/175, Memo, Major Evans, 21 August 1855.
36. 'Return of Navvies from the Crimea', *Dublin Evening Mail* (1 June 1855), p. 4; 'The Late Assault on Police by Navvies', *Morning Advertiser* (25 June 1855), p. 7.

37. G.F. Chadwick, 'The Army Works Corps in the Crimea', *Journal of Transport History*, Vol. VI, No. 3 (May 1964), pp. 129–30.
38. Ibid., p. 130.
39. Ibid., pp, 130–1.
40. 'Murderous Assault on the Police by Crimean Navvies', *Canterbury Journal* (23 June 1855), p. 2.
41. Chadwick, 'Army Works Corps', pp. 131–4.
42. Ibid., p. 140.
43. 'Military Floating Factory', *Leeds Times* (8 September 1855), p. 7.
44. Chadwick, 'Army Works Corps', pp. 132 and 134.
45. 'Our Army in the Crimea', *Yorkshire Gazette* (19 January 1856), p. 4.
46. Chadwick, 'Army Works Corps', p. 137.
47. Ibid., pp. 134–5; WO 28/175, Report, Harry Jones to General Simpson, 18 September 1855.
48. Douglas and Ramsay (eds), *Panmure Papers*, Vol. I, p. 429.
49. Ibid., Vol. I, p. 256.
50. Chadwick, 'Army Works Corps', p. 135.
51. 'Railway Wagons &c. for the Crimea', *Leeds Times* (28 July 1855), p. 6.
52. 'Our Winter Prospects in the Crimea', *Bell's Weekly Messenger* (8 September 1855), p. 2.
53. 'State of the Roads', *North British Agriculturalist* (15 August 1855), p. 10.
54. Robins (ed.), *Romaine's Crimean War*, p. 203.
55. 'The Balaklava Railway', *Kentish Mercury* (8 September 1855), p. 3.
56. Douglas and Ramsay (eds), *Panmure Papers*, Vol. II, p.16.
57. Ibid., p. 38.
58. Robbins, 'Balaklava Railway', p. 40.
59. *Dublin Evening Telegraph* (8 September 1855).
60. TNA, WO 28/175, Memo, Requesting a 'Pile Driver' now in Sebastopol, 24 September 1855.
61. TNA, WO 28/175, Memo, 'Permission wanted to take out stone from . . . the Redan', 21 November 1855.
62. TNA, WO 28/175, Memo, 'Recommending the establishment of saw mills', 20 November 1855.
63. TNA, WO 28/175, Memo, 'Waggons required to convey stones', 12 October 1855.
64. Chadwick, 'Army Works Corps', pp. 135–6 and 138.
65. TNA, WO 28/175, Memo, the old road, 5 November 1855; Memo, Evans, the old road, 9 November 1855.
66. Chadwick, 'Army Works Corps', p. 136.

NOTES

67. 'The War', *Bradford Observer* (30 August 1855), p. 7.
68. *Morning Chronicle* quoted by *Yorkshire Gazette* (1 December 1855).
69. *Manchester Courier* (20 October 1855).
70. 'From our Own Correspondent', *Daily News* (27 November 1855), p. 5.
71. 'Incidents of the War', *Stroud Journal* (15 December 1855), p. 6.
72. 'Hurricane in the Crimea', *Yorkshire Gazette* (22 December 1855), p. 4.
73. Institute of Civil Engineers (ICE), London, CID 32943, Letters from G.O. Mann in the Crimea (October 1855–May 1856), p. 2, letter dated 8 October 1855.
74. Ibid., pp. 3–4, letter dated 26 October 1855.
75. Ibid., p. 4.
76. Ibid., p. 5, letter dated 2 November 1855.
77. 'Locomotive Engine for Balaklava', *Leeds Intelligencer* (8 September 1855), p. 5.
78. *Leeds Mercury* (22 September 1855).
79. 'The War', *Kentish Gazette* (27 November 1855), p. 2.
80. Robbins, 'Balaklava Railway', p. 40.
81. ICE, CID 32943, Mann Letters, p. 8, letter date 28 December 1855.
82. Ibid., p. 9, letter dated 4 January 1856.
83. *Daily News* (7 December 1855).
84. Minart, 'Lettres écrites pendant la campagne de Crimée', p. 363.
85. H. Jack, *Locomotives of the LNWR Southern Division* (Sawtry: Railway Correspondence and Travel Society, 2001), pp. 100–1.
86. Dawson, *Grand Crimean Central Railway*, p. 76; see also Jack, *Locomotives*, p. 101 and Jack, emails, 14 August 2018 and 15 August 2018.
87. 'The First Locomotive for the Crimea', *Falkirk Herald* (11 January 1855), p. 2.
88. 'Locomotives in War', *The Engineer* (24 November 1899), p. 532; H. Jack, 'Clement Stretton Railway Historian?', *Railway Archive No 18* (2008), pp. 66–70. Whilst considered to be a reputable source and expert in his own lifetime, Stretton has since been proved to be very unreliable and prone to not letting facts, or the absence thereof, get in the way of telling a good story: he made things up.
89. Robins (ed.), *Romaine's Crimean War*, pp. 192 and 224–5; Memo, Harry Jones, 18 September 1855.
90. TNA, WO 28/175, Memo, McMurdo, 16 November 1855.
91. Dawson, *Grand Crimean Central Railway*, pp. 81–3.

Chapter 10

1. Letter, Lord Panmure, Land Transport Corps, 14 September 1855; TNA, WO 28/175, McMurdo to General Simpson, 14 October 1855.
2. TNA, WO 33-2-B, Lieutenant Colonel E.R. Wetherall, Report on Land Transport, 5 December 1855.
3. TNA, WO 33-2-B, Colonel E.R. Wetherall, 'Memorandum on the Establishment Required for the Land Transport Corps', 14 December 1855.
4. Sweetman, 'Military Transport in the Crimean War', pp. 87–9; Massé, *Predecessors of the Royal Army Service Corps*, pp. 30–2.
5. 'The Land Transport Corps', *The Globe* (29 January 1856), p. 4.
6. 'The Land Transport Corps', *North British Agriculturalist* (2 January 1856), p. 10.
7. Massé, *Predecessors of the Royal Army Service Corps*, pp. 30–2.
8. Sweetman, 'Military Transport in the Crimean War', pp. 89–91; Massé, *Predecessors of the Royal Army Service Corps*, pp. 37–8.
9. TNA, WO 28/175, Memo, McMurdo to Airey, requesting timber for hut, 24 July 1855.
10. TNA, WO 28/175, Memo, McMurdo, supplying the Maltese Drivers with warm clothing, 11 October 1855.
11. *Reports From Commissioners*, Appendix, pp. 185–6.
12. Ibid., p. 186.
13. TNA, WO 28/175, Memo, McMurdo, sheepskin coats, 29 October 1855; Memo, McMurdo, warm clothing for native drivers, 15 November 1855.
14. *Reports from Commissioners*, Appendix, p. 186.
15. Ibid., pp. 186–8.
16. TNA, WO 28/175, Memo, McMurdo, requesting to be supplied with tools, 5 October 1855; McMurdo, requisition of tools, 11 October 1855; McMurdo, respecting a requisition for two stable huts, 11 October 1855.
17. Ibid., Memo, McMurdo, requisition for hospital huts, 29 October 1855; Memo, Wetherall, hospital marquees having been blown down, 2 December 1855.
18. TNA, WO 28/175, Memo, McMurdo, nails wanted, 15 November 1855; Memo, Lieutenant Colonel Evans LTC, requisition 1,000,000 feet of planking, 17 November 1855.
19. ICE, CID 32943, Mann Letters, p. 8, letter dated 28 December 1855.
20. TNA, WO 28/175, Memo, McMurdo to Airey, 'applies for 200 Turkish Army Labourers', 23 July 1855.

21. TNA, WO 28/175, Memo, McMurdo, proposing the construction of roads, 8 August 1855.
22. M. Springman, *Sharpshooter in the Crimea. The Letters of Captain Gerald Goodlake VC* (Barnsley: Pen & Sword, 2005), p. 161.
23. Chadwick, 'Army Works Corps', pp. 134–5.
24. Chadwick, 'Army Works Corps', p. 135.
25. TNA, WO 28/175, Memo, 'Wagons for road making', 4 September 1855; Memo, '10 wagons can be given for road making', 11 September 1855; Memo, 'Carts and wagons for road making purposes', 20 September 1855; Memo 'Carts can be supplied', 21 October 1855; Memo, lumber wagons for Captain Goodlake, 28 September 1855.
26. TNA, WO 28/175, Memo, Powell to McMurdo, 12 October 1855; Memo, McMurdo 'The road now making alongside the railway', 18 September 1855.
27. TNA, WO28/175, Memo, 'On the Subject of Transport for Huts', 24 September 1855.
28. 'Land Transport Corps. Required', *Sun* (17 January 1856), p. 1.
29. Chadwick, 'Army Works Corps', pp. 136–7; 'Preparations to Depart', *Manchester Courier* (3 May 1856), p. 4.
30. 'From the Correspondent of the Daily News', *Wigan Observer* (6 October 1855), p. 3.
31. Ibid.
32. TNA, WO 28/175, Memo, Head Quarters, 25 September 1855.
33. TNA, WO 28/175, Memo, McMurdo to Simpson, 17 September 1855.
34. Y.E. Aydin, email, 30 January 2021. Turkish Archives, HR.MKT.126-7, purchase of trees, 5 November 1855.
35. C. Robins, 'Steam Tractors and "Tracked" vehicles in the Crimean War', *Journal of the Society for Army Historical Research*, Vol. 92, No. 370 (Spring 2014), pp. 103–8.
36. *A Series of Reports on Stores of Various Kinds supplied for service during the War With Russia* (London: George E Eyre & William Spottiswoode, 1859), pp. 34 and 74.
37. Dawson, *Grand Crimean Central Railway*, p. 84.
38. ICE, CID 32943, Mann Letters, p. 8, letter dated 28 December 1855.
39. Ibid., pp. 9–10, letter dated 26 January 1856.
40. *Caledonian Mercury* (29 December 1855), citing the *Morning Chronicle*.
41. 'The Mud and Wet – Miserable Conditions of the Horses', *Manchester Courier* (29 December 1855), p. 4.
42. TNA, WO 33-2-B, Codrington to Panmure, 10 December 185.

43. TNA, WO 28/175, Memo, Lieutenant General H.W. Barnard, Land Transport, 30 December 1855.
44. 'Winter and the Land Transport Corps', *Fifeshire Journal* (3 January 1856), p. 2.
45. 'The Land Transport Corps', *Manchester Daily Examiner & Times* (5 January 1856), p. 9.
46. 'A Contemporary reminds us', *Daily News* (4 January 1856), p. 4.
47. 'The Land Transport Corps', *The Examiner* (12 January 1856), pp. 2–3.
48. *Reports from Commissioners*, Appendix, p. 188.
49. 'Despatches from Gen Codrington', *Daily News* (15 January 1856), p. 2.
50. Shepherd, *Crimean Doctors*, Vol. 2, pp. 587–8.
51. S.M. Goldie (ed.), *Florence Nightingale. Letters from the Crimea 1854–1856* (Manchester: Manchester University Press, 1997), p. 272.
52. Ibid.
53. *Report to the Right Hon. Lord Panmure . . . of the Sanitary Commissioners* (London: Harrison & Sons, 1857), p. 179.
54. Ibid., pp. 179–80ff.
55. 'Allied forces in the Crimea. Despatches from Sir W Codrington', *Manchester Courier* (12 January 1856), p. 3.
56. 'Traffic on the Balaklava Railway', *Manchester Courier* (9 February 1856), p. 4.
57. 'Camp, Sebastopol, February 16', *Bolton Chronicle* (8 March 1856), p. 2.
58. 'Our Army in the Crimea', *Cumberland Pacquet* (29 April 1856), p. 7; 'The Crimea', *Northern Daily Times* (10 May 1856), p. 2.
59. 'Assault on Wife by her Husband', *Morning Advertiser* (28 April 1856), p. 7.
60. Douglas and Ramsay (eds), *Panmure Papers*, Vol. II, pp. 184, 195, 214 and 227.
61. Y.E. Aydin, email 30 January 2021, İ.MMS. 7-276, sale of Balaclava Railway, 17 May 1856.
62. Ibid., HR.SYS. 1356-22, sale of Balaclava Railway, 30 May 1856.
63. Douglas and Ramsay (eds), *Panmure Papers*, Vol. II, p. 236.
64. 'The British Army in the Crimea', *Morning Chronicle* (26 April 1856), p. 5.
65. 'The Crimea: Clearing out of the Allies', *Cumberland and Westmorland Advertiser* (15 July 1856), p. 3; *John Bull* (2 August 1856), p. 4 citing the *Morning Herald*; Y.E. Aydin, email 30 January 2021, A.MKT. MHM. 18-58, 17 March 1857.

66. Robbins, 'Balaklava Railway, pp. 41–2; M. Robbins, 'The Balaklava Railway: A Footnote', *Journal of Transport History*, Vol. 2, No. 1 (May 1955), pp. 51–2.
67. 'Triumphal Entry of the Guards', *Lloyd's Weekly Newspaper* (13 July 1856), p. 4; 'Portsmouth', *Hampshire Chronicle* (2 August 1856), p. 5.

Conclusion

1. Spiers, *Engines for Empire*, p. 42.
2. C. Philips, *Civilian Specialist at War: Britain's transport experts and the First World War* (London: University of London Press, 2020), Chapter 7.

Select Bibliography and Sources

Archive Sources

Herefordshire Record Office
General Sir R. Airey, Crimean Papers E47/G/IV/A.

Institute of Civil Engineers, London
Letters Godfrey Oates Mann from the Crimea, CID 32943.

John Goodchild Collection, West Yorkshire History Centre, Wakefield
Denby Grange Colliery, Misc. Papers, JG001097, JG001078.

Manchester Regiment Archives, Ashton-under-Lyne
Ensign J. Clutterbuck, Mss. Acc. MR1/16/1.

National Army Museum, London
General Sir R. Airey, Mss. Acc. 1962-10-94.
Driver H. Clarke, Mss., Acc. 1964-02-33.
Captain A.M. Earle, Mss., Acc. 1994-03-153.
General J.B.B. Estcourt, Mss., Acc. 1962-10-95.

The National Archives, Kew
Land Transport Corps, WO 28/175
Land Transport, WO 33/2B/8, Colonel Wetherall.
Regulations, Army Works Corps, WO /33/2B/5.
Remonstration by the Duke of Newcastle regarding land transport, WO 43/973.

University of Nottingham Library, Special Collections
Letters regarding Crosskill Portable Railway, Mss. Ne C 10337/1–3.

SELECT BIBLIOGRAPHY AND SOURCES

West Yorkshire Archive Service, Bradford
J. Studholme-Brownrigg, Crimean Letters, Acc. SpSt.

Wigan Archives, Edward Hall Collection
War Department Official letter book: Crimea Quartermaster General's Department, December 1854–June 1855, Acc. EHC/16.

Parliamentary Reports
Report of the Commissioners appointed to inquire into the Regulation affecting the Sanitary Condition of the Army, London: George & Edward Eyre and William Spottiswoode, 1858.
Report of the Committee Appointed to inquire into the Commissariat Department with Evidence and Appendix, London: Harrison & Sons, 1858.

Published Diaries and Letters

Calthorpe, S., *Letters from Head-Quarters of the Realities of the War in the Crimea*, 2 vols, London: John Murray, 1856.
Campbell, C.F. *Letters from Camp to his relatives during the Siege of Sebastopol*, London: Richard Bentley & Son, 1894.
Douglas, G. and G.D. Ramsey (eds), *The Panmure Papers. Being selections from the correspondence of Fox Maule, second Baron Panmure . . .*, 2 vols, London: Hodder & Stoughton, 1908.
Fitzherbert, C. (ed.), *Henry Clifford VC, his letters and sketches from the Crimea*, London: Michael Joseph, 1956.
Goldie, S.M. (ed.), *Florence Nightingale. Letters from the Crimea 1854–1856*, Manchester: Manchester University Press, 1997.
Hamley, E.B., *The story of the Campaigns of Sebastopol*, Edinburgh: William Blackwood & Sons, 1855.
Kelly, C., *Mrs Duberly's War. Journal & Letters from the Crimea*, Oxford: Oxford University Press, 2008.
Luscombe, W. (ed.), *Cadogan's Crimea*, New York: Atheneum, 1980.
Minart, Capitaine, 'Lettres écrites pendant la campagne de Crimée par les frères Charles, Alfred et Édouard Minart', *Carnet de la Sabretache*, Vols 8 and 9 (1909 and 1910).
Panmure, Lord, *Sidney Herbert, Lord of Lea. A memoire*, London: John Murray & Co., 1906.
Peard, G.S., *Narrative of a Campaign in the Crimea*, London: Richard Bentley, 1855.
Percy, A. *A Bearskin's Crimea: Colonel Henry Percy VC*, Barnsley: Pen & Sword, 2007.

Robins, C. (ed.), *Romaine's Crimean War. The letters and journal of William Govett Romaine*, London: Army Records Society, 2005.

Robinson, F., *Diary of the Crimean War*, London: Richard Bentley & Co., 1856.

Springman, M., *Sharpshooter in the Crimea. The Letters of Captain Gerald Goodlake VC*, Barnsley: Pen & Sword, 2005.

Sterling, A.C., *The Highland Brigade in the Crimea*, London: John Macqueen, 1897.

Stuart, B. (ed.), *Soldier's Glory, being 'Rough Notes of an old soldier'*, Tunbridge Wells: Spellmount, 1991.

Vanson, General É., *Crimée Italie Mexique. Lettres de campagnes 1854–1867*, Paris: Berger-Levrault et Cie, 1905.

Wrottesely, Lieutenant General G.E., *The life and Correspondence of Field Marshal Sir John Fox Burgoyne, Bart.*, London: Richard Bentley & Son, 1873.

Secondary Sources: Books and Papers – Crimean War

Beckett, I.F.W., *The Victorians at War*, London: Hambledon & London, 2003.

Burroughs, P., 'An Unreformed Army?', in D. Chandler and I. Beckett (eds), *The Oxford Illustrated History of the British Army*, Oxford: Oxford University Press, 1994.

Chadwick, G.F., 'The Army Works Corps in the Crimea', *Journal of Transport History*, Vol. VI, No. 3 (May 1964).

Dawson, A.L., 'British Army Perception of French Army Support Services during the Crimean War (1854–1856)', unpublished M.Res Thesis, University of Leeds, 2012.

Dawson, A.L. 'The French Army and British Army Reforms', Conference proceedings, *Charting the Crimean War: Contexts, Nationhood, Afterlives*, National Army Museum, London, 28 June 2013.

Dawson, A.L., *Letters from the Light Brigade*, Barnsley: Pen & Sword, 2014.

Dawson, A.L., 'The French Army and British Crimean War Reforms', in *19: Interdisciplinary Studies in the Long Nineteenth Century*, 2015 (20).

Dawson, A.L., *Real Warhorses*, Barnsley: Pen & Sword, 2016.

Dawson, A.L., *The Siege of Sevastopol, 1854–1855*, Barnsley: Frontline, 2017.

Dawson, A.L., *The Grand Crimean Central Railway*, Stroud: Amberley Books, 2019.

Fisher, G., 'Failure of the Ambulance Corps in the Crimean War', *Journal for the Society of Army Historical Research*, Vol. 91, No. 367 (Autumn 2013).

Gouttman, A., *La Guerre de Crimée 1853–1856. La Première Guerre Moderne*, Paris: Éditions Perrin, 2006.

Gouttman, A., 'Objectif Sebastopol', *Napoléon III Magazine*, No. 1 (Janvier–Mars 2008).

Griffith, P.G., *Military Thought in the French Army 1815–1851*, Manchester: Manchester University Press, 1989.

Hibbert, C., *The Destruction of Lord Raglan*, London: Pelican, 1963.

Lambert, A.D., *The Crimean War: British Grand Strategy against Russia 1853–1856*, Manchester: Manchester University Press, 2011.

Massé, Lieutenant Colonel C.H., *The Predecessors of the Royal Army Service Corps 1757–1888*, Aldershot: Gale & Polden, 1948.

Shepherd, J.A., *The Crimean Doctors*, 2 vols, Liverpool: Liverpool University Press, 1991.

Spiers, E.M., *The Army and Society 1815–1914*, London: Longman, 1980.

Spiers, E.M., *Radical General: Sir George de Lacy Evans 1787–1870*, Manchester: Manchester University Press, 1983.

Spiers, E.M., *Engines for War. The Victorian Army and its use of Railways*, Manchester, Manchester University Press, 2017.

Strachan, H.F.A., 'Soldiers, Strategy and Sebastopol', *The Historical Journal*, Vol. XXI, Part 2, 1978.

Strachan, H.F.A., *Wellington's Legacy: Reform of the British Army 1830–1854*, Manchester: Manchester University Press, 1984.

Sutton, D.J., *Wait for the Waggon: The Story of the Royal Corps of Transport and its Predecessors 1794–1993*, Barnsley: Leo Cooper, 1998.

Sweetman, J., 'Military Transport in the Crimean War, 1854–1856', *English Historical Review*, Vol. 88, No. 346 (January 1973).

Sweetman, J., *War and Administration*, Edinburgh: Scottish Academic Press, 1984.

Railways

Baxter, B. and D. Baxter, *British Locomotive Catalogue 1825–1923. Volume 2a London & North Western Railway*, Ashbourne: Moorland Publishing Co. Ltd, 1978.

Cooke, B., *The Grand Crimean Central Railway*, Knutsford: Cavalier House, 1990.

Dawson, A.L., *The Grand Crimean Central Railway*, Stroud: Amberley Publishing, 2019.

Jack, H., *Locomotives of the LNWR Southern Division*, Sawtry: Railway Correspondence and Travel Society, 2001.

Luard, Captain C.E., 'Field Railways, and their General Application in War', *Journal of the Royal United Services Institute*, Vol. XVIII (1874).

Robbins, M., 'The Balaklava Railway', *The Journal of Transport History*, Vol. 1, No. 1 (May 1953).

Robbins, M., 'The Balaklava Railway. A Footnote', *The Journal of Transport History*, Vol. 2, No. 1 (May 1955).

Index

Page numbers in **bold** refer to illustrations

Balaklava Railway
accidents 102–4, 156–9, 163–4
Balaklava Depot 88, **88**, **153**, **154**
carries sick and wounded 112–13
construction begins 81–93
cost 72
horses 87, 90, 92, 100–2, 109, 174–5
inclines 81, 87, 90, 91, 92, 98, 100, 102, 104, 105, **105**, 106, 108, 109, 112, 116, 155, 156–7, 160, 164, **165**, **166**, 176, 177, 181, 182, 184, 190, 191
labourers 92–3, 107
locomotives 92, 152, 180–5, 209, 214
  Alliance 181–2, 183, 214
  Bury type 184–5, **185**
  Swan 183
  Victory 182–3, 214, 218
navvies 72–81, 76–81, **74**, **76**, **78**, **79**, 94, 95, **96**, 96–8, 168
  pay 73
  recruitment 76–7
  travel to Crimea 77–81
  uniform 77

officers 152–5
  Clancy, Ensign (14th) 152–3
  Collinwood, Captain (21st) 152
  Grace, Lieutenant (57th) 152–3
  Lamb, Lieutenant (50th) 152
  Powell, Major (39th) 113, 152–3, 163–4, 166, 176, 188, 201
  Rance, Ensign (14th) 153
operation 155–6, 186–92, 188–92
  crossing keepers 191–2
  guards 189–90, 192
  locomotive drivers 190
  speed 191
Railway Board 81, 85, 87
railway, general 110, 118, 203, 205–10, 214, 216, 217–18, 221–2
relaid 172–80
ropes and capstans 87, 90
Sardinian branch 178–80
scheme presented 71–3
sold to Turkey 216–18
starts work 109
stationary engines 75, 87, 91, 92, 98, 105, **105**, 106, **165**, **166**, 181, 183

253

track and materials 75, 78, 100
  gauge 91
waggons 87, **88**, 90, 91, 102, **103**, 108, **108**, 109, 113, 114–15, 161, 162, 163–7, **165**, 175–6, 190, 203, 209–10, 215, 221

British Army
Board of Ordnance 11, 12–13, 14
Chasseur (factory ship) 171–2, 187
commanders 4–7
commissariat 10–12, 34–42, 107, 114, 162, 188
contract system 13–15
  provision of forage 40–1
  provision of fuel 40
  provision of rations 40
logistics 4–21
  horses 19–21, 194, 216
  remounts 19–21
losses at sea 50
losses through overwork 50–4, 120, 208, 209–10, 211–12
roads and road building 40, 41–2, 201–8, 220, 221
staff 7–10
Staff Certificate 8
transport 16–19, 120, 219–22
  animals 35–7, 45, 128–9, 130–2, 135, 194–6, 198–9, 211–12, 216
  ambulances 17–18, **18**
  Corps of Drivers 35–6, 43–4
  hired Turkish wagons 35–7, 42
  Royal Waggon Train **14**, 16, 123
  waggons and carts 35–7, 42–3, 44–5, 131–2, 187, 199, 204–6, 208, 211
units
  1st (Royal) Dragoons 50
  1st (Royal) Regiment 46

2nd (Royal North British) Dragoons 51
4th Dragoon Guards 50–1
6th Inniskilling Dragoons 50–1, 53
8th Hussars 81
17th Lancers 118
21st (Royal North British Fusiliers) 47
28th Regiment 58
39th (Dorsetshire) Regiment 92–3
47th (Lancashire) Regiment **15**
68th (Durham) Light Infantry **14**, 57
71st (Highland Light Infantry) 156–9, **158**, 160, 161
Ambulance Corps 120, 142–51, 206
  ambulance mules 148–50, **151**, 206
  ambulances 17–18, **18**, **143**, 144, 145, 148
  Hospital Conveyance Corps 18, 143
  Medical Staff Corps 19
  merged with LTC 151
  officers
    Grant, Major John 144, 147, 150, 151
    Piggot, Captain John 144, 147, 151
Army Works Corps 166, 168–73, 173, 176–7, 186, 201, 203, 205–7, 216, 220, 221
  duties of 169–70
Land Transport Corps 104, 112, 119, 120–41, 176, 186, 193–4, 195–7, 199, 204–8, 209, 210–12, 216, 219, 220, 221

254

duties of 127–8, 135–6
Military Train 195
mutiny in Bristol 139–41
organisation 123–7, 195–6
sickness 136–8, 211–13
uniform **121**, 124–5, **125**, **129**, 136–7

French Army
command and officers 22–5
commissariat (*Intendance Militaire*) 25–6, 57, 120, 122
   bread ovens 32–3
   system of supply 31–3, 48
method of promotion 23–4
écoles
   Cavalerie (Saumur) 29–30
   État Major 8
   Militaire (St Cyr) 25
   Veterinaires 29–30
remounts and horses 29–30
   government studs 30
roads and road building 42, 175, 202, 219
staff (*Corps d'État Major*) 25
transport (*Train*) 26, 27–9, 44
tents 46, 47
   loss in fire at Varna 32–3
units
   27e Régiment de Ligne 106, 159, 184
   Corps du Génie 42, 202
   Service de Santé Militaire 142
   Train d'Artillerie 28, 128
   Train des Équipages 26, **27**, 27–9, 44, 56–7, 111, 120, 127, 212
      Mulets d'Ambulance 111–12, **113**, **147**, 148, **149**
   Train Auxilliaire 29, 127

Train du Parc du Génie 28, 128
Troupes d'Administration 26
Zouaves **31**
waggons, carts and caissons 29, **42**, 44, **45**, **210**

Personalities: British
engineers
   Beatty, James 72, 73, 76, 86, 87, 88, 100, 101, 102, 103, 104, 107, 108, 109, 114, 115, 116, 117–18, 152, 159, 160, 168, 173, 174, 177–8, 180, 186, 203, 218
   Boydell, James **207**, 208
   Campbell, Donald 73, 75, 81, 88, 152, 168, 180, 210, 217
   Crosskill, William 69–71
      patent waggons 44–5
      portable railway 69–71
   Doyne, William Thomas 170, 171, 173, 174, 176, 177–8, 203–4
   Kellock, John 152
   Mann, Godfrey Oates 180–1, 201, 208–9
   Paxton, Sir Joseph 68, 95, 168, 169, 170
   Peto, Brassey and Betts 68, 71, 72, 73, 76, 174
      Betts, Edward 69, 72
      Brassey, Thomas 69
      Peto, Sir Samuel Morton 59, 68–9, **69**, 72, 115
nursing staff
   Nightingale, Florence 213–14
   Seacole, Mary 212–13, **213**
officers
   Airey, General Sir Richard 7, 9, 41, 55, 82, 83, 93, 102, 112, 114, 122, 132, 145, 162, 166, 203

Barker, RA, Captain George 85
Bell, Lieutenant Colonel Sir George 46
Boxer, Admiral Edward 84
Brown, General Sir George 4, **5**, 6
Burgoyne, RE, General Sir John 6, 41, 63, 73, 86, 220
Cambridge, Prince George, Duke of 6
Campbell, Major General Sir Colin 85
Cathcart, General Sir George 6
Clifford, Captain Henry 96, 97
Codrington, General Sir William 175–6, 183, 194, 195, 210, 214, 217
de Lacy Evans, General Sir George **5**, 6, 18
Drake, Deputy Commissary General William 10, 85–6, 87, 104
Duberly, Fanny (wife of paymaster, 8th Hussars) 81, 83
Earle, Captain Maxwell 9, 83
Elphinstone, RE, Lieutenant Howard 85, 91
Estcourt, General Sir James B.B. 7, **8**, 9, 20, 56, 130, 134
Filder, Commissary General Sir William 10, **10**, 11, 35–41, 49, 53, 74, 82, 85, 104, 114, 116–17, 118, 162, 220
Goodlake, VC, Captain Gerald 113, 163–4, 203, 204, **204**
Hall, RE, Major 88, 90
Hamiliton-Gordon, Lieutenant Colonel Alexander 83, 85
Hardinge, General Sir Henry, CinC 6, 54, 122
Heath, RN, Captain Leopold 85, 87

Hodge, Lieutenant Colonel 50–2
Jones, RE, General Sir Harry 168, 174, 186
Lucan, George Bingham, Earl of 6, 50, 53, 54, 55
McMurdo, Lieutenant Colonel William 104, 107, 112, 114, 119, **119**, 122–3, 124, 126, 128, 129, 130–1, 132–3, 134, 136–7, 150, 152, 162, 166, 176, 183, 186–7, 193, 196–8, 203, 204, 206–8
Nolan, Captain Louis Edward 20, 21
Raglan, FitzRoy James Somerset, Lord 3, **5**, 6, 9, 11, 37, 41, 49, 52, 53, 74, 81, 85, 87, 97, 109, 111, 112, 113, 118, 131, 160, 168
Romaine, William Govett, Judge Advocate General 81, 85, 87, 101, 103–4, 105, 109, 118, 126
Scarlett, General Sir James 52
Simpson, General Sir James 9, 133, 173, 174
Smith, Dr Andrew 17, 142, 143, 144, 145, 147
Sterling, Lieutenant Colonel Anthony 85, 88, 89, 91, 94, 96–7, 102
Wellington, Arthur Wellesley, Duke of 4, 6, 61
Wetherall, Lieutenant Colonel Edward Robert 187, 193–4, 198, 208
politicians
  Aberdeen, Lord, Prime Minister 2, 72, 123
  Newcastle, Duke of, Secretary of State at War 2, 43, 59, 72, 74, 75, 79, 97, 194, 220

Palmerston, Lord, Prime Minister 2, 134, 217
Panmure, Lord, Secretary of State for War 8, 56, 128, 168, 173, 175–6, 187, 195, 210, 216, 217
Trevelyan, Sir Charles 11, 43, 51, 74

Personalities: French
Allonville, *Général* Armand-Octave-Marie d' 30
Bonaparte, *Général* Prince Joseph-Napoléon 23
Bonaparte, Napoléon III, Louis-Napoléon 1, 2, 3, 32, 61, 222
Bosquet, *Général* Pierre 23, **24**, 269
Canrobert *Général* François Certain 23, **23**, 26, 38
Larrey, Baron Dominique 17, 19, 142, 146
Martimprey, *Général* Édouard de 32
Minart, *Sous Lieutenant* Alfred 106, 159–60, 184
Minart, *Lieutenant* Charles 106
Morris, *Général* Louis-Michel 23
Saint-Arnaud, *Maréchal* Jacques Leroy de 3, 22, **23**, 32
Vanson, *Lieutenant* Emile 97, 160
Vico, *Lieutenant Colonel* Jean-Pierre **24**, 56–7

Places and Events
Balaklava 38, 41, 76, 81, 82, 84, 86, 87, 88, 97, 100, 103, 108, 110, 176, 184, **198**, 202, 206
Diamond Wharf 100, 101, 107, 108, **189**, 190–1
Ordnance Wharf 87, 101, **191**
Post Office 86, 88, **89**
Constantinople 1, 37, 80
Great Storm (14 November 1854) 46–9
    Allied camps destroyed 46–8
    loss of forage 49–50
    loss of winter clothing 48
Kadikoi 41, 81, 86, 87, 98, 101, 102, 103, 107, 110, **111**, 114, 115, 176, 181, 184, 206
Depot 107, 108, 114, 127, 162
Varna (Depot) 36, 37

Railways
general 60–7
Liverpool & Manchester Railway 60–1, 60
    carries troops 62
Russian 66
use of railways by British army 62–3
use of railways by French army 63–6
use of railways in Crimean War 66–7, 170, 218